The wonderfully successful ...*For Teachers* series now includes seven titles. These books are very popular both for individual teacher reference and as the foundation for an in-service. The following titles are now or soon to be available:

Title	ISBN	Price
Macs For Teachers	1-56884-601-0	19.99 (with disk)
The Internet For Teachers	1-56884-600-2	19.99 (with disk)
Mac Multimedia For Teachers	1-56884-603-7	24.99 (with CD)
The World Wide Web For Teachers	1-56884-604-5	24.99 (with CD)
A Clarisworks Reference For Teachers	1-56884-853-6	24.99 (with CD)
America Online For Teachers	1-56884-697-5	24.99 (with CD)
PCs For Teachers	1-56884-602-9	24.99 (with CD)

Quantity discounts up to 40 percent off list are available to schools that order directly from IDG Books Education Group. Please call 800-434-2086 for information or mail a school purchase order to IDG Books Education Group, 2103 East Southlake Blvd., Southlake, TX 76092

MACS® FOR TEACHERS™

by Michelle Robinette

"This special Printing of *Macs For Teachers* has been modified as part of a special Apple Computer Bundle. You'll find the bonus disk files mentioned in this book on the Educator Advantage CD."

IDG Books Worldwide, Inc.
An International Data Group Company

Foster City, CA ♦ Chicago, IL ♦ Indianapolis, IN ♦ Braintree, MA ♦ Southlake, TX

Macs© For Teachers™

Published by
IDG Books Worldwide, Inc.
An International Data Group Company
919 E. Hillsdale Blvd.
Suite 400
Foster City, CA 94404

Library of Congress Catalog Card No.: 95-76826

ISBN: 1-56884-601-0

Printed in the United States of America

10 9 8 7 6 5

1B/SS/QT/ZW/IN

Distributed in the United States by IDG Books Worldwide, Inc.

Distributed by Macmillan Canada for Canada; by Computer and Technical Books for the Caribbean Basin; by Contemporanea de Ediciones for Venezuela; by Distribuidora Cuspide for Argentina; by CITEC for Brazil; by Ediciones ZETA S.C.R. Ltda. for Peru; by Editorial Limusa SA for Mexico; by Transworld Publishers Limited in the United Kingdom and Europe; by Al-Maiman Publishers & Distributors for Saudi Arabia; by Simron Pty. Ltd. for South Africa; by IDG Communications (HK) Ltd. for Hong Kong; by Toppan Company Ltd. for Japan; by Addison Wesley Publishing Company for Korea; by Longman Singapore Publishers Ltd. for Singapore, Malaysia, Thailand, and Indonesia; by Unalis Corporation for Taiwan; by WS Computer Publishing Company, Inc. for the Philippines; by WoodsLane Pty. Ltd. for Australia; by WoodsLane Enterprises Ltd. for New Zealand.

For general information on IDG Books Worldwide's books in the U.S., please call our Consumer Customer Service department at 800-762-2974. For reseller information, including discounts and premium sales, please call our Reseller Customer Service department at 800-434-3422.

For information on where to purchase IDG Books Worldwide's books outside the U.S., contact IDG Books Worldwide at 415-655-3021 or fax 415-655-3295.

For information on translations, contact Marc Jeffrey Mikulich, Director, Foreign & Subsidiary Rights, at IDG Books Worldwide, 415-655-3018 or fax 415-655-3295.

For sales inquiries and special prices for bulk quantities, write to the address above or call IDG Books Worldwide at 415-655-3200.

For information on using IDG Books Worldwide's books in the classroom, or ordering examination copies, contact the Education Office at 800-434-2086 or fax 817-251-8174.

For authorization to photocopy items for corporate, personal, or educational use, please contact Copyright Clearance Center, 222 Rosewood Drive, Danvers, MA 01923, or fax 508-750-4470.

 is a trademark under exclusive license to IDG Books Worldwide, Inc., from International Data Group, Inc.

About the Author

Native Georgian Michelle Becker Robinette developed an interest in computers during her first year as an elementary school teacher when an Apple IIe was placed in her classroom. There were no instructions to follow — just a computer. She taught herself and eventually incorporated technology into the everyday functioning of her classroom. Eight years later, Michelle has now moved on to the bright new world of the Mac and is currently the technology coordinator for a large elementary school in metro Atlanta. She enjoys helping teachers overcome their "techno-phobia" and is constantly working to merge technology and curriculum in an effort to make the computer a part of the education process — not a subject within itself.

When she's not at the keyboard, Michelle has her hands full caring for her four-year-old daughter Jessie (who is already very computer literate, thank you), her two-year-old son John-Michael (who loves dancing to old John Cougar Mellencamp CDs), and her husband John (whom Michelle describes as "too good to be true").

In an earlier life (her early twenties), Michelle earned a degree in journalism from Georgia State University (which, to her parents dismay, she never used — until now) and spent a couple of wild and crazy years as an NFL cheerleader for the Atlanta Falcons. She later earned her teaching credentials from the University of Georgia and went on to receive her Masters and Specialist degree in education.

If Michelle could have it her way, every parent would spend a day as a teacher in order to fully appreciate the demands of the job — a rainy day without a recess break!

Welcome to the world of IDG Books Worldwide.

IDG Books Worldwide, Inc., is a subsidiary of International Data Group, the world's largest publisher of computer-related information and the leading global provider of information services on information technology. IDG was founded more than 25 years ago and now employs more than 7,700 people worldwide. IDG publishes more than 250 computer publications in 67 countries (see listing below). More than 70 million people read one or more IDG publications each month.

Launched in 1990, IDG Books Worldwide is today the #1 publisher of best-selling computer books in the United States. We are proud to have received 8 awards from the Computer Press Association in recognition of editorial excellence and three from Computer Currents' First Annual Readers' Choice Awards, and our best-selling ...*For Dummies*® series has more than 19 million copies in print with translations in 28 languages. IDG Books Worldwide, through a joint venture with IDG's Hi-Tech Beijing, became the first U.S. publisher to publish a computer book in the People's Republic of China. In record time, IDG Books Worldwide has become the first choice for millions of readers around the world who want to learn how to better manage their businesses.

Our mission is simple: Every one of our books is designed to bring extra value and skill-building instructions to the reader. Our books are written by experts who understand and care about our readers. The knowledge base of our editorial staff comes from years of experience in publishing, education, and journalism — experience which we use to produce books for the '90s. In short, we care about books, so we attract the best people. We devote special attention to details such as audience, interior design, use of icons, and illustrations. And because we use an efficient process of authoring, editing, and desktop publishing our books electronically, we can spend more time ensuring superior content and spend less time on the technicalities of making books.

You can count on our commitment to deliver high-quality books at competitive prices on topics you want to read about. At IDG Books Worldwide, we continue in the IDG tradition of delivering quality for more than 25 years. You'll find no better book on a subject than one from IDG Books Worldwide.

John J. Kilcullen

John Kilcullen
President and CEO
IDG Books Worldwide, Inc.

Dedication

To my 3 Js:

John, Jessie, & John-Michael.

Credits

**Senior Vice President
and Publisher**
Milissa L. Koloski

Associate Publisher
Diane Graves Steele

Brand Manager
Judith A. Taylor

Editorial Managers
Kristin A. Cocks
Mary Corder

Product Development Manager
Mary Bednarek

Editorial Executive Assistant
Richard Graves

Editorial Assistants
Constance Carlisle
Chris Collins
Kevin Spencer

Production Director
Beth Jenkins

Production Assistant
Jacalyn L. Pennywell

**Supervisor of
Project Coordination**
Cindy L. Phipps

Supervisor of Page Layout
Kathie S. Schnorr

**Supervisor of Graphics
and Design**
Shelley Lea

Reprint/Blueline Coordination
Tony Augsburger
Todd Klemme
Patricia R. Reynolds
Theresa Sánchez-Baker

Media/Archive Coordination
Leslie Popplewell
Melissa Stauffer
Jason Marcuson

Associate Project Editor
Bill Helling

Editor
Diane L. Giangrossi

Technical Reviewer
David Pogue

Associate Project Coordinator
Sherry Gomoll

Project Coordination Assistant
Regina Snyder

Graphics Coordination
Gina Scott
Angela F. Hunckler
Carla Radzikinas

Production Page Layout
Cameron Booker
Elizabeth Cárdenas-Nelson
Maridee V. Ennis
Laura Puranen
Anna Rohrer

Proofreaders
Jenny Kaufeld
Dwight Ramsey
Robert Springer

Indexer
David Heiret

Cover Design
Kavish + Kavish

Acknowledgments

First and foremost, I thank my creator who has proven over these past few years that he has a plan for me. He charts the path and I'm just along for the ride. Thanks for this interesting side journey.

I married the most wonderful guy in the world. John is my best friend, and this book couldn't have been written without his help and support. Thanks for being Mommy *and* Daddy over these past few months.

To Jessie and John-Michael: Mommy's finished the book. Now we can go to the beach!

My parents instilled in me the desire to learn and encouraged all my dreams (even the crazy ones). Mom and Dad, I'm finally using the journalism degree you paid for.

I will forever be in debt to Professor Brenda Manning at the University of Georgia for her inspired teaching — and for changing my life with her lessons on the power of positive thoughts.

Thanks to all the inspired folks at Gwinnett County Public Schools. I need to specifically thank Robin Gerlach, Pam Willis, Debbie DeFrieze, Linda Dillard, John Dalton, Rob Younge, Bard Williams, and principals extraordinaire Gary Fairley (for giving me my wings) and Nancy Samples (for allowing me to soar).

My closest friends have been very patient while I've been chained to my computer. Please forgive me Angela, Joan, Shannon, and the rest of the "inner circle." I've missed you guys!

I now turn my attention to all the fine people at IDG Books.

My editor, Bill Helling, is the kindest man a writer could ever hope to work with. His skill and expertise corrected many a mistake, and his kind manner made criticism seem like a redirected compliment. Bill made writing my first book both fun and relatively painless. In addition to all this, he's also a dedicated Dad. I hope we will work together again soon!

I have made a new circle of IDG friends across the country. To Megg Bonar and Suki Gear (my new California girlfriends), and Judi Taylor (my new Indy friend), thanks for believing in this project and being my cheerleaders! Let's do lunch in San Francisco one day. Thanks to Jim Kelly for holding my hand (from September 'til January) and not giving up on my idea. I also need to thank John Kilcullen, David Solomon, Milissa Koloski, Diane Steele, and anyone else who helped get this book on paper! IDG has the coolest employees in the world. I'm honored to be a part of this fine group.

And, of course, I send unlimited thanks to David Pogue, who provided the original inspiration for this book.

(The publisher would like to give special thanks to Patrick J. McGovern, without whom this book would not have been possible.)

Contents at a Glance

Cartoons at a Glance

By Rich Tennant

page 171

page 133

page 67

page 247

page 278

page 199

page 158

page 261

page 227

page 9

Table of Contents

Foreword

· ·

Since the first time I was asked what I wanted to be in life, my answer has always been "an engineer like my father and an elementary school teacher like Miss Skrak (my 4th and 5th grade teacher)." I started Apple Computer largely by accident. The initial intent was to build a machine for a technical person (myself). But the usefulness of such modestly priced computers for average people has caused great changes in homes and in business — as well as in education. For the last several years I have spent almost full time supporting the local public schools while contributing equipment and technical support. I have, with a small staff, taught year-long courses for 5th through 8th graders, as well as for teachers.

Computers were simple machines in 1977, but they can be incredibly complicated to use and understand nowadays. To many students, the computer is as interesting and fun as a video game. Provide a computer and some software and, presto, the students will line up to use it. But today's students should be taught *how* to use the computer: to vary the look of text, to use fonts correctly, to align paragraphs and columns automatically, to include graphics, to emphasize items by various methods. And not to go crazy with all these capabilities.

The students learn much of this if motivated. But they lapse into sloppiness creating works no better than those created with a typewriter if they don't feel that computer quality has value. The big obstacle here is the teacher.

Teachers with normal (or *minimal*) computer experience don't assign tasks in a way applicable to computer solutions. For example, having the students create a computer timeline to demonstrate a unit on Egyptian history doesn't always come to mind for teachers. Also, most teachers cannot evaluate student work in terms of whether or not proper computer techniques were used. It is not uncommon to find teachers admiring a font stew or a rainbow decoration of colors — amazed that it's even possible. With just a little experience, teachers discover that such techniques are often a very *simple* way to add effect to a paper.

You can never learn enough about using your computer — which changes every time a new operating system is introduced. And I find it intimidating for newcomers (*teachers* included) to have tons of software that they don't yet know how to use dumped on them.

Miss Skrak always made me feel proud about my scientific and mathematics knowledge. I credit her for strengthening my education values. My parents told me that adults had done a pretty poor job with the world in a lot of ways — and that we students attend school to learn from mistakes and make a *better* world. They told me how elementary school teachers earn less money than many other types of workers. I felt my teacher was worth more than that. I grew up caring about and helping others, like teachers and childhood heroes do. I particularly cared about young people and their world.

Allocation of funds for computers is tight where I live. My district is lucky to have me. California ranks 47th in per capita spending on schools, and it's getting worse due to legislation of the past. I occasionally see cases where the schools get equipment — but not the staff training or funding to keep it maintained. Because the importance of the computer in education from elementary school through college is obvious, it may be time for school boards to reprioritize expenditures and requirements. But the ultimate question is how schools can obtain more funding, since computer costs are on top of funds required to teach every bit of material being taught when I was in school.

The materials covered by this book are very appropriate, and I am honored to write this foreword. The programs discussed represent the most commonly used ones in our schools — and are exactly the ones I use and teach.

Steve Wozniak
Co-founder of Apple Computer

Introduction

1 am one of you.

I've spent the last eight years in the classroom — I know how important your job is, I know that you are a well-educated individual, I know how hard you work, and I know how difficult it is to fit one more thing into your daily schedule. I'm also aware of how underappreciated you sometimes feel. (And there is very little incentive these days to spend time learning something new.) It seems to me that every time a school system jumps on a new bandwagon, trains staff members, and gives them time to master a new concept, the system turns around and decides to go in another direction. Remember the phonics-vs-sightreading debate? Remember open classrooms?

A wonderful veteran teacher I had the pleasure of working with once said, "It's all a big circle; every ten years or so ideas resurface, and they just put a new name on them." I really believe that she is right — in most cases. However, *that's just not going to happen with technology. It is here to stay, and if you don't decide to join in this movement, you may eventually be left behind!*

I recently left the classroom to become the technology coordinator for the elementary school in my neighborhood. I thought I'd landed the perfect job. The description called for me to preview software and hardware, train teachers, oversee our three computer labs, and come up with plans to make relevant ties between curriculum and technology. The school was only a mile from my home. And the best part of all — I had an office *and* a phone.

If you're not a teacher, you couldn't possibly appreciate that final tidbit of information.

College graduate that I am, I decided to research and pool all my resources. Guess what? Every piece of published work out there was aimed at the business executive who sometimes has those one-hour-or-more lunch breaks and an assistant to screen out interruptions so that they can sit and read about their new computer and all the wonderful things they can spend their money on to make it really work for them.

Let me stop for a moment and examine this last sentence in teacher terms:

Business World	Teacher's World
Real lunch break	25 minutes max
Eat with colleagues in restaurant	Eat in cafeteria with 100 or more students
Ever-present assistant	Maybe an aide once a week for 30 minutes
Expense account	A what?

And here is the age-old answer we're always given if we complain about our jobs: *"But you have summers off!"*

Don't you just love that response? Let's see. After taking a graduate course or two in order to maintain my credentials, participating in the staff development that wasn't required (but was *strongly suggested* by the administration), and spending two weeks before school starts getting my room ready because pre-planning week was filled with everything but planning time, I probably only have about two weeks *off* in the summer.

And now they've put a computer in your room. Or maybe a beautiful new computer lab that cost thousands of dollars has been installed in your school. What are you going to do?

My Rationale

That, my fellow educators, is why I've decided to write this book.

I want to tell you what *you* need to know, not what civilians need to know, about computers. I want to spare you weeding through those lofty computer manuals with vocabulary that could have been invented either by my four-year-old (mouse pad, screensaver, icon, floppy disk) or a rocket scientist (megabyte, partition, disk cache, PRAM).

These manuals accompany every piece of software you purchase. And then you have the five or six manuals Apple included with your computer. Of course, we all have time to read these tomes that were probably written by someone who has never even stepped foot in the classroom! In all honesty, less than half of each of these masterpieces is necessary reading.

When I first became interested in computers, I had no one to tell me the shortcuts or walk me through even the simplest procedures. Now I get a real thrill out of showing teachers ways to make their lives easier. I've noticed that most people in education who know a little about computers tend to treat the topic as some big secret that only a select few are allowed to know.

Above all, I want you to walk away from this book feeling comfortable with technology and its uses in the world of education. I want you to spread the word about technology, the Mac, and how it has helped you become a much better teacher.

My Objectives

I've designed this book to do the following:

- ✔ explain high-tech vocabulary in teacher terms
- ✔ make your day-to-day paperwork a breeze
- ✔ enhance your curriculum through technology
- ✔ help you get the most out of a classroom Mac or a Mac Lab

And, if you are comfortable with the preceding concepts, I'll take you a step or two beyond conventional computing.

The Lesson Plan

In **Chapter 1**, I'll assume that you have a Mac and printer (or access to these in your school), and that the Mac is installed (put together and plugged in). Don't worry; you can complete this first task on your own. The Mac is very easy to put together, and I know that you are an educated individual who is capable of reading and following simple directions. Macs even have symbols to help you match cables with the proper ports. In this first chapter, I explain how to turn your Mac on and how to use the mouse. I also describe the menu bar, go over some basic Macintosh syntax, and tell you how to turn your Mac off.

Chapter 2 covers some of the computer terminology that *techno-nerds* throw out to make the rest of us feel inferior: memory, hard disks, floppies, and so on. I also give you a list of words that are often overheard in computer circles and have no relevance to the world of education.

In **Chapter 3,** you'll be on your way. It's like the first day of school! I teach you all about folders, icons, and keyboard shortcuts. I can almost guarantee that you will keep working and fly right through this chapter.

Chapter 4 sifts through the confusing world of software and checks out a few of the desk accessories found in the Apple menu. You also learn the cornerstone of all human endeavor — Cut and Paste.

After all the work you've done, in **Chapter 5,** you finally learn how to put it on paper. I'll tell you all you need to know about the different types of printers and how to make them work.

I'm sure you'll keep working on into **Chapter 6** and **Chapter 7,** where you are introduced to *ClarisWorks* and the wonders of word processing. I help you create a personalized letterhead along with my all-time great time-saver, a lesson-plan template that allows you to throw away your lesson-plan book .

Chapter 8 teaches you how to use the spreadsheet function in *ClarisWorks*. Spreadsheet knowledge lets you create customized checklists.

In **Chapter 9,** you create a database for your class. After you create this database, I explain the mail-merge capabilities that allow you to send the same letter (with a personalized greeting) to each parent in your class.

Chapter 10 examines the major software categories: skill-and-drill, productivity, multimedia, and simulation.

CD-ROM technology is the newest wave to hit educational shores. In **Chapter 11,** I tell you everything you need to know about this acronym and share some ways to use it in the educational setting.

I discuss some of the *hot topics* in educational technology in **Chapter 12.** The topics highlighted include portfolio assessment, grade-book software, and keyboarding programs.

Turn to **Chapter 13** and make a copy for your technology coordinator or principal. This list of software titles is super! (I had to weed through tons of trash software to get to the treasures.) It *is* possible to get a lot for a little money.

In **Chapters 14 and 15,** I help you fake your way through the two programs found in just about every school: *KidPix2,* and *The Writing Center.*

In **Chapters 16** and **17,** I discuss modems and on-line services in the school setting. I also take you on a quick tour of America Online.

In **Chapter 18,** I give hints on using one Macintosh in a classroom full of students. At first, I thought this task was an impossibility. However, we teachers can be very creative when it comes to time and space.

Chapter 19 deals with the computer-lab situation and is worth reading even if your school doesn't have a lab. Who knows? You may become the crusader who persuades the PTA to make the investment!

Chapter 20 holds some ideas on getting your local community and board of education excited and involved in your technology pursuits.

Scanners, touch screens, and QuickTake cameras are just a few of the cool additions that any school's technology inventory would welcome. **Chapter 21** covers the neat things that you may like to add as you become more techno-literate.

Great deals and my favorite publications are listed in **Chapter 22.** I've included detailed lists with addresses and phone numbers.

Appendix A holds a lesson from every curriculum area, for use in either the classroom or lab. These lessons can be adapted for any grade level. Sharing these lessons is my way of creating a springboard. Teachers are smart; just plant a seed of information and watch it grow. I'd love to hear back from any of you who really take off with these lesson plans and go in all kinds of directions.

Appendix B, "Troubleshooting," was written by my new buddy, David Pogue. He is the author of *Macs For Dummies,* 3rd Edition (IDG Books Worldwide, 1995) and can answer just about any question you may have concerning your Mac or software.

In **Appendix C,** you'll find down-to-earth, easy-to-understand definitions for all those over-used techno-terms.

Appendix D holds visual references you'll want to cut, copy, and laminate — and keep beside your computer. I've provided printouts from *KidPix 2* and *The Writing Center.*

Why Mac?

Personally, I use the Mac for economic reasons. Macs are in my school system, and, therefore, I have easy access to hardware and software. Apple computers are number one in educational circles and will probably continue to be for many years to come. And a Mac is very easy to learn and use on a daily basis — even for adults.

Macintosh is tops in education for many reasons. Above all, it is the easiest computer to operate. Children seem to pick things up much more quickly than adults — including colds, frogs, and other unmentionable objects. After reading this book and learning the basics, you'll find your students pushing you toward new heights in computers and technology.

You are a teacher because you love children, you love imparting knowledge, and you want to have a stake in our future. Computers and technology are going to be a large part of this future.

The Final Bell

I appreciate the fact that you lead a busy life and have very little time for business or pleasure reading. Keeping that in mind, I will try to make this book succinct, informative, and enjoyable. And who knows? Maybe those classrooms of the future we keep reading about will really exist one day. And you, my friend, will be a few steps ahead of the game.

Conventions Used in This Book

Teacher Approved — This icon highlights items or activities that I highly approve of and feel would be worthwhile additions to your classroom environment.

Techno Terms — This icon brings your attention to information that's crucial to basic computer operation — but I'll give it to you in easy-to-understand language.

Heads Up — Wake up and pay attention! This is critical information for teachers. No sleeping or daydreaming allowed during the lesson.

Learning Link — This icon points out great ways to integrate curriculum and technology.

Try This — This one points out some real *hands-on* learning activities. You know, the kind of stuff we do everyday in our classrooms.

Ode to Pogue

David Pogue is an *incredible* man.

I realized this last summer while reading *Macs For Dummies*. He took an intimidating subject and turned it into an enjoyable learning experience. His wit and humor kept me going and eventually turned me into a computer addict.

After reading his book, I decided to give the genius a call — that's right, I just picked up the phone, dialed New York City information, and asked for the number. He not only accepted my phone call but was very warm and polite as well. Our discussion soon led to the need for more computer information for teachers. And thus a book was born — this book!

David agreed to be my accomplice in crime. We devised a plan to create a book that had the Dummies style and delivery, without calling it a Dummies book. (I explained that teachers wouldn't think very highly of that label.) And without hesitation he agreed to give whatever assistance was needed to create this literary masterpiece.

You see, David is a MacGod. In the kingdom of Mac, he knows all and sees all. It is rare to find someone with his high level of knowledge who is still willing and patient enough to share it with others. In that sense, David is a teacher. In fact, he's been one of the best teachers I've ever encountered.

I had supreme confidence in my own abilities in the field of education and using the Mac to enhance curriculum. What I needed was David to hold my hand (and allow a wee bit o' plagiarism) through the technical aspects of Mac use, care, and feeding. I hope some of his wit and wisdom have rubbed off on me over the past few months of our relationship — and if you enjoy this book, you have him to thank for the initial inspiration.

Some excerpts that appear are taken directly from *Macs For Dummies*, 3rd Edition (IDG Books Worldwide, 1995). Appendixes B and C, and large portions of Part I, are paraphrased from this same supreme work.

Part I
For the First-Time Mac User

The 5th Wave   By Rich Tennant

"Well, the first day wasn't bad—I lost the 'Finder', copied a file into the "Trash' and sat on my mouse."

In this part...

There are at least four ways to become "one of those teachers who knows about computers." (We all have a few of these technically-literate individuals in our school, and our feelings for them usually range from contempt to sheer admiration.) You could wait for your school to provide some type of inservice that would probably be taught after school when you are usually busy grading papers, picking up your kids, or taking the dog to the vet. You could read the manuals that came with the Mac, which are almost as exciting as a PTA meeting. You could even enroll in a class taught at a local computer center and pay big bucks for information that mainly addresses the needs of the business Mac user. The final way (and, in my opinion, the *ideal* way) to learn about using the Mac is to read this book!

Have you made a decision?

In this part, you'll be given the respect you deserve. I won't bother you with information you don't need. Instead, I'll give you the basics — the bare bones required to help you get up and running on the Mac — and nothing else.

Well, I may throw in a little teacher humor every now and then.

One last thought . . .

You *can* do this. Think about what you are expected to be on a daily basis in your personal and professional life: mother/father, cook, chauffeur, accountant, custodian, wardrobe expert, laundry specialist, counselor, planner, curriculum creator, entertainer, artist, decorator. The list is endless.

This computer stuff is a piece of cake compared to those responsibilities!

Chapter 1

A Bare-Bones Approach
to Mac Basics

● ●

In This Chapter

▶ How to turn on the Mac and what you hope happens

▶ Using the mouse and the mouse practice program

▶ Menu bars

▶ The desktop: icons, windows, and Macintosh syntax

▶ Using multiple windows and multiple views

▶ Shutting down

▶ Top Ten Differences between your Mac and your students

● ●

1 know how frustrating it can be to have a new student, a new set of text books, or a new piece of classroom equipment thrust upon you. It's not that you don't welcome the new addition; it's just that things had been going too smoothly. The thought of accommodating the newcomer is both frustrating and overwhelming.

The student will be fine. Just pair him up with your most sociable child. By the end of the day, they'll be fast friends. The text book may look brand new, but you'll probably find very few changes once you get past the glossy, new, graphically inviting cover — which allowed the publisher to call it a new edition and charge your school system double the original cost. Finally, kind friend, trust me when I tell you that the computer is just as easy to conquer. And you'll have fun at the same time!

It's sitting there waiting to meet you. So think happy thoughts, roll up your sleeves (or put on your reading glasses), and do it!

Switching the Mac On

In this very first lesson, you'll be asked to locate the On button. To keep life interesting, Apple has decreed that This Switch Shall Be in a Different Place on Every Different Mac Model. Fortunately, after you know where yours is, it'll pretty much stay in that spot for as long as you own your Mac.

There are five possible places you'll find the power switch. Here goes:

A keyboard button	Every Mac keyboard has this key in the upper-right corner. It has a left-pointing triangle on it:
	On many of the world's Macs, this key turns the machine on. If yours doesn't, you must have one of the other on-switch locations.
Back-panel switch	Feel around on the ends of your Mac's back panel. On many Macs, especially smallish or inexpensive ones, there's a plastic rocker switch back there. If you look at it, the On position is marked by a straight line, and the Off position is marked by a circle. Nobody can ever remember which is which. You may want to think of it this way: the *O* stands for *Off*. (Of course, it also stands for *On* . . . and they wonder why people are intimidated by computers?)
Round front-panel button	A couple of models (610, 6100) have a round nub of an On/Off button on the front panel, on the right side.
Back-panel pushbutton	PowerBook laptops only. If your model number begins with a 1, you have to flip open the back panel, which is a pain. You'll then see the round, concave power button. (If your PowerBook model number begins with a 5, you turn it on with the triangle-labeled key on your keyboard.)
Keyboard pushbutton	PowerBook Duos only. There's a rubber capsule-shaped button on the keyboard; it's your On switch. (There's an identical button on the back.)

Was your hunt for the elusive On Switch successful? Then turn the Mac on! You should hear a ding or a chord, and after a few seconds, an image appears on the screen.

What you hope to see

After a few seconds, you should see this cute little smiling computer.

A few seconds after that, you are given a pleasant "Welcome to Macintosh" message. Your *desktop* should appear. Or, if your school has already installed a protection program *(At Ease)*, you see something that looks like a file folder. If you see this file folder, ask someone in your school for the password that will get you to the desktop — and have this person disable *At Ease* for you.

Great Job! You are ready to go: Skip forward to "The First Day of School."

What you may see

The very first time you switch on a new Mac, there's a chance that you'll see a disk with a blinking question mark, as shown in the following figure.

The Mac, in its own charming, universal, picture-based language of love, is trying to tell you that it can't find a disk to start up from. More specifically, it can't find an electronic *System folder,* which is where the Mac's instructions to itself live. It's the same as your being absent for a day and forgetting to leave plans for a substitute. (I'm sure none of you would ever do such a thing!)

If you see the blinking question-mark icon, you've just met your first computer problem. Now is a good time to dog-ear the pages of Appendix B, "Trouble-shooting." This problem and many others are explained — and solved — for you there.

You need to give the Mac a disk containing a System folder, or it will sit there like an idiot and blink at you until the warranty expires. The easiest way to provide it with a System folder is to locate those white-labeled floppy disks that came with the Mac. (They don't, alas, come with Performa models.) The one that contains a System folder is called Disk Tools. Insert the disk into the slot on the front of the computer — metal side first, label side up. And then read Appendix B for the full troubleshooting scoop.

The First Day of School

Well, you've done it! The machine is on. It wasn't that hard, was it? Now, take some time for you and your Mac to get better acquainted.

Using the mouse

The mouse is the gray, soap-sized plastic box on the desk beside your keyboard. Having trouble visualizing it as a rodent? Think of the cord as its tail, and (if it helps you) draw little eyeballs on the sloping side facing you.

Now then, roll the mouse across the desk (or mouse pad), keeping the cord pointed away from you. See how the arrow pointer moves across the screen? For the rest of your life, you'll hear that pointer called the *cursor*. And now you know that those technically literate teachers are not referring to the kid with the advanced vocabulary when they use this computer term.

Try lifting the mouse off the desk and waving it around in midair like a remote control. Nothing happens, right? The mouse only controls the cursor when it's on a flat surface. (A ball on the bottom of it detects movement and moves the cursor accordingly.) That's a useful feature because it means that you can pick the mouse up when your run out of desk or mouse pad space, but the cursor will stay in place on the screen. Only when you set the mouse down and begin to roll it again will the cursor continue moving.

One day, while working with a group of first graders in the lab, I came upon a sweet little girl who was slowly rolling the mouse up her leg. When I asked why she had the mouse on her leg, she replied, "I needed to get to the bottom part of my picture and I ran out of room. My leg's longer than that mouse pad — and it still works!"

People who use a mouse for the first time sometimes think that they are stuck when they get to the edge of their mouse pad. Simply pick that baby up and move it over.

What's on the menu?

Let's do some real computing here.

1. Move the cursor up to the white strip at the top of the screen and touch the arrow on the word Special.

   This white strip is called the *menu bar*. Pointing to something on the screen in this way has a very technical term: *pointing*. (I told you this would be a piece of cake!)

2. Now put your index finger on the square button on the mouse and press the button down. Hold it down. Don't let go.

   If it all went well, you should see a list of commands drop down from the word Special, as shown in the following figure. Keep holding down the button.

```
Special
Clean Up Desktop
Empty Trash...

Eject Disk        ⌘E
Erase Disk...

Restart
Shut Down
```

Congratulations — you've learned how to *click* the mouse (which is yet another term you can now use in front of those computer-nerd colleagues). You've also learned how to pull down a menu (the list of commands).

3. Try letting go of the mouse button: The menu disappears.

You have only one more mouse skill to master — *drag*. The act of moving the mouse with the button down is called dragging. This movement is useful in the menu bars when you want to make a selection from the menu.

Let's try the act of dragging.

1. Point your mouse at the word Special on the menu bar.

2. Now here comes the tricky part: Click and hold down the mouse button. While you are holding down the mouse button, pull down the menu.

   As you pull down the menu, your options are highlighted.

The only commands that don't get highlighted are the ones that are dimmed, or "grayed out." They're dimmed because they don't make any sense at the moment. For example, if there's no disk in the floppy-disk drive, choosing Eject Disk wouldn't make any sense, so the Mac makes it gray, which means it's unavailable to you.

3. Roll the mouse all the way down to the words Shut Down so that they're highlighted, as shown in the following figure.

4. If you've had enough for one session, release the mouse button — the Mac turns itself off.

If you are ready for more, and you want to slog ahead with this lesson, don't let go of the button yet. Instead, slide the cursor off the menu in any direction and *then* let go of the mouse button. The menu snaps back up like a window shade, and nothing happens. (You invoke a menu command only when you release the mouse while the cursor is *on* a command.)

The mouse practice program

If you are a true teacher, you know the benefits of observation. So do the folks at Apple, and they've provided computer owners with a guided tour to help you better understand your machine.

Stop now and find the Macintosh Basics disk that came with your computer (or the Mouse Practice program that came with your Performa or Powerbook). *It may have come pre-installed on your Mac, in which case you'll see it on your hard drive.*

The Macintosh Basics disk is a clever, animated introduction to the Mac, and it shows you America's favorite computer skills (the ones you just learned): pointing, clicking, and dragging.

Because the Macintosh Basics disk does such a good job of teaching you the basics of Macintosh, I won't bother rehashing them further. So, if you don't have this program on your hard disk, I'll just show you how you use the Macintosh Basics disk:

1. Turn on your Mac, if you haven't already done so.

2. Insert the Macintosh Basics disk into the floppy disk drive (metal side first, label side up).

   When the disk is about 90 percent of the way in, the Mac grabs it and slurps it inside.

3. Open the Macintosh Basics (or Mouse Practice) folder, if necessary, by pointing to it and quickly clicking the mouse button twice.

4. Point to the little Macintosh Basics man (or Mouse Practice Woman) and double-click *that*.

From there, just follow the instructions on the screen. Turn down the corner of this page, and you can pick up here when you're ready to go on.

The Desktop: a.k.a. the Finder!

I don't know about your desk, but I certainly couldn't interchange the word Finder with my desktop. It's impossible to find anything on top of that piece of furniture. As a matter of fact, I'm not sure if I should call it a desk at all — I never sit behind it and work, because I never have the time!

Powerbook mouse buttons

If your Mac is a laptop Mac, you're probably halfway to the bookstore to return this book. Yes, it's true; your computer doesn't have a mouse. Instead, it has a *trackball* (which is essentially an upside-down mouse) or a *trackpad*. The principle is the same: Roll the ball away from you, and the cursor moves up the screen. Instead of a square mouse button, you have two crescent-shaped buttons nestled against the ball or pad. (If you've got two buttons, they're identical in function.)

I won't mention this distinction again, because if you're smart enough to have bought a Powerbook, you're smart enough to translate future references to the mouse into trackball terms.

Other than the fact that there's a Trash can, nobody's really sure why they call this "home base" screen the *desktop* — or the *Finder*. Move the mouse to the File menu and hold the button down. See the word Find? (If not, read the sidebar "All systems are go.")

This command instantly roots through all your stuff and locates any file you ask for. Thus the name: the Finder. Used in a sentence, you might hear it like this: "Well, no wonder you don't see the Trash can. You're not in the Finder!"

Moving Things Around on the Desktop

So now you've mastered the mouse! Take a look at the Mac screen. (Once again, if you see what look like two file folders, ask someone in your school to disable *At Ease*.) You've already encountered menus (those words File, Edit, View, and so on, at the top of the screen).

Near the upper-right corner of the screen, you should see an *icon* (a small symbolic picture). Icons represent everything in the Mac world, and they all look different: One represents a letter you wrote, another represents the Trash can, another represents a floppy disk you've inserted. Here are some examples:

You can move an icon by dragging it.

1. Point to the Trash icon.

2. Drag it to a new position. (Move the mouse while the button's down.)

Hey, this isn't so technical after all!

All systems are go

You know how your reading series comes out with a new version every few years? Well, Apple does the same thing: It keeps making minor changes to its computers, trying to make them better (and providing more incentive to buy them).

You've already encountered the System folder, which holds software the Mac needs for itself. The trouble is, in 1991 Apple came out with a newer version of this software, called System 7. (It replaces the older version, which, with great originality, was called System 6.)

System 7 has lots of terrific features, especially for the beginning Mac user. Every Mac sold since early 1991 is equipped with System 7.

If you bought your Mac used, or if you bought it some time ago and you're only now starting to learn it, then you might have System 6. It's easy to tell which System you have: Look in the upper-right corner of the screen. Do you see the little computer icon? If so, you have System 7. If not, you have System 6.

In general, I'm going to assume that you're using System 7 (or 7.01 or 7.1 or 7-point-anything). I'll try not to leave System 6 users in the lurch, though.

For now, if you don't see the Find command in the File menu, you should see its System 6 equivalent, Find File, under the Apple menu, which is marked by the Apple logo at the left side of the menu bar. It serves the same purpose as System 7's Find command.

Icons, Windows, and Macintosh Syntax

Point to the hard-disk icon (a rectangular box) in the upper-right corner of the screen. A hard disk is like a massive floppy disk. It's the filing cabinet that contains all your work, all your files, and all your software.

So how do you see what's in it? Where do you get to see its table of contents?

It turns out that any disk icon can be opened into a *window,* where you'll see every item inside listed individually. The window has the same name as the icon you opened. (It may already be open. If there's a window open on your screen, choose Close from the File menu. Choose Close again and again until no windows are open on your screen.)

Before we proceed, though, it's time for a lesson in Macintosh syntax. No, don't moan; it's nothing like English syntax. In fact, everything you do on the Macintosh has this format: Noun-Verb. Not much poetic nuance, but it's sure easy to remember.

Let's try a noun-verb command, shall we?

1. Click the hard-disk icon in the upper-right corner of the screen.

   It should turn black, indicating that it's *selected.* Good job — you've just identified the *noun.*

2. Move to the File menu and choose Open.

You guessed it! Open is the *verb.* And sure enough, your hard disk *opens* into a window, where you can see its contents.

Did any of that make sense? In the world of Macintosh, you always specify *what* you want to change (using the mouse), and then you use a menu command to specify *how* you want it changed. You'll see this pattern over and over again: *Select* something on the screen and then *apply* a menu command to it.

Look over the contents of your hard-drive window. See the following figure. (Everybody's got different stuff, so what you see on your screen won't exactly match these illustrations.) You can do all kinds of neat things to a window. They're worth learning because you're going to run into windows everywhere once you start working.

CLOSE BOX - Click here to close the
window. It's the same as choosing
Close from the File menu.

TITLE BAR - Drag anywhere in this
striped area to move the entire window.

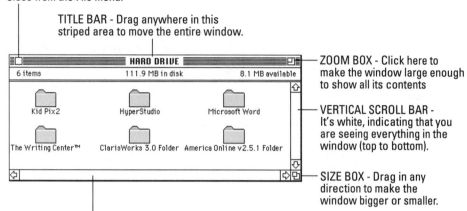

ZOOM BOX - Click here to
make the window large enough
to show all its contents

VERTICAL SCROLL BAR -
It's white, indicating that you
are seeing everything in the
window (top to bottom).

SIZE BOX - Drag in any
direction to make the
window bigger or smaller.

HORIZONTAL SCROLL BAR - It's white, indicating that you're seeing
everything in the window (left to right). If there were something off to
either side, the bar would be gray. Then you would click the arrows to
adjust your view, or use the sliding square.

Go ahead and try some of the little boxes and scroll bars. Click them. Tug on
them. Open the window and close it again. No matter what you do, *you can
never hurt the machine by doing "the wrong thing."* That's the wonderful thing
about the Macintosh: It's the Nerf appliance.

Now try this. Make sure your hard drive window is open. See the System folder?
Even if you don't, here's a quick way to find it: Quickly type **SY** on your keyboard.

Presto: The Mac finds the System folder (which happens to be the first thing
that begins with those letters) and highlights it, in effect dropping it in front of
you, wagging its tail. (If not, absorb the wisdom in the sidebar "Those keyboard
shortcuts didn't work?")

Try pressing the arrow keys on your keyboard: right, left, up, down. The Mac
highlights neighboring icons as you do so.

Take a look at what's in the System folder. Of course, using your newfound noun-verb method, you could (1) click the System folder to select it and then (2) choose Open from the File menu.

But that's the sissy way. Try this power shortcut: Point to the System folder icon so that the tip of the arrow cursor is squarely inside the picture of the folder. Keeping the mouse still, click twice in rapid succession.

If all went well, your *double-click* succeeded in opening a new window, showing you the contents of the System folder. (If it didn't work, you probably need to keep the mouse still or double-click faster.)

Remember this juicy golden rule: *Double-clicking* an icon is the same as opening it. The precious moments and treasured calories you save by using this short-cut will add up rapidly.

Using Multiple Windows and Multiple Views

Multiple windows and a great view add value to any home. The same is true with your Mac. However, unlike your beautiful new home, the Mac allows you to alter your view to best suit your needs. (If only I could alter the view of my neighbors' garage and unkempt yard as easily!)

Those keyboard shortcuts didn't work?

If typing letters of an icon name doesn't seem to do anything, it's because you're using System 6. This is a System 7 feature. So is selecting icons using the arrow keys.

I feel at this point that I should tell those of you still operating with System 6 that's it time to spend a little money and upgrade your system software.

It's virtually impossible to purchase new software to run on your Mac if it isn't equipped with at least System 7 or higher. So go tell your administrative types that you need to spend a little more of their money to join the rest of us who are living in the 90s.

Multiple windows

Right now, you should have *two* windows open on the screen: the hard-drive window and the System-folder window. (The System-folder window may be covering the first one up; they're like overlapping pieces of paper on a desk.)

1. Click the title bar of the System-folder window and drag it downward until you see the hard-drive window behind it. See the following figure.

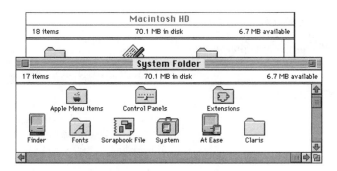

2. Take a stress-free moment to experiment with these two windows: Click the back one to bring it forward and then click the one that *was* in front to bring it to the front again.

If you need any more help fooling around with these windows, the Macintosh manual has a complete tutorial.

Multiple views

There's one more aspect of windows that will probably make the type A personalities squirm with delight. Up until now, you've been viewing the contents of your disk as a bunch of icons. Nice, but wouldn't it be neat to see things alphabetically?

1. Make sure the System folder is the active window (the one in front).

   We're going to use the System folder because it's got a lot of stuff in it. Remember how to choose a command from the menu?

2. Locate the View menu at the top of the screen. From it, choose by Name. (That's *by,* with a lowercase *b.*)

   Suddenly, the big icons are replaced by a neat alphabetical list of the window's contents.

For would-be weenies only (non-essential info)

When you view a window's contents in a list, each folder *within* the window is marked by a tiny triangle. The triangle points to the right.

You can open one of these folders-within-the-folder in the usual way, if you wish — by double-clicking. But it's much more satisfying for neat freaks to click the *triangle* instead. In the following figure, the before-and-after view of the Control Panels folder (inside the System folder) shows how much more organized you can be.

When you click the triangle, in other words, your window becomes like an outline. The contents of that subfolder are indented. To *collapse*, or close the folder, click the downward-pointing triangle.

One more trick: See the words Size and Kind (at the top of the window)? Click either of these words. Instantly, the Mac re-sorts everything in the window, based on the word you clicked. Example: Click Size, and you'll see the largest files first.

Top Ten Differences between Your Mac and Your Students

1. Your Mac never plays in the bathroom.

2. Your Mac always remembers what you told it the day before.

3. Your Mac doesn't have parents to make your life *interesting*.

4. Your Mac doesn't ask about recess every five minutes.

5. Your Mac never has excuses; it always finishes its work on time.

6. Your Mac gets along well with others.

7. Your Mac never loses its work.

8. Your Mac has never heard of *Power Rangers* or *Beverly Hills 90210*.

9. Your Mac follows directions.

10. Your Mac always speaks to you politely.

Chapter 2
High-Tech in Teacher Terms

*W*arning: The text you are about to read is not a reflection of me or my personality. My editor made me include this information. I had to do it!

Feel Free to Skip This Chapter

When was the last time someone told you that? I look at this chapter in the same way I do the endless stream of memos that are sent from the district office; it's worth scanning now, but it isn't crucial in your development as a computer aficionado. Later, you may want to come back and read it on a more detailed level — and by then it will all make more sense.

I must also apologize ahead of time because I promised you that I would only include the *essential* stuff. This information isn't essential, but it is worth knowing at some point. And it will allow you to converse at a much higher level with the other techno-wizards at your school.

Storing Things with Floppy Disks

Human beings, for the most part, store information in one of two places. Either we retain something in our memory, or, if it's too much to remember, we write it down on an envelope that gets lost between school and home.

Computers work pretty much the same way as humans (except they don't have a supply of envelopes). They can either store what they know in their relatively pea-brained *memory*, which I'll cover in a moment, or they can write it down. A computer writes stuff down on disks.

The most common kind of disk is the *floppy disk*. Don't ask me why they still refer to these as "floppy." In truth, these disks are quite rigid. Those of you who were around during Apple's IIe days know all about the large 5 ¼-inch floppies that truly were "floppy" and easy to bend or damage. The disks I'm referring to here are only 3 ½ inches and made of hard plastic.

Inside the protective hard shell, is a circle of the same shiny brown stuff that tapes are made out of. Instead of recording a Public Television special to share with your class at a later date, the computer records your documents: a letter to the superintendent, your class grades, or your first novel.

Floppy disks come in several capacities, but even the largest one holds only about 1,000 pages' worth of data. That may seem like a lot, but that's just text. Pictures, for instance, take up much more space; that same floppy disk can probably only hold one or two color pictures. You can see that floppies aren't very handy for storing lots of information.

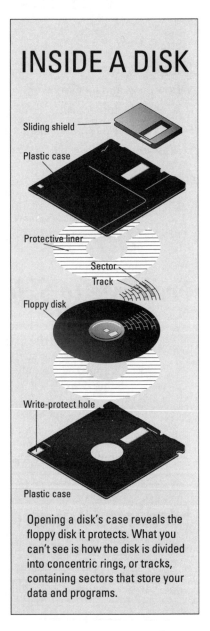

INSIDE A DISK

Sliding shield

Plastic case

Protective liner

Sector

Track

Floppy disk

Write-protect hole

Plastic case

Opening a disk's case reveals the floppy disk it protects. What you can't see is how the disk is divided into concentric rings, or tracks, containing sectors that store your data and programs.

The Hard Disk

Nearly every Mac has an even better storage device built inside it: a *hard disk.* The concept of a hard disk confuses people because it's hidden inside the Mac's case. Since you can't see it or touch it, it's sort of conceptual — like beta-carotene or retirement accounts, I guess. But it's there, and a hefty chunk of you Mac's purchase price pays for it.

Hard disks differ from floppy disks in a few critical ways. A hard disk delivers information to the computer's brain about ten times faster than a floppy and costs about 500 times as much as a floppy. (Floppies are dirt cheap.)

Why all this talk of disks? Because this is where your life's work is going to live when the computer is shut off.

Don't be confused if you hear (or see) the words *hard drive* and *hard disk* used interchangeably — they're the same beast.

Memory

Those of you who don't have children are probably a great deal smarter than the rest of us. Enjoy the ability you now possess to complete a task or a thought without interruption. Being able to remember where you last laid your keys or to remember the last paragraph you read is a privilege that seems to disappear when you enter the world of parenting.

Students have remarkable memories. However, their memories seem to be more selective. How is it that they remember to put snack money in their pockets each morning yet forget their homework?

The Mac's memory is powerful, but when it is turned off at night, it forgets everything. It becomes a dumb, metal-and-plastic doorstop. That's because a computer's memory, just like yours, is kept alive by electrical impulses. When you turn off a Mac, the electricity stops. (Fortunately, few things can turn off a person, except possibly nosepicking — a common classroom occurrence — which fortunately has no long-term effect on our memories.)

Therefore, each time you turn on a Mac, it has to re-learn everything it ever knew, including the fact that it's a computer, what kind of computer it is, how to display text, and so on. It's like the first day of school when the kids seem to have forgotten everything over the summer.

When you turn on the Mac, there's a whirring and blinking; the hard disk inside begins spinning. When it hits about 3,600 rpm, the Mac starts reading the hard disk (or, if the analogy helps you, it "plays" the disk like a record player). It finds out : "Hey, I'm a Mac! And this is how I display text!" and so on. It's reading the hard-disk and copying everything it reads into memory. (If only students could re-learn their information as quickly as the Mac!) Without the hard disk, the Mac is like someone with a completely hollow skull — and we've all met that type.

Your Mac's memory doesn't hold as much as your hard disk: the hard-disk is used for long-term permanent storage of lots of things, and memory is used for temporary storage while you work on one thing at a time.

Who's Meg?

You often hear computer jocks talk about megs. Trust me — they're almost certainly not discussing Meg Ryan or Meg Tilly. Meg is short for *megabyte*.

What is highly confusing for most beginners — and it took me forever to keep straight — is that memory (fast, expensive, temporary) and hard-disk space (permanent, slower) are measured in the same units: megabytes. A typical Mac has between two and eight megs of memory (silicon chips), but between 80 and 500 (or even more!) megs of hard-disk space (spinning platters).

Sinking in the sea o'terminology

OK, here's your life preserver. Hold on and read. If you're like me, you'll end up coming back to this passage a number of times before it's all completely straight in your head.

Megabyte: A unit of memory or storage capacity, nicknamed *meg* or abbreviated MB. One meg equals 1,024 kilobytes, or K; a K is about the equivalent of one page from that oh-so-exciting history textbook.

What is RAM?

I'll make this very simple: RAM is memory (Random Access Memory).

Putting It All Together

OK. Now that you know where a computer's information lives, let me take you on a tour of the computer's guts. If we were going on a school field trip, you'd be getting on the comfortable yellow bus at this point, and I'd be telling you to keep your hands inside the window at all times.

When you turn on the Mac, the hard disk spins, and the Mac copies certain critical information into its memory.

So far, the Mac only knows that it's a computer. It doesn't know anything else that's stored on your hard disk; it doesn't know about the grades from your second-period English class or the children's book you've been writing — yet.

To get to any of this work, you need to transfer this information from your hard disk into memory. In simple terms, you have to open the file. (Remember double-clicking from Chapter 1?) Once opened, the file is in memory and ready for you to manipulate to your heart's content.

You can enter grades and average them, delete sentences from your book, or type a letter to a worried parent. Remember, you are making all these changes while the document is in memory. If your three-year-old daughter comes in demanding attention and accidentally pulls the plug on your computer, the screen will go blank and the changes you've made will disappear forever. You are left with only the original copy that was on your hard disk.

The message here is SAVE, SAVE, SAVE!

Saving is a very simple process that every Mac program comes equipped to offer. Most people use this command every five or ten minutes so that their work is always up-to-date and preserved on the disk. You can save your work to your hard disk or floppy disk. It is also important to make backups (on floppies) of everything on your hard disk in the event that you will someday experience the inevitable hard-drive crash. (You learn how to use this save command in Chapter 3.)

Differences between Memory and a Hard Disk

1. You usually buy memory two or four megabytes at a time. Hard disks usually come in 160-, 250-, and 500-meg sizes (and on up).

2. Memory comes on chips — little brown mini-circuit boards. A hard disk is a big box made of metal (and sometimes housed in plastic).

3. You can only install memory inside the computer (something you usually hire a local guru to do). A hard disk may be either inside the Mac (an internal hard drive) or a separate box you just plug into the back (an external hard drive).

4. Memory delivers information to the Mac's brain almost instantly. The hard disk sometimes seems to take forever.

5. Memory is sometimes referred to as RAM. A hard disk has no abbreviation.

6. Not every Mac has a hard disk (some people still use very old models with nothing but floppy disks). But every Mac has memory.

7. When the Mac is reading some information off the hard disk, a little light flickers on and off (usually on the front of your Mac or on the case of an external hard disk). You can't tell when the Mac is getting information from RAM.

8. As a very general rule, RAM costs about $35 per megabyte, and hard-drive space averages about $2 per meg.

9. Memory's contents disappear when you turn off the computer. A disk's contents stay there until you deliberately throw them away.

Ready for Action

Enough chalk talk. Let's take ourselves out of the classroom and have some fun!

Hop on the bus, boys and girls. We're going on an interactive field trip of sorts. In the next chapter you are going to put your fingers to the keyboard, move your mouse, and manipulate your computer environment.

Chapter 3

Doing Windows and Getting Floppy (Not Sloppy)

● ●

In This Chapter

▶ All about folders, windows, and icons

▶ Learning keyboard shortcuts

▶ Taking out the trash

▶ Working with floppy disks

▶ Top Ten Disk and Window Tips

● ●

*M*anipulative. Now here's a word we've never heard! Let's see. We use manipulatives in math, and the kid in the third row uses his manipulative behavior to annoy me — and, oh yes, my own children can be very manipulative when playing my husband and me against each other.

This type of manipulative behavior is quite different from that manipulative stuff you learned for the computer, however. I'm now going to show you how all the clicking and dragging you've been doing is, in fact, leading up to something useful.

Foldermania

It has been said that your hard disk is like the world's largest filing cabinet. It's where you store all your stuff. But a filing cabinet without filing folders would be about as convenient to handle as a kindergartner without a *potty pass*.

The *folders* on the Mac screen don't occupy any space on your hard drive. They're electronic fictions whose sole purpose is to help you organize your stuff. The Mac provides an infinite supply of them. Want a folder? Do this: From the File menu, choose New Folder.

File	
New Folder	⌘N
Open	⌘O
Print	⌘P
Close Window	⌘W
Get Info	⌘I
Sharing...	
Duplicate	⌘D
Make Alias	
Put Away	⌘Y
Find...	⌘F
Find Again	⌘G
Page Setup...	
Print Desktop...	
Go To At Ease	

Ooh, tricky, this machine, eh? A new folder appears. Note that the Mac gracefully proposes *untitled folder* as its name. (Kinda like when you get a new student in your class and for weeks you say things such as "my *new student* is really doing well.")

Notice something else, though? The name is highlighted in black. Remember our earlier lesson? Highlighted = selected = ready for you to do something. When text is highlighted, the Mac is ready for you to replace it with anything that you type. In other words, you don't even have to backspace over it. Just type away.

1. Type *Third Grade*. Press the Return key.

    The return key tells the Mac that your naming spurt is over.

    Now, to see how folders work, create another one.

2. Choose New Folder from the File menu again.

    Another new folder appears, once more waiting for a title.

3. Type *Class List*. Press Return.

You are going to create one more empty folder. But by this time, your wrist is probably weary from the from trek back and forth to the File menu. Don't you wish there were a faster way to make a folder?

There is.

Keyboard Shortcuts

Pull down the File menu, but don't select any of the commands in it yet. See the weird notation to the right of some of the commands?

File	
New Folder	⌘N
Open	⌘O
Print	⌘P
Close Window	⌘W
Get Info	⌘I
Sharing...	
Duplicate	⌘D
Make Alias	
Put Away	⌘Y
Find...	⌘F
Find Again	⌘G

Get used to them. They're *keyboard shortcuts,* and they appear in almost every menu you'll ever see. You're by no means obligated to use them, but you should understand that they let you select certain menu items without using the mouse.

When you type, you press the Shift key to make a capital letter, right? They call the Shift key a *modifier key* because it turns ordinary, well-behaved citizen keys like 3 and 4 into wild symbols like # and $. Welcome to the world of computers, where everything is much more complicated. Instead of having only one modifier key, the Mac has three of them!

Unimportant info regarding other menu symbols

Besides the little keyboard-shortcut symbols at the right side of a menu, you'll occasionally run into a little downward-pointing arrow or a sideways-pointing arrow, like these:

What these arrows are telling you is that the menu is so long, it doesn't even fit on the screen. The arrow is implying that there are still more commands in the menu that you're not seeing. To get to them, carefully roll the pointer along the menu all the way to that downward- or sideways-pointing arrow. Don't let it scare you: The menu commands will jump upward, bringing the hidden ones into view.

Look down next to your spacebar. There they are: In addition to the Shift key, one says Option, one says Control, and another either says Command or has a little ⌘ symbol on it. It's that little cloverleaf symbol that appears in the File menu. Next to the New Folder command, it's ⌘-N. That means:

1. While pressing the ⌘ key down, press the N key.

   Bam! You've got yourself another folder.

2. Type *2nd Quarter Grades* and press Return.

   You've just named your third folder. So why have you been wasting a perfectly good afternoon (or whatever part of the day it is in your time zone) making empty folders? So that you can pretend you're getting organized.

3. Drag the Class List folder on top of the Third Grade Folder.

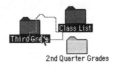

Make sure that the tip of the arrow actually hits the center of the Third Grade folder so that the folder becomes highlighted. When it turns black, let go of the Class List folder — and watch it disappear into the Third Grade folder. (If your aim wasn't good, you'll now see the Class List folder sitting next to the Third Grade folder; try the last step again.)

4. Put the 2nd Quarter Grades folder into the Third Grade folder in the same way — by dragging it on top of the Third Grade folder.

5. Double-click the Third Grade Folder.

   Yep. Opens right up into a window, and there are your two darling folders nestled sweetly where they belong. If you were to double-click one of them you'd open another window.

   OK, so how do you get them out again? Do you have to drag them individually? That would certainly be a bummer if you had 50 folders in the Third Grade Folder.

   It turns out there are several ways to select more than one icon at a time.

6. Click above and to the left of the Class List folder. Without releasing the mouse button, drag down and to the right so that you enclose both folders with a dotted rectangle.

   If you are using System 7, then each icon turns black as the dotted rectangle encloses it. (Otherwise, nothing turns black until you release the mouse button.) In any case, release the mouse button when you've got both icons enclosed.

   Now that you have several folders selected, you can move them *en masse* to another location.

This was a somewhat unproductive exercise, of course, because we were working with empty folders. It gets much more exciting when you start working with your own documents. All these techniques work equally well with folders and with documents.

Taking out the Trash

There's one more icon-manipulation trick you'll probably find valuable.

1. Close the Third Grade folder by clicking its *close box.*

   The close box is that little box in the upper left-hand corner of the window, by the way. (You could also go to the File menu and choose Close Window, but why make it harder?)

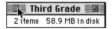

2. Drag the folder on top of the Trash can in the lower-right corner of the screen.

Don't let go until the Trash can actually turns black (when the tip of the arrow cursor is upon it). When you do let go, notice how the Trash can bulges, a subtle reinforcement of how important it thinks it is. (I've experienced students with this same posture just before they utter answers that are completely off-base.) Anyway, this is how you throw things out on the Mac: Just drag them on top of the Trash can.

If you need to rescue something, just double-click the Trash to open its window; drag whatever-it-was right back onto the screen.

So if putting something into the Trash doesn't really delete it, how do you delete it? Choose Empty Trash from the Special menu.

Note: If you are using System 6, then the Trash can doesn't sit there, bulging, until you Empty Trash. It gets emptied automatically when you turn off the Mac, and sometimes sooner.

Having Fun with Floppies

For our next trick, you're going to need a floppy disk. If you didn't buy a box of blank disks with your Mac, you're going to need some eventually. If you don't have a blank disk handy, you can use one of the white System disks that came with your Mac.

1. Put the disk into the disk-drive slot.

The Mac gulps it in with a satisfying *kachunk*. If it's a brand new disk, you'll see the following message:

> This disk is unreadable by this Macintosh. Do you want to initialize the disk?
>
> Name: [untitled]
>
> Format: [Macintosh 1.4 MB ▼]
>
> [Eject] [Initialize]

Go ahead. Click Initialize. (If you're asked whether you want to make it single-sided or double-sided, select double-sided — unless you're going to be sending this disk to someone who bought a Mac in 1984 and immediately moved to Borneo.) You're then asked to name the disk: type a name, click OK, and then wait about 45 seconds while the Mac prepares the disk for its new life as your data receptacle.

If it's *not* a new disk — for example, if you're using one of the disks that came with your Mac — the floppy-disk icon shows up on the right side, just beneath your hard-disk icon.

To see what's on the disk, double-click the icon. As you've no doubt tired of hearing repeated, a double-click on a disk icon opens its contents window.

This is important stuff: In your lifetime, you'll do a lot of copying from floppy disks *to* your hard drive (such as when you buy a program and want to put a copy of it on your hard drive.) If you are smart, you'll also do a lot of copying onto floppies from your hard drive (such as when you make a backup copy of all your work, in preparation for the inevitable day when something will go wrong with your hard disk).

2. Double-click your hard-disk icon.

   If its window was closed, it now opens. If the window was open but hidden behind the floppy-disk window, the hard-disk window comes to the front.

3. Drag the Class List folder on top of the floppy-disk icon.

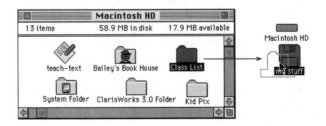

If you already trashed your Class List folder, no big deal. Choose New Folder from the File menu (or press ⌘-N) to create a new folder. Drag that instead.

The point is that, on a Macintosh, making a copy of something is as easy as dragging it to the disk you want it copied onto. You can also drag it into the disk's window (if it's open) instead of onto its icon.

Copying something *from* floppy *to* your hard disk is equally easy. Open the floppy-disk window (by double-clicking the floppy-disk icon). Then drag whatever icons you want onto the hard-disk icon (or onto the hard-disk window).

For example, in the following illustration, two files are being copied from a floppy disk — not just into the hard-disk window, but into a *specific folder* on the hard disk:

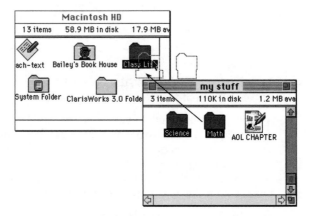

OK. So you've made a copy of your third quarter math grades, or you've just copied this week's lesson plans onto your hard disk. Now what? How do you get the disk out?

Well you wouldn't be alone in guessing that you use the Eject Disk command in the Special menu. But you'd be sort of wrong. The Eject Disk command does spit out the disk — but it leaves the disk's icon on the screen so that the Mac thinks it's still available. The minute you try to go on with your work, the Mac will start displaying messages demanding that you give the disk back to it.

A much better way to get rid of the disk is to select it (noun) and choose Put Away (verb) from the File menu. That makes the disk pop out, *and* its image disappears from the screen.

Top Ten Window, Disk, and Trash Tips

"I don't do windows," you say? After reading the following tips, you'll find windows so easy to do that you may even consider cleaning the Venetian blinds.

1. To rename an icon or disk, click carefully on its name. Wait for a second or so, until a rectangle appears around the name. That's your cue to type away, giving it a new name. Press Return when you're done.

   It works a little differently in System 6. Just click an icon and start typing. No rectangle, no waiting.

2. If you're looking at a windowful of file icons, you can select one by typing the first couple of letters of its name.

3. Don't forget that you can look at a window's contents in a neat list (choose "by Name" from the View menu). Once in a list view, when a folder is highlighted, you can press ⌘-→ to expand it (as though you'd clicked the triangle to view its contents) and ⌘-← to collapse it again.

4. In System 7, every time you choose Empty Trash from the Special menu, the Mac asks you if you're absolutely sure. If you'd prefer it to simply vaporize the Trash contents without asking, select the Trash icon. Choose Get Info from the File menu and click the "Warn before emptying" checkbox so that the X disappears.

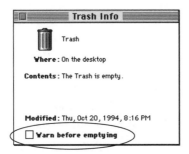

5. If you're trying to make a copy of a floppy disk, and you have only one floppy-disk drive, you'll find that the Mac can only copy a little bit at a time. It winds up asking you to insert one disk, then the other; one disk, then the other . . . until your wrists are swollen and bleeding.

A better, faster idea: Copy the entire disk to your *hard disk,* eject the floppy, insert the blank floppy, and then copy the stuff from the hard disk to the new floppy. Using the hard disk as an intermediate holding tank in this way eliminates the disk swapping. (Just trash the superfluous copy from your hard disk when it's all over.)

6. If you have a very important document, you can prevent it from getting thrown away by accident. Click its icon. Choose Get Info from the File menu. Select the Locked checkbox. Now, even if you put it in the Trash and try to empty the Trash, the Mac will simply tell you that there's a locked item in the Trash, which it won't get rid of.

7. You already know how to copy a file from one disk to another. You can copy it on the *same* disk, too. Click the icon and choose Duplicate from the File menu.

   Or, while pressing the Option key, drag the icon onto a new window or folder.

8. Isn't it frustrating to open a window that's too small to show you all of its contents?

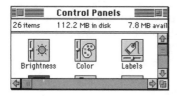

Of course, you could spend a weekend fussing with the scroll bars, trying to crank the other icons into view. Or, using error-and-trial, you could drag the lower-right handle (the resize box) to make the window bigger.

There's a much quicker solution. Click the *zoom box* in the upper-right corner of the window. The Mac automatically makes the window *exactly* large enough to show all of the icons.

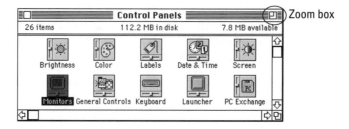

9. You don't have to be content to leave the Trash stranded way down there at the bottom of your screen. You can move it anywhere you want, just by dragging it. That's especially handy if you're lucky enough to have one of those screens the size of a Cineplex Odeon and don't feel like packing a week's worth of supplies every time you want to make a Journey to the Trash Corner.

10. You don't have to eject disks and clean up your windows before you shut down the computer. The disks pop out automatically, and the windows will be right where you left them the next time you turn on the Mac.

Chapter 4

Getting Some Work Done

● ●

In This Chapter

▶ What software is for those who care

▶ Tips on purchasing software

▶ Using the desk accessories

▶ Selecting, copying, and pasting text

▶ Using the application menu

● ●

*U*nless you actually bought (or received) some software when you got your Mac, you won't be able to do much more than admire the Mac's contribution to your decor. So, unless you purchased a Performa (a model that comes loaded with software) or you are using the computer in your school (which, I hope, is loaded with some great programs already), get ready for a spending spree.

Of course, every Mac comes with some software. For example, each Mac comes with the System software (those white floppy disks) that it needs for its own internal use. It also comes with some mini-programs, like the Calculator and the Note Pad, called *desk accessories*. But the rest is up to you.

Buying Software

It's time to spend some more money. Software, for the most part, is expensive. For example, the world's most popular Mac word-processing program is *Microsoft Word,* and the lowest price I've seen for it is $280. (However, in Chapter 13, I'll introduce you to some really great deals that are available only for educators.)

If you are on a budget (what teacher isn't?) and don't much care about being in the vanguard, you can get a lot of power in the form of an integrated program like *ClarisWorks* or any other program whose name ends with 'Works.

ClarisWorks is number one in the educational market; most school systems can enter into bulk purchase plans with Claris to help make the program even more affordable. *ClarisWorks* is my personal recommendation for any teacher, and Part II of this book will give you ideas on how to use this multi-purpose program.

Where to get software

You can buy software two ways: at a store and via mail order. Software stores give you a better dose of reality which is something we can all use: You get to pick up and heft the actual box, tap a live human being on the shoulder to ask questions, ask other customers what they've had luck with, and so on. In some stores you can even try out the software on a real Mac, so you won't wind up buying something you don't need. As in the computer-hardware world, a good software dealer is an excellent resource.

Mail-order companies have different kinds of advantages: Many of them take returns even after you've opened the box; many of the companies offer huge discounts to educators; they don't charge sales tax; and so on. And, of course, you don't have to fire up the minivan — you get your order the next day (the overnight shipping charge is usually $3 per order). I admit that I love getting my order the very next day; MacWarehouse and I have a very good relationship.

See Chapter 23, "Great Deals and Great Reads," for information on vendors.

What to buy

Software companies quickly discovered the magic behind slick packaging and major marketing campaigns. Don't be fooled. In the beginning of my computer pursuits, I wasted many a dollar on the software found within flashy ads and brochures. Experience has since taught me to trust my colleagues.

Computer magazines are second on my list of resources — *Mac Home Journal, Family PC, Macworld,* and *MacUser* are all very reliable.

Schools systems, along with the teachers within these venerable institutions, are strapped for money. Big news, right? Therefore, getting the most for your money is important. When I say the most, I mean in the form of quality, rather than quantity. A school full of poor, unused software is worth nothing in comparison to a school that owns one or two great pieces of software used by all the students regularly.

How to buy

In the school setting, you have many options for purchasing software: single copy, lab pack, site license, or a bulk-purchase agreement.

- ✔ **single copy** — You get one copy; you may use it on only one computer.

- ✔ **lab pack** — The size of these packages is based on the software company (from 5-15 copies).

- ✔ **site license** — This license allows the user to load the software on a large number of computers (20-50) specified by the software company. (Most site licenses used to be unlimited, but this has changed in recent years.)

- ✔ **bulk-purchase agreements** — Many large school systems enter into agreements with major software companies to provide their schools with software and *really* reduced rates. (My system is able to purchase any Claris product made for $38 per copy.)

You always need to do your math and figure out the price you'll be paying per copy of the software. Some of the multiple-unit packages are a great deal — others aren't.

Your very first software

Several menus appear across the top of the screen. Remember these? As you get to know the Mac, you'll discover that their wording changes from program to program. Right now, they say File, Edit, View, Label, and Special; in a word processor, they might say File, Edit, Font, Size, and Format. The menu names (and commands listed in those menus) are tailored to the function of the software.

Software pirates

Remembering that software is a copyrighted item is very important. When you purchase a software program, you are only allowed to use that software on one computer (or the specified number of computers if you've purchased a lab pack or site license). You can't share your program with a friend or load it on your computer at home — that's illegal. Software piracy is a huge problem today. Register your software purchases and honor the terms of your registration agreement.

One menu is *always* on your screen, though: the Apple menu, which is the at the left edge of the menu bar. Among other things, this menu provides immediate access to some useful mini-programs known as desk accessories. *Desk accessories* are sure-fire, non-threatening, and fun — perfect for your first baby steps into the world of using software.

Desk Accessories

Let's start with something simple. Move your cursor up to the Apple menu () and choose Calculator. The Calculator pops up in a tiny window of its own.

The Calculator

Using the mouse, you can click the little calculator buttons. The Mac will give you the correct mathematical answer, making you the owner of the world's heaviest and most expensive pocket calculator.

What's neat is that you can also type the keys on your *numeric keypad*, the block of number keys on the right side of your keyboard. As you press these real keys, you can watch the *on-screen* keys in the Calculator window get punched accordingly.

Leave the calculator open on the screen. You may want to click on its title bar and move it to the side.

The Note Pad

Now go back to the menu again. This time choose Note Pad. Instantly, the world's most frill-free word processor appears on the screen.

I like to use the Note Pad while I'm writing; I leave myself reminders of points I want to be sure to include later in the text. Once you open Note Pad, simply access it by going to the Finder icon (upper-right corner) and highlighting its name.

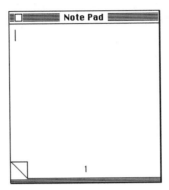

You'll learn more about word processing in the next section. For now, we're just going to do some informative goofing around. With the Note Pad open on your screen, type a math problem like this:

37+8+19*3-100

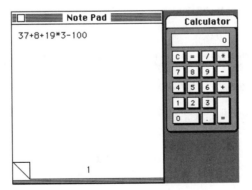

In the computer world, the asterisk * means "times," or multiply. If you make a mistake, press the big Delete key at the upper-right corner of your keyboard. This means "Backspace."

Now, by dragging the Note Pad's title bar, move it so that you can see the Calculator window, too. You're going to use two programs at once, making them cooperate with each other — one of the most remarkable features of the Mac.

Selecting text

This is about to get interesting.

1. Using the mouse, carefully position the pointer at the left side of your equation (top).

2. Press the button and drag to the right (middle). Release the mouse when you've highlighted the entire equation (bottom).

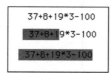

You just selected some text. Remember in Chapter 1 when you selected an icon and then used a menu command? Struggling, as always, to come up with a decent analogy, I likened this *select-then-operate* sequence to building a noun-verb sentence.

Well, it works just as well with text as it does with icons. You've highlighted, or selected, some text — so the Mac now knows what the noun is — what it's supposed to pay attention to. All you have to do is select a verb from one of the menus. And our verb *du jour* is Copy.

The cornerstone of human endeavor: Copy and Paste

Choose Copy from the Edit menu.

The fire alarm sounds, children scream, the building empties . . . and absolutely nothing happens with your computer, as far as you can tell.

Menu refresher

"Choose Copy from the Edit menu." If that sentence stumps you, remember that you place the pointer on the *word* Edit at the top of the screen. Press the mouse button to make the list of commands appear; don't let go. Move the pointer down the list until you reach the word Copy, which becomes highlighted. Release the mouse button. That's how you *choose* a command from a *menu*. And I won't say another word about it.

Behind the scenes, though, something very useful occurred. The Mac looked at the selected equation and memorized it, socking it away into an invisible storage window called the *Clipboard*. (If only children had such an invention on which to store their multiplication facts!) The Clipboard is how you transfer stuff from one window to another, as well as from one program into another. (Some programs even have a Show Clipboard command, in which case I take back the statement about the Clipboard being invisible.)

You can't see the Clipboard at this point. But in a powerful act of faith, you put your trust in me and believe that it contains the highlighted material (the equation).

The Application menu

Do you see the tiny Note Pad icon at the right end of your menu bar? It's next to that question mark thing.

the Application menu

This icon actually represents a menu — the Application menu. It lists all the programs you have running at once: the Note Pad, the Calculator, and the famous Finder (or desktop).

You multitasking maniac! And you thought grading papers during bus call was a difficult combination.

Choose Calculator from the Application menu.

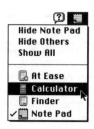

The Calculator window comes to the front, and the icon in the upper right changes to look like a Calculator.

Those of you still awake will, of course, object to using the Application menu to bring the Calculator forward. You remember all too plainly from Chapter 1 that simply clicking in a window brings it to the front, an act that would have required less muscular effort.

Right you are; watch for a bonus in your paycheck. However, learning to use the Application menu was a good exercise. There are going to be many times in your life where the program that's in the front covers up the entire screen. So *then* how will you bring another program forward, big shot? That's right. You won't be able to *see* any other windows, so you won't be able to click something to make it active. You'll have to use the Application menu.

In any case, the Calculator is now the active application (*active* just means it's in front). Now then, do you remember that intricate equation that's still on the Mac Clipboard? Instead of typing an equation into the Calculator by punching keys, let's just *paste* it in.

1. Press the Clear key on your Mac keyboard, or click the C button on the Calculator.

   You just cleared the display. We wouldn't want your previous diddlings to interfere with this tightly-controlled experiment.

2. From the Edit menu, choose Paste. Watch the Calculator!

   If you looked in time, you saw the number keys flashing like Las Vegas at midnight. And with a triumphant beep (sometimes), the Mac displays the answer to your math problem.

Did you get what just happened? You typed out a math problem; a word processor (the Note Pad) copied it to the Clipboard and pasted it into a number-cruncher (the Calculator). Much of the miracle of the Mac stems from its capability to mix and match information among multiple programs in this way.

It's a two-way street, too. You can paste this number back into the word processor.

1. From the Edit menu choose Copy. But wait! Something was already on the Clipboard. Where is the Mac to put this new copied info?

   On the Clipboard, of course. And whatever was there before (your equation) gets nuked. The Clipboard contains exactly one thing at a time — whatever you copied most recently.

2. From the Application menu, choose Note Pad (or just click the Note Pad window).

3. The Note Pad is now the active application. Type this:

   Dear Mrs. Jones: The total cost for the lens your son broke during our visit to the planetarium will be $

   Stop after the $ sign. Move the mouse up to the Edit menu.

4. From the Edit menu, choose Paste.

   Bingo! The Mac pastes in the result from the Calculator (which it had been keeping ready on the Clipboard).

   Incidentally, whatever's on the Clipboard stays there until you copy something new or until you turn off the machine. This means you can paste it over and over again.

5. For a second time, choose Paste from the Edit menu.

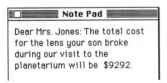

By now, you're probably cradling your wrist, which no doubt aches from all those trips to the menu. Although what you're about to learn is, technically speaking, a *power-user technique*, it will save you all kinds of time and chiropractor bills.

You don't have to use the menu to issue a command like Copy or Paste. If you wish, you can use a keyboard shortcut to do the same thing. You may remember having used the ⌘ key in Chapter 3 to issue commands without using the mouse.

And how are you supposed to remember which letter key corresponds to which command? Well, usually it's mnemonic (great spelling-bee word): ⌘ + P for Print, ⌘ + O for Open, and so on. But you can cheat; try it right now. Pull down the Edit menu, but don't let go of the mouse button.

There's your crib sheet (I've seen a few of those in my days!), carefully listed down the right side of the menu. Note that the keyboard shortcuts for all four of these important commands (Undo, Cut, Copy, Paste) are adjacent on the keyboard: Z X C V.

C is Copy. And V, right next to it, is Paste. Let go of the mouse button and try it.

1. While holding down the ⌘ key, type V.

   Bingo! Another copy of the Clipboard stuff (92) appears on your Note Pad.

   (In the future, I'll just refer to a keyboard shortcut like this as "⌘-V".)

2. Press ⌘-V again.

   Yep, that kid really did some damage when he shot that rubber band across the planetarium. The lens he broke on the telescope will cost $92,929,292 to replace. However, the planetarium has agreed to a 10-percent down payment, with the balance to be paid over the next 50 years. In other words, let's *undo* the last 92 pasting.

3. From the Edit menu, choose Undo.

   The most recent thing you did — in this case, pasting the fourth 92 — gets undone.

I bet this kid wishes there were an Undo key in real life!

Remember, though, that Undo only reverses your most recent action. Suppose you (1) copy something, (2) paste it somewhere else, and then (3) type some more. If you choose Undo, only the typing will be undone (step 3), not the pasting (step 2).

The Apple menu has some other DAs, too. (No, not District Attorneys. Like everything in the Mac world, it's cooler to call something by its initials. DA = desk accessory.) Play around with the other items: the Puzzle, the Alarm Clock, Key Caps, and all that other stuff. (Consult your Macintosh owner's manual for more details — it's not crucial info at this point.)

Control Panels

One item in your Apple menu *isn't* a DA. It says Control Panels, and all it does is open up your Control Panels folder. What exactly is your Control Panels folder? Well, it's a folder that lives inside your System folder containing a bunch of icons, each controlling some aspect of your Mac. Go ahead and choose it from the menu to make this window appear:

Everybody's got a slightly different set of Control Panels, so your screen may look a little different. In any case, I'll show you around one Control Panel, then you can take it from there.

1. Quickly type *GE* on your keyboard.

   Remember this handy trick? You can select one icon in a folder just by typing the first couple of letters of its name. In this case, you get the General Controls window.

2. Double-click on General Controls.

   The General Controls window opens. It looks like . . . well, rather like a control panel. These controls govern the way your Mac works; you can customize your working environment, to a certain extent. (The System 7.5 and Performa controls look slightly different.)

The Desktop Pattern is the shading that fills the background, behind the windows and stuff. You can change the design.

When you type (as in the Note Pad), the Mac marks your place with a blinking *insertion point*. These buttons control how fast it blinks, in the event that the blinking rate has been triggering inconvenient seizures.

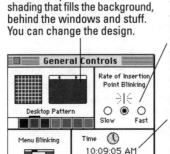

Click a number to change the time. Usually, when you buy a Mac, it's set to California time, so double-check this.

Click "24 hr." if you are a military-type person who wakes up at 0600 hours each morning.

Click a number to change the date.

When you choose a command from a menu (and release the mouse), the command blinks. This setting controls how many times. How did we *live* before we had this?

3. All right. Close the General Controls window by clicking the close box in the upper-left corner; enough fooling around. It's time to get some work done. (If I only had a nickel for every time I've said that.)

Fortunately, *working* on the Mac is almost as much fun as goofing off — and your students will tell you the same thing!

Chapter 5

A Quiet Talk about Printers

In This Chapter

▶ What the different types of printers are and how much they cost

▶ What fonts are and how to load them

▶ How to print

*Y*ou've done all this work, and now it's time to print. I must first tell you that this subject could become *very* deep. If, after reading this chapter, you feel the need for more knowledge on printers and fonts, please get *Macs For Dummies*, 3rd Edition. David Pogue goes into much more detail on the subject. I will try to give you the information you need right now, however. The extra stuff is worth learning about later on, if you're the curious sort.

A Primer on Printers

Printers come in all kinds of configurations and prices. You can spend next to nothing and get a printer whose printouts are so jagged that they look like something scribbled by an angry middle-schooler. Or you can spend a thousand clams or so and get a printer whose printouts look like they were typeset.

The three types of printers I will discuss are:

- ✔ dot-matrix
- ✔ inkjet
- ✔ laser

Dot-matrix: low-cost, low-quality

I'm talking about the Apple ImageWriter II. If you were a teacher during the 80s, your school was probably full of these babies (mine still is). It's called a *dot-matrix* printer because it prints by firing little pins against a ribbon that strikes the paper. The resulting collection of dots forms the letters.

These printers are in many of our schools because they are cheap and they were the first ones available to work with those wonderful Apple IIc and Apple IIe computers — computers that were often our first introduction to the world of computing. If your school has just begun to purchase Macintosh computers, those same printers that are connected to your IIe or IIc machines will work with your new Macs. They will serve you well until your budget has room for upgrades.

The ImageWriter is slowish and so noisy that people regularly buy mufflers for them. The print quality isn't anything to write home about — yet it is a good machine for the school setting. The ImageWriter uses ribbons that are considerably cheaper than ink cartridges (and you can also purchase color ribbons). The ImageWriter uses *pin-fed paper* (attached sheets of paper with little holes running along each side) that you can load and then have fed out of the box. Pin-fed paper keeps you from constantly having to reload paper.

Inkjet: low-cost, high-quality, low-speed

Inkjet printers create a printed image by spraying a mist of ink on the paper.

Yes, Virginia, there *is* a high-quality inkjet printer that won't bleed you dry: the Apple StyleWriter. Its quality almost matches a laser printer's. It's very small, very lightweight, and almost silent. (That's more than I can say for some students.) You can feed all kinds of nonliving things through it: labels, envelopes, tagboard, whatever. And it costs less than $300.

So what's the catch? Well, for people who are used to laser printers, the StyleWriter II's speed — two pages per minute — seems pretty slow. (They shouldn't complain; the original StyleWriter only printed half a page per minute!) Still, the StyleWriter II is so compact, quiet, and inexpensive — and it prints grays so beautifully — that it's hard to resist.

Note, however, that inkjet-printed pages smear if they ever get the least bit damp; the printing isn't laser-crisp if your stationery is even slightly absorbent.

Laser: high-cost, high-quality

If you can afford to pay something like $1,200 for a printer, though, some real magic awaits you: *PostScript laser printers*. Don't worry about the word PostScript for now. Just look for the word PostScript in the printer's description, as if it were some kind of seal of approval.

A PostScript laser printer can print any text, in any style, at any size, at any angle — and everything looks terrific. PostScript laser printers can also print phenomenal-looking graphics, like all the diagrams in Macintosh magazines. They're quick, quiet, and hassle-free. Most can print envelopes, mailing labels, and paper up to legal-size (but not tagboard).

You still have your ImageWriter?

Many schools choose to keep their ImageWriter printers. Strange, you may think? Well, these printers are already in the school, for one thing. And they are very inexpensive to maintain. You can purchase a ribbon for an ImageWriter for about $5 while a cartridge for an inkjet printer will run about $25 — and the toner cartridge for a laser printer will set a school back about $75! (But don't forget that the number of copies — and their quality—will vary according to whatever you choose.)

Keeping an ImageWriter also allows students to print in color for a much lower cost than color printing on the other printers. A color ribbon for an ImageWriter runs about $15. No, the quality isn't as good. But it's better than just settling for black on white.

It's not hard to understand why a school opts for the noisy yet inexpensive ImageWriter. And when photocopies are made from Image-Writer-produced pages, the copies turn out beautifully.

Oh, How I Love Those "Fancy" Letters

If you have a computer-friendly co-worker who has been producing some incredible-looking parent letters or student handouts, you've probably noticed some pretty "fancy" lettering on those documents. To computer nerds, those "fancy" letters are better known as *fonts*. Printers call these letters *typefaces*. OK, so you get the picture — in the world of Apple, different styles of letters are called fonts.

Your computer comes loaded with some basic fonts. Under System 7 those fonts are:

Chicago	Courier	Geneva
Helvetica	Monaco	New York
Palatino	Συμβολ	Times

Fonts are fun

The basic set of fonts that came with your Mac let you accomplish some amazing stuff because you not only can change the size of your letters, you can also change the style and color.

We'll get to the how-to portion later in Chapter 7. Right now I just want you to be aware of the possibilities that await you.

Every word-processing program in use today allows the user the flexibility of choosing a font style and making changes within that style. Notice the different ways I've altered the fonts in the following figure.

Chicago	<u>Chicago</u>	Chicago
Helvetica	Helvetica	<u>**Helvetica**</u>
Palatino	Palatino	*Palatino*

You can also purchase additional fonts from any software vendor. There are literally thousands of different fonts out there — and they are very cheap.

As a teacher, fonts allow you to make what your students or their parents read fun, exciting, and eye-catching. How many of us look twice at those boring memos that are written in standard print? However, a memo like the following one is easy to create and will make someone want to read it simply because of the way it looks.

Parents:
Don't forget about our spring carnival this Saturday. I hope to see you there!
Thanks!
Mrs. Robinette

Parents

Don't forget about our spring carnival this Saturday. I hope to see you there!

Thanks!
Mrs. Robinette

Knowing a little about fonts makes you look at a page in a magazine or an ad in the newspaper in a new way. You start to notice the creativity behind the advertising game and how fonts express different feelings.

Too cool!

Signature Software will create a font based on your own handwriting. The company sends you a special form to fill out (see the insert in the back of this book for ordering information). By using the samples you provide them, they then produce a font based on either your cursive or manuscript style — and even add a signature to the font that you can access by a combination of keystrokes.

This type of font will let you add personal touches to newsletters or notes home without ever picking up a pen! Wouldn't this service come in handy when you're writing thank-you notes to every child the day before Christmas break?

My name is Michelle.

I have two beautiful children.

Loading a new font

So you decide to go out and buy some of the nice fonts you've been looking at. How do you get them onto your machine?

It's easy. If you are using System 7 (which I hope most of you are by now, because System 7.5 is already on the market), quit all your programs.

1. Insert your new disk into the computer. Double-click the icon of the disk to open it.

   You should see a number of little suitcases, each one labeled with the name of a font that you've purchased.

2. Now open up your hard drive (double-click the hard-drive icon in the upper-right corner of your screen) and find your System folder.

   You don't have to open this folder; simply decide which fonts you'd like and drag them over to the System folder.

3. When the System folder is highlighted, let go of the mouse.

   Remember, do not open the System folder. Simply drag the suitcase on top of the folder until it is highlighted and release the mouse. (I'm really a teacher. See how I repeat the information I want you to remember?)

   You'll see a message alerting you that the Mac is going to install the font for you. Just smile, wave, and click OK. Wasn't that easy?

How to Print

Bet you haven't had a lesson with that title since about first grade. (Unless, of course, you teach first grade.)

Plugging in a 'Writer

If you bought an ImageWriter, StyleWriter, or other 'Writer, a cable (printer-to-Mac) probably came with the printer. It's a no-brainer to connect them; there's only one possible place to plug the cable into the printer. The other end goes into the back of the Mac. There's a little round jack with a printer icon. (It's next to the jack with the telephone icon.) Of course, you also need to plug your new appliance into the wall.

Plugging in a laser printer

If you bought a laser printer, believe it or not, you probably did *not* get a cable with it. It's kinda like textbook adoptions; someone shows you all the great things that *can* come with the package — and your school system purchases only the books. Like those workbooks you wanted, the cable's not included. Don't ask me why.

When Apple invented the LaserWriter, they charitably recognized that not every company (or school) could afford a $4,000 printer to sit beside each desk. They had a great idea, though: a system where several Macs could all plug into the same printer.

Ladies and gentlemen, I hereby introduce you to the word *network*.

The wires and connectors that attach these Macs to a single shared printer (and which, by the way, can also connect Macs to each *other*) are called LocalTalk. These connectors aren't cheap; the last time I looked, a pair of connectors (what you need for *one* Mac and *one* printer) was about $75.

Soon thereafter, competitors got into the act with rival connectors such as PhoneNet and ModuNet. There were two brilliant concepts behind these rival wiring systems. First, they were much less expensive than Apple's product. Second, they used ordinary phone wire to connect the connectors. (Apple's LocalTalk requires special cables.) If you decide to move your printer into the next room, no big deal — just buy a longer piece of phone wire from Radio Shack.

This information is all relevant only if you believe that you *must* have a network in order to plug a Mac into a laser printer. And, in fact, that's exactly what the salespeople would like you to believe. But here's another money-saving tip: You only need all that fancy wiring *if* you plan to share your laser printer with other Macs.

If it's just for you, your Mac, and a cup of coffee on the desk, get a plain old ImageWriter II cable for $15. After all, one Mac and one printer hardly qualify as a *network*.

Anyway, if you do get the more expensive connectors, plug one connector into the back of the printer and the other into the printer jack in the back of the Mac. Then connect the connectors using LocalTalk cable or phone wire, as appropriate. And if you're just going to use an ImageWriter cable, see the preceding section, "Plugging in a 'Writer."

The whole *networking* concept is wonderful for schools and I'll talk a little more about this in Chapter 19.

Letting the Mac know it has company

The hardest part of printing on a Mac comes at the very beginning — an unfortunate fact for the novice who simply wants to get going.

When you first plug a printer into the Mac, it's like a kid on the first day of school — not smart enough to notice it has a new friend. You have to tell the Mac explicitly. We'll get to that stuff in a moment.

Imagine that you work in a big school with lots of technology money; you have three different kinds of printers and a four dozen Macs, and they're all wired together into a giant network. You want to print something. You have to be able to tell the Mac the following stuff:

- ✔ what *kind* of printer you want to use (laser, StyleWriter, whatever)
- ✔ if there's *more than one* of each printer connected to the network
- ✔ which *printer(s)* you have connected

That long-winded explanation was supposed to help you understand why there's a desk accessory in your Apple menu called the *Chooser*. Using this gadget, you can specify what kind of printer — and which one — you want to use.

If you're a one-person operation, of course, this stuff is utterly superfluous. But you have to go through it, anyway. What the heck — maybe your school will get that multi-million dollar technology grant, and you'll know exactly what to do!

The Chooser

Once the Mac is connected to the printer, turn both machines on and follow these steps:

1. Choose Chooser from the menu. You should see something like this:

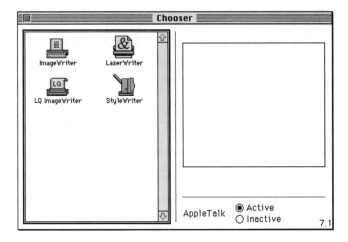

Your screen may look different, of course. The icons that appear in the left half of the window depend upon which *printer drivers* have been placed in your System folder. A printer driver is a little piece of software that teaches the Mac how to communicate with a specific printer. Its name and its icon match the printer itself, as you can sort of tell from the preceding figure.

2. If you see a printer driver icon in the Chooser window that matches your printer, you're in luck! Click it.

   If you selected a laser printer, you should see its name show up in the *right* side of the Chooser window, as shown here:

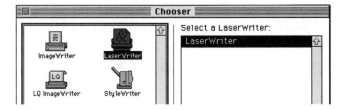

Good going! Everything's coming up roses. If the names of several printers show up on the right, then you're either part of a school network with several printers or you're an unexpectedly wealthy individual. Congratulations.

If you don't see *any* icons in the left half of the Chooser window, somebody's probably taken them out. No matter — re-install all these icons by running the Installer on your original white System-software disks (or the startup compact disc). Now you can repeat this Chooser business, and everything should go fine.

If things still aren't going well — for example, if you click the driver icon but your printer's name doesn't show up in the right side of the window — see Appendix B of this book, "Troubleshooting."

Anyway, once you click a printer driver icon, a couple of things happen. If you're selecting a laser printer, you'll be told to turn on *AppleTalk*. AppleTalk is related to LocalTalk, the networking system described previously; remember that if you have a laser printer, you're supposedly part of a network even if just one Mac is attached to it. So make sure the little AppleTalk setting (in the lower-right corner of the dialog box) is active if you have a laser printer. Conversely, make sure AppleTalk is *inactive* if you have a StyleWriter.

3. Close the Chooser.

But when you close the Chooser, you'll get a soon-to-be-annoying alert message:

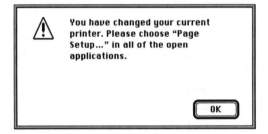

It tells you (as if you didn't know) that you've just changed to a new printer. Its advice, though, is sound.

4. Choose Page Setup from your File menu after you select a printer driver. A dialog box appears.

5. Don't *do* anything in this box; just click OK.

You've just introduced the Mac to its new printer. All of this is a one-time operation, by the way. Unless you have to switch printers or something, you'll never have to touch the Chooser again.

Background printing

In the Dark Ages of the 1980s, when you printed something, the printer's soul took over your Mac's body. You couldn't type, you couldn't work, you couldn't do anything but stare at the screen that said "Now printing." It was a dark and stormy era, a time of wild children waiting for their stories to print. Only when the paper came out of the printer were you allowed to use your computer again.

Since then, some clever Apple engineer figured out how to allow *background printing*. When you use this handy feature, the Mac sends all the printing information at a million miles an hour into a *file* on your hard disk and immediately returns its attention to you and your personal needs.

Then quietly, behind the scenes, the Mac shoots a little bit of that file at a time to your printer. It all happens during the microseconds between your keystrokes and mouse clicks, making it seem as though the Mac is printing in the background. In time, the printer receives all the information it needs to print, the paper comes gliding out, and you've been able to keep working the whole time.

In practice, there are a few background-printing realities to consider. First of all, a document takes much longer to print in the background than it would if the Mac devoted all of its brainpower to printing. Similarly, making your Mac concentrate on two things at once also bogs down what you're doing: While something's being printed in the background, you can outtype your word processor, windows seem to take longer to open, and so on. Finally, background printing isn't available for ImageWriters (unless you buy a program called a *spooler*, especially designed for the ImageWriter).

Turning the Background Printing feature on and off is easy. Select Chooser from the menu. In the lower-right side of the box, you'll see the On/Off buttons. Go for it.

If it's 2:00 on a Friday afternoon, and you need to print your five-page parent letter as quickly as possible, turn off background printing.

After all that: How you actually print

OK. Suppose you've followed all the directions and the printer is plugged in (and via the Chooser, the printer has been introduced to the Mac). You've created a beautiful document using some really cool fonts. The moment has arrived. You actually would like to *print* the thing.

1. Choose Print from the File menu.

DeskWriter	3.1	OK

Quality:
- ⦿ Best
- ○ Normal
- ○ Draft

Pages:
- ○ All
- ⦿ From: 3 To: 3

Copies:
2

Page Order:
- ☐ Print Back to Front

Cancel
Preview
Help

This dialog box appears; it looks different depending on your printer, but the one pictured here is what you see if you have a 'Writer:

You can specify how many copies you want by clicking and typing in the Copies box.

The main thing you do in this dialog box is tell the Mac which pages of your document you want it to print. If you just want page 1, type a 1 in *both* the From and To boxes. If you want page 2 to the end, type 2 into the From box and leave the To box empty.

Some printers (Lasers and 'Writers) give you the option of printing "back to front." This means that when you pick up your pile of printed papers, the first page of text will be on top.

2. Click OK.

   You did it, my friend!

Canceling printing

If you want to interrupt the printing process, ⌘-period does the trick — that is, while pressing the ⌘ key, type a period. Several times, actually. Even then, your printer will take a moment (or page) to respond to you.

Using the Tab key in dialog boxes

Now would be a good time to mention what the Tab key does in dialog boxes such as the Print dialog box. Suppose you want to print two copies of page 3. Instead of using the mouse to click in each number box on the screen, you can just press Tab to jump from box to box.

Part II
Making a Teacher's Life Easier

The 5th Wave   By Rich Tennant

"A BRIEF ANNOUNCEMENT CLASS — AN OPEN FACED PEANUT BUTTER SANDWICH IS NOT AN APPROPRIATE REPLACEMENT FOR A MISSING MOUSEPAD."

In this part...

*E*verything in education is centered around the children — and justifiably so. However, it sure would be nice if a few perks were thrown in every once in a while for those of us down in the trenches.

For example, I'll never forget the day my school cafeteria added baked potatoes to the teachers' lunch bar. We were all so excited! Looking back, it seems ridiculous, but it also proves how deprived we poor teachers sometimes are. Something as simple as a baked potato provided us happiness and conversation for weeks. (And we became oh-so-creative with our toppings.)

Imagine what would happen if teachers were *always* allowed to leave the school for lunch.

ClarisWorks is much like that baked potato that I so artfully loaded on my lunch tray last year. It will cause you to chatter excitedly for days as you show colleagues your incredible creations and brag about how much easier day-to-day tasks have become. And like the potato, *ClarisWorks* has everything you need in one neat package. How's that for stretching an analogy?

Later in this book, we will discuss the wonderful things your *students* can do with this spud of a program. But right now, I want to give *you* a well-deserved perk.

In this part, I show you a variety of ways in which ClarisWorks can make your professional (and maybe personal) life easier. You'll learn about the world of word processing, templates, and databases — and I'll take you step-by-painless-step through the creation of each document.

Chapter 6
An Overview of ClarisWorks

- -

- -

*Y*ou know all the Macintosh basics. Now it's time to get busy.

I hope you took my suggestion and ordered *ClarisWorks*. If not, stop now and get yourself a copy of any 'Works program (*ClarisWorks, Microsoft Works, Great Works,* and so on). They are all very similar. I will admit that all of the activities in the next three chapters can be completed on just about any 'Works program. Use the program you prefer. Then make the necessary adjustments. (I just prefer *ClarisWorks*.)

What is ClarisWorks?

ClarisWorks is Swiss-army-knife software. Just look at all you get, even if you don't know what they are yet: a word processor, a database, and a spreadsheet. Now how much would you pay? But wait. You also get a graphics program that can even serve as a basic page-layout system. And if you call now, they'll even throw in a little communications program (to use if you own a modem — a phone hook-up for your Mac).

All these modules are neatly bundled into a single program. You can write a letter and put a graphic in it, or you can design a flyer that has a little spread-sheet in it, and so on. This section will be worth reading, even if you don't own *ClarisWorks* yet, because *ClarisWorks* works exactly like most other Mac programs.

Marvelous Modules

As I mentioned earlier, *ClarisWorks* has it all. Here's a brief description of each module:

Word Processing — You know that a word-processing document is something you type: a memo, lesson plans, and newsletters.

Drawing — This is *ClarisWorks'* version of *MacDraw*. In this kind of document, you toy around with lines, shapes, and colors to produce logos, maps, classroom layouts, diagrams, and other important visuals.

Painting — This is *ClarisWorks'* version of *MacPaint* or *Photoshop*. Painting is another way of making graphics. Unlike the Drawing mode, where you can create only distinct circles, lines, and squares, the Painting tools let you create shading, freeform spatters, and much more textured artwork.

Database — An electronic index-card file, very much like *FileMaker*. You type in your lists — household expenditures, record collections, classroom books — and the program sorts them, prints them, finds certain pieces of info instantly, and so on.

Spreadsheet — A computerized ledger sheet, almost exactly like *Excel*. It crunches numbers, for example, and it calculates your car's mileage per gallon, your bank account, how much of the phone bill your teenage daughter owes — that kind of thing.

Communications — You need this kind of program if you want to use your modem for dialing up local "electronic bulletin boards," pay-by-the-hour information services like CompuServe, or your local school's computer system. (You can't use a program like this to dial up America Online or eWorld. Instead, you have to use a special program provided by those companies.)

To make *ClarisWorks* strut its stuff, I'll show you in the following chapters how to create a class-list database, personalized stationery, customized checklists, lesson-plan templates (templates are stationery documents that remain constant and let you add changes to them each time you pull them up), and much more! But first, let's continue with our overview.

Installing ClarisWorks

If you are working on a computer at your school, you more than likely have *ClarisWorks* on your hard drive. You can thus feel free to jump ahead to "*ClarisWorks* Boot Camp."

If you're not sure, open your hard drive (double-click the icon) and take a look. If you don't see *ClarisWorks* in your window, you need to install it. Don't worry; the installation process is very simple.

1. Find the *ClarisWorks* disk labeled "Disk 1" or "Installer."

2. Put that baby into your disk drive and wait for the icon to appear on your desktop.

3. Double-click the disk icon. You should see a window containing a picture that looks like this:

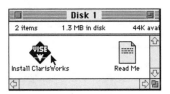

4. Double-click the Installer.

   Note: Most new programs come with an Installer program loaded onto the disk. This program puts all the necessary components of a program into their proper places on your hard disk (System folder, Control Panels, and so on). On larger programs, the Installer even lets you customize the installation. This gives you the freedom to leave off certain features that you don't feel are necessary for your current computing needs. (Wouldn't it be nice if we had the option of customizing our class lists?)

5. You have a college degree — simply follow the directions as they appear on the screen to install this program onto your hard disk.

   Installation will take some time. Go check your messages or let the dog out. The computer will tell you when (or if) it needs another disk and will even show some type of graph indicating where it is in the process of your installation.

   When you return, you'll see another message telling you that installation was successful. (Don't you love that positive feedback?)

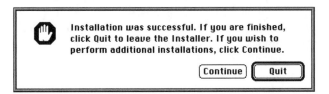

ClarisWorks Boot Camp

I want to take this time to review a few *ClarisWorks* basics with you.

The New Document dialog box

This dialog box appears each time you open *ClarisWorks,* and it gives you a variety of choices. Look at your two choices on the left: Start with a Blank Document and Start With an Assistant or Stationery.

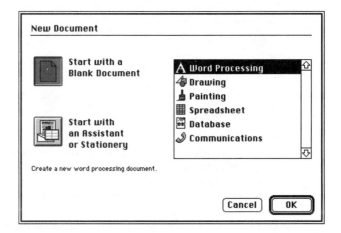

Start with a Blank Document means what it says. You are starting from scratch with nothing to guide you.

Start With an Assistant or Stationery will give you assistance in creating a variety of pre-designed *ClarisWorks* documents or let you go right to a statio-nery item you've already created (maybe your weekly lesson-plan form).

So what is stationery? When you create a document that you know you will be using again and again (like your lesson-plan form), *ClarisWorks* gives you the option of saving this document as *stationery:* Each time you open your lesson-plan form, a copy of the original appears, ready for you to fill in. The original is never altered, and you don't spend unnecessary time re-entering items that recur every week. Saving a document as stationery is an option each time you save something in *ClarisWorks*.

The word-processing rulers

We'll go into each of these controls in Chapter 7. For this overview, I want you to be aware of the incredible amount of control *ClarisWorks* gives you. Isn't this great? My typewriter sure didn't make writing this easy!

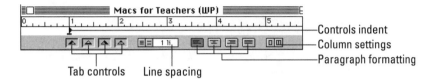

Tab controls   Line spacing

Controls indent
Column settings
Paragraph formatting

The Open dialog box

This dialog box appears when you choose Open from the File menu. You use this box when you want to retrieve saved work. If your work is saved on a floppy disk, simply put the disk in the computer after this box appears. The computer will then read the disk. The disk's contents will appear in the scrollable window.

If your work is saved on your hard drive, you may have to do some digging to find out exactly where it is saved.

If you saved your work in a *ClarisWorks* folder, it should appear when you choose Open from the File menu. Simply highlight the name and click Open (or double-click the name).

A folder   A document   A stationery document

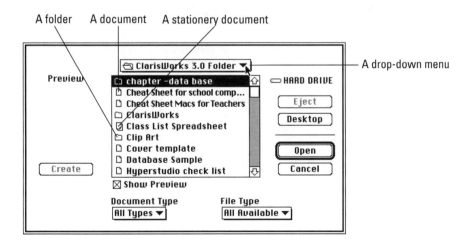

A drop-down menu

If you saved your work on the hard drive, pull down the drop-down menu (also called a pop-up menu!) at the top of the dialog box. Then choose Hard Drive. The hard-drive contents will appear in your scrollable window. Just find your work!

We'll practice this procedure in Chapter 7.

The View buttons

In the lower-left corner of the *ClarisWorks* screen, you'll find an odd-looking array of controls:

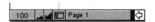

As you can tell, *ClarisWorks* makes it extremely easy to blow up your work. (Obviously, I mean *magnify it;* destroying it is up to you.) A quick click on either of those little mountain buttons makes your work appear smaller or larger. Or jump directly to a more convenient degree of magnification by using the percentage pop-up menu. Click and hold where it says 100. A list of percentages appears for you to choose from. You won't be changing the size of the actual printed work — only how it's displayed on the screen.

The final control (to the right of the mountains) lets you view or hide the tool palette. These tools are used primarily in the drawing and painting modules of *ClarisWorks*.

The Save dialog box

Saving a document is a very important skill. (We will review it in Chapter 7, of course!) Let me take this opportunity to introduce you to the Save dialog box.

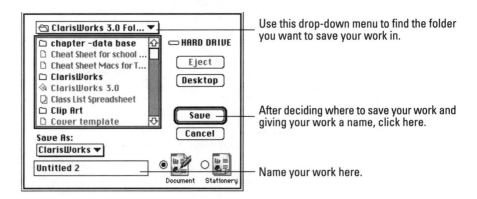

After you've typed something wonderful (and you choose Save from the File menu), your demanding computer requires that you give your masterpiece a title. In its manipulative way, the computer also asks that you store that document someplace.

You run into this not-very-graphic, not-very-helpful, not-very-user friendly Save box more often than Apple's designers would probably like to admit — once for every single document you create, actually.

Saving to a disk

In schools, many computers are set up to require you to save your work to a disk. If that's the case, simply insert the disk when this dialog box appears. The disk's contents (if any) will appear in the scrollable box. Then type in the name of your file and click Save.

Saving to a folder

Other schools set up a folder on the hard drive for each teacher. If that's the case, you may have to do a little digging to find your folder.

If your folder is inside *ClarisWorks*, it should show in the dialog window immediately after you choose Save from the File menu.

If the folders are kept on the desktop, click the Desktop button (or choose Desktop from the drop-down menu at the top of the box). You should see your folder as one of the choices in the scrollable window.

If the folders are kept on the hard drive, pull down the drop-down menu at the top of the box and choose Hard Drive. Find your folder and open it (double-click it, or highlight it and click the Open button). Now you are ready to save to your folder.

An easy way to avoid learning this stuff

This business about the "Save Where?" dialog box is, as anybody will tell you, the most confusing thing about the Mac. After years of experience, a few professional beginners (including myself) have adopted the following cheat — and we never lose another file.

Whenever you save a file, you are faced with the Save dialog box. Name your file, and then click the Desktop button. Only then should you click the Save button.

Go ahead and ask — "What's the point?"

Easy. When you're done working for the day and you return to the desktop, you won't have to wonder what folder your document's icon fell into. Your new file will be sitting right there, on the desktop — in plain sight.

At this point, it's child's play to drag the icon into the folder where you want it.

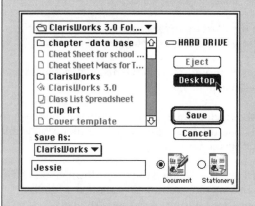

So, let's get busy! Jump into chapters 7, 8, and 9 where we will put all this information into practice.

Chapter 7

The Wonderful World of Word Processing

● ●

In This Chapter

▶ Your very first word-processing lesson

▶ Saving your work for posterity

▶ Retrieving a document

▶ Creating templates for a letterhead and lesson plans

● ●

*W*ell, here it is, folks, the reason most people use the computer: word processing. Don't let the name fool you. You aren't actually processing the words into anything . . . you're typing. Not only that, you are typing without a little bottle of white-out at your side.

Word processing is typing made easy. So go ahead and have some fun.

Supply List for Word Processing 101

As your instructor, I'm going to ask you to come to class prepared. Don't worry — you're not going to need to take a trip to the local mall or computer store.

This supply list is short and simple. You need two folders. (Not folders you can hold in your hands — electronic folders.) These folders can be found free, right now, at your local menu bar.

1. Choose New Folder from the File menu. (Make sure you're in the Finder or Desktop.)

2. When the folder appears, it is ready to have a name typed in. Name this first folder *School Stuff.*

3. Now, repeat the whole process — but this time name the folder *Funny Anecdotes*.

4. Finally, let's drag the Funny Anecdotes folder into the School Stuff folder.

(You know. Click the mouse button — and hold it down — when your pointer is on the Funny Anecedotes folder. Then drag it to the School Stuff folder and release the mouse button.)

5. You are set up and ready to begin your word-processing lesson.

Word Processing 101

Find the *ClarisWorks* icon on your hard disk. It may be inside a folder, which you can open by double-clicking. In any case, once you find the program icon, double-click it; you'll be presented, after a moment, with a menu screen that looks like this (if you have version 3.0):

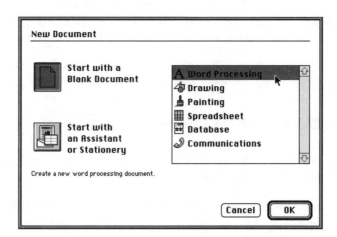

Choose word processing. You then see a blank screen and some changes on your menu bar.

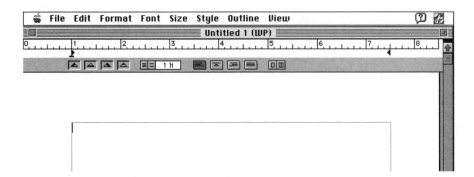

Rules of word processing

The first rules of typing on a computer are going to be tough to learn, especially if, like me, you've been typing since high school. But they're super crucial. Here they are:

✔ **Don't press the Return key at the end of each line.**

I'm dead serious here. When you type your way to the end of a line, the next word will automatically jump down to the next line. If you press Return in the middle of a sentence, you'll mess everything up.

✔ **Put only ONE space after a period.**

This was a hard one for me to swallow too. But it's true!

If that last statement gives you uncontrollable muscular facial spasms, I don't blame you. After all, I'm telling you to do something that you were explicitly taught not to do by your sharp-tongued, high school typing teacher.

Nonetheless, don't put two spaces after a period. Typewriters print letters onto paper by slapping tiny metal blocks against a ribbon, and every block (every letter) is the same width — including the space. But on a Mac, every letter has a different width. Look how much wider this W is than this I, for example. On the Mac, a space is already extra wide, thus saving you that precious calorie you would have exerted to press the spacebar a second time.

Why aren't you supposed to hit Return at the end of each line?

First time in print! Here's an actual example of the kind of mess you can get into by pressing Return after each line of text.

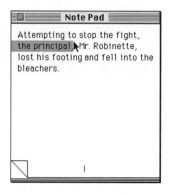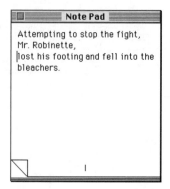

At left: the original passage. Suppose you decide to remove Mr. Robinette's title, "the principal," because everybody already knows what kind of guy he is. But suppose you'd been foolish enough to press Return after each line of text. If you remove those highlighted words, the words "Mr. Robinette" flop back to the left side of the line, but the rest of the sentence stays where it is, looking dumb. On the other hand, if you hadn't put Returns into your text, you'd get the figure below, where everything looks peachy.

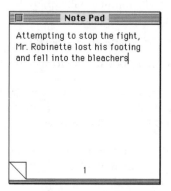

There are a few other rules, too, but breaking them isn't serious enough to get you investigated by the school board. So dig in. Make sure you have a blank piece of electronic typing paper in front of you.

You should see a short, blinking vertical line at the beginning of the typing area: the *insertion point.* It's called the insertion point because it shows you where the letters will appear when you start to type.

Type the passage below. If you make a typo, press the Delete key, just like Backspace on a typewriter. Don't press Return when you get to the edge of the window. Just keep typing, and the Mac will create a second line for you. Believe.

The teacher's screams could be heard throughout the school as the student attempted to recapture his snake and return it to the aquarium.

See how the words automatically wrapped around to the second line? This feature is called, with no small originality, *word wrap.*

But suppose, as your novel is going to press, you decide that this sleepy passage really needs some spicing up. You decide to insert the word *terrified* before the word *screams.*

Remember the blinking cursor — the insertion point? It's on the screen even now, blinking calmly at the end of the sentence. If you want to insert text, you have to move the insertion point.

There are two ways to move the insertion point. First, try pressing the arrow keys on your keyboard. You can see that the up- and down-arrow keys move the insertion point from line to line, and the right- and left-arrow keys move the insertion point across the line. Practice moving the insertion point by pressing the arrow keys.

If the passage you want to edit is far away (on another page, for example), using the arrow keys to move the cursor is inefficient. Your fingers would be bloody stumps by the time you finished. Instead, grab that mouse:

1. Using the mouse, move the cursor (which, when it's near text, looks like this |) just before the word *screams.* Click the mouse.

> The teacher's |screams could be heard throughout the
> school as the student attempted to recapture his snake and
> return it to the aquarium.

This is as confusing as word processing ever gets — there are two little cursors, right? There's the blinking insertion point, and this one⏐, which is called an I-beam cursor. In fact, they're quite different. The blinking insertion point is only a marker, not a pointer. It always shows you where the text typing will appear. The I-beam, on the other hand, is how you move the insertion point to a different location; when you click with the I-beam, you set down the insertion point.

2. Type the word *terrified.*

The insertion point does its deed, and the Mac makes room on the line for the new word. A word or two probably got pushed onto the next line. Isn't word wrap wonderful?

So much for inserting text: You click the mouse (to show the Mac where) and then type away. But what if you need to delete a bunch of text? What if you decide to edit out the first half of our sample text?

Well, unless you typed the challenging excerpt with no errors, you already know one way to erase text — by pressing the Delete key (which is called Backspace on some keyboards). Delete (or Backspace) takes out one letter at a time, just to the left of the insertion point.

That's not much help in this situation, though. Suppose you decide to take out the first part of the sentence. It wouldn't be horribly efficient to backspace over the entire passage just so you could work on the beginning.

Instead, you need a way to edit any part of your work, at any time, without disturbing the stuff you want to leave. Once again, the Macintosh method (noun-then-verb) saves the day:

1. Using the mouse, position the I-beam cursor at the beginning of the sentence.

This takes a steady hand. Stay calm.

2. Click just to the left of the first word and keep the mouse button pressed down. Drag the I-beam cursor to the end of the word *as.*

As you drag, the text gets highlighted, or selected.

> The teacher's screams could be heard throughout the school as the student attempted to recapture his snake and return it to the aquarium.

If you're especially clever and forward-thinking, you'll have selected the blank space after the word *as,* as well.

All right. In typical Mac syntax, you've just specified what you want to edit, by selecting it (and making it turn black to show it's selected). Now for the verb.

3. Press the Delete key.

Bam! The selected text is gone. The sentence looks pretty odd, though, since it doesn't begin with a capital letter.

4. Using the mouse, position the cursor just before (or after) the letter *t* that now begins the sentence. Drag it sideways across the letter so that it's highlighted.

> the student attempted to recapture his snake and return it to the aquarium.

Here comes another ground rule of word processing, See how you've just selected, or highlighted, the letter *t?* The idea here is to capitalize it. Of course, using the methods for wiping (and inserting) text that you learned earlier, you could simply remove the *t* and type a *T*. But since you've selected the *t* by dragging through it, replacing it is much easier.

5. Type a capital *T*.

The selected text gets replaced by the new stuff you type. That, in fact, is another ground rule: *Selected text gets replaced by the new stuff you type.* As your Macintosh proficiency builds, keep that handy fact in mind; it can save you a lot of backspacing. In fact, you could select 400 pages of text and then hit one single key to replace all of it. Or you could select only one letter but replace it with 40 pages of typing.

Hint: If you make a change that you didn't mean to make, go to the Edit menu and choose Undo. This step will undo the last action taken.

Take a moment now for some unsupervised free play. Try clicking anywhere in the text (to plant the insertion point). Try dragging through some text. If you drag perfectly horizontally, you select text just on one line (below left). If you drag diagonally, you get everything between your cursor and the original click (below right).

> Breathlessly, he ran into the workroom only to find a line of ten other teachers waiting for the copy machine. His eye began to twitch uncontrollably as he realized the parent letter would not be going home that afternoon.

> Breathlessly, he ran into the workroom only to find a line of ten other teachers waiting for the copy machine. His eye began to twitch uncontrollably as he realized the parent letter would not be going home that afternoon.

You *de-select* (or, equally poetically, *un-highlight*) text by clicking the mouse. Anywhere at all.

Try pointing to a word and then double-clicking the mouse: You've easily selected exactly that word and without having to do any dragging.

As you experiment, do anything you want with any combination of drags, clicks, double-clicks, and menu selections. It's nice to know — and you may want to prepare a fine mahogany wall plaque along these lines:

Nothing you do with the mouse or keyboard can physically harm the computer.

Oh sure, it's possible to erase a disk or wreck one of your documents or something, but none of that requires a visit to a repair shop. You can't break the computer by playing around.

Form and format

One of the most important differences between a typewriter and its replacement — the personal computer — is the sequence of events. When you use a typewriter, you set up all the formatting characteristics before you type: the margins, the tab stops, and (for typewriters with interchangeable type heads) the type style.

But the whole point of a word processor is that you can change anything at any time. Many people type the text of an entire letter (or proposal or memo) into the Mac and then format it. When you use a typewriter, you may discover, after typing the entire first page, that it's slightly too long to fit, and your signature will have to sit awkwardly on a page by itself. With a Mac, you'd see the problem and nudge the text a little bit higher on the page to compensate.

Word processing has other great advantages:

- no cross-outs
- easy corrections that involve no white-out and no retyping
- a permanent record of your correspondence that's electronic, not paper
- a selection of striking typefaces (fonts) at any size
- paste-in graphics

I think it's safe to say that once you try it, you'll never look back.

The return of Return

With all the subtlety of a Mack truck, I've taught you that you're forbidden to use the Return key at the end of a line. Still, that rectangular Return key on your keyboard is important. You press Return at the end of a paragraph, and only there.

To the computer, the Return key works like a letter key — it inserts a return character into the text. It's just like rolling the paper in a typewriter forward by one notch. Hit Return twice, and you leave a blank line.

The point of Return, then, is to move text higher or lower on the page. Check this example, for instance.

The Return character moves text down on the page. So, if you want to move text up on the page, drag through the blank space so that it's highlighted. Then press Delete. Of course, what you've done is to select the usually invisible Return characters. If you delete them, the text slides up the page. (See the sidebar, "Seeing the unseen," if you need to satisfy your curiosity right now.)

Combine this knowledge with your advanced degree in Inserting Text. (Remember? You click to place the blinking insertion point and then type away.) You can see how you make more space between paragraphs or push all the text of a letter down on the page.

Appealing characters

Another big-time difference between word processing and typing is all the great character formatting you can do. You can make any piece of text bold, italic, underlined, all of the above, and more. You also get a selection of great-looking typefaces (fonts) — only a few of which look like typewriter stuff.

Here's the scheme for changing some text to one of those character formats: noun-verb. Sound familiar? Go for it.

1. Select some text by dragging through it.

   Remember, you can select a single word by double-clicking it. To select a bunch of text, drag the cursor through it so that it turns black. You've just identified what you want to change.

   ClarisWorks keeps its Bold, Italic, and Underline commands in the Style menu.

2. From the Style menu, choose Bold.

   You can apply several of these formats to the same text, too, although you won't win any awards for typographical excellence. Try changing the typeface also. The various fonts are called things like New York, Chicago, Times, and Geneva. To change the font, go to the Font menu and take a look at your choices. The final trick involves changing the size of your text. You can do this by going to the Size menu. Your font will look its best if you choose only from the sizes that are written in an outline or hollow-style format — not those written in solid. Trust me on this one; it will print, yes, but it won't look as good as it could.

   ```
   New York 12 point plain
   New York 14 point bold italic
   New York 18 point plain shadow
   New York 24 point plain outline
   ```

   By applying a variety of styles and varying the size, a single font can appear in many different ways. Before you know it, those parents are going to be waiting eagerly for the next school notice, just to see your font creativity.

Seeing the unseen

I said that returns are usually invisible. However, every time you press the Return key, the Mac actually does plop down a symbol onto your screen. Same thing with the Spacebar. Same with the Tab key.

In *ClarisWorks,* the command to see these neat symbols falls under the Edit menu in the Preferences category. Choose Preferences from the Edit menu and you should see another screen with lots of choices. There are some neat choices here, but none is truly crucial. I've been talking about invisible characters. Notice the box that reads Show Invisibles. Click this box to see all those neat characters. Otherwise, leave it blank — and only the computer will see them.

Come back and play with the other preferences when you find some time.

Font-crazed kids

Be warned, kids go crazy with these options. I guess we don't give them enough choices or creative outlets these days. Who knows? Anyway, after introducing the concept of character formatting, I usually let them have an entire period to get familiar with their options. Then, when it's time to put what they've learned into practice, I find it best to set a few limitations. Otherwise they will spend the entire work period playing with character formatting instead of generating a product.

Formatting paragraphs

Where type styles and sizes can be applied to any amount of text, even a single letter, *paragraph formatting* affects a whole paragraph at once. In *ClarisWorks*, these styles are easy to apply. Clicking four times within a paragraph will highlight the entire passage. Then by choosing any of the four justification options located just below the menu bar, you can have your text become left-justified, right-justified, centered, or fully justified. You can also determine the amount of space between each line. Take some time now to play with your options before going on to the next exciting lesson.

Left justified

Teaching is one of the hardest and most important jobs in the country. Being a good teacher takes time effort and dedication. One has to be willing to give with little in return in the way of pay. The rewards come in the smiles and eagerness to learn a new skill. Being remembered as a good teacher is almost as important as being remembered as a good parent. In both cases you have a direct impact on the future of our country.

Right justified

Teaching is one of the hardest and most important jobs in the country. Being a good teacher takes time effort and dedication. One has to be willing to give with little in return in the way of pay. The rewards come in the smiles and eagerness to learn a new skill. Being remembered as a good teacher is almost as important as being remembered as a good parent. In both cases you have a direct impact on the future of our country.

Centered

Teaching is one of the hardest and most important jobs in the country. Being a good teacher takes time effort and dedication. One has to be willing to give with little in return in the way of pay. The rewards come in the smiles and eagerness to learn a new skill. Being remembered as a good teacher is almost as important as being remembered as a good parent. In both cases you have a direct impact on the future of our country.

Full justification

Teaching is one of the hardest and most important jobs in the country. Being a good teacher takes time effort and dedication. One has to be willing to give with little in return in the way of pay. The rewards come in the smiles and eagerness to learn a new skill. Being remembered as a good teacher is almost as important as being remembered as a good parent. In both cases you have a direct impact on the future of our country.

Setting tabs/using the ruler

Claris made these jobs easy when it created *ClarisWorks*. Take a look at this ruler:

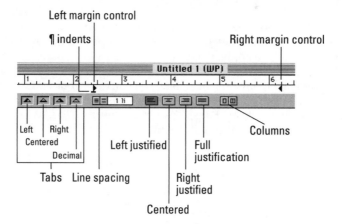

The solid black triangles on the left and right control the indents. Simply click and slide the triangles to the desired position.

Tabs are nearly as easy. Choose the type of tab marker you desire (left, centered, right, or decimal) and click the triangle that represents that type of tab. As you click, drag the triangle to the desired position. You can set as many tabs as you need; the little triangles simply reappear when you drag one off.

You can hide this ruler by choosing Hide Rulers from the View menu.

Guide to power typing

Because you *can* format text after you've typed it doesn't mean you *have* to. Most users get used to the keyboard shortcuts for the common style changes, like bold and italic. They're pretty easy to remember: In *ClarisWorks,* you get bold by pressing ⌘-B, and italic with ⌘-I.

What's handy is that you can hit this key combo just *before* you type the word. For example, without ever taking your hands off the keyboard, you could type ⌘-B once to turn bold *on* for the next burst of typing and ⌘-B again to turn it off — all without ever having to use a menu.

Please Save Me!

No, I can't save you from that conference with the parent who "used to be a teacher" and seems to think she can handle things better than you. But I can save you from the severe bouts of depression suffered by those who simply create and print . . . only later to find small, yet crucial, errors — such as incorrect spelling. Teachers *never* make spelling mistakes. And if they do, there's always a parent ready to circle this gross error and bring it to their attention.

It may terrify you — and it probably should — to find out that you've been working on an imaginary document. It's being preserved only by a thin current of streaming electricity. It doesn't exist yet, to be perfectly accurate, except in your Mac's *memory.*

You may recall — if you happened to wade through Chapter 2 — that *memory is fleeting.* (Specifically, I mean computer memory. Yet, isn't it amazing how so much of this terminology applies to students?) In fact, the memory is wiped away when you turn the Mac off — or when your curious toddler thinks the little red light on the surge protector switch needs to be pushed. At that moment, anything that exists on the screen is gone forever.

Therefore, it is very important to save, save, save. When you save your work, the Mac transfers it from transient, fleeting, electronic memory onto the good, solid, permanent disk. There your work will remain, safely saved. It will still be there tomorrow. It will still be there next week. It will still be there ten years from now, when you're ready to retire and write your memoirs.

In *ClarisWorks* the save command is located in the File menu. Try to save the wonderful sentence you typed about the teacher and the snake.

From the File menu, choose Save.

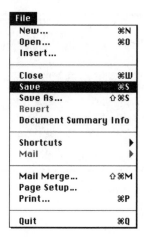

You are now presented with a *dialog box*, because the computer needs to have a little chat with you before proceeding.

What the Mac wants to know is: "Under what name would you like me to file this precious document?"

And how do you know this? Because in the blank where it says Save As, there's a proposed title that's *highlighted* (selected already). And what do you know about highlighted text? *Anything you start typing will instantly replace it.*

The Mac, in its cute but limited dialogy way, is trying to tell you that it needs you to type a title. Go ahead, do it. Type *Snake Episode*.

At this point, you could just click the Save button. The Mac would take everything in perilous, fleeting memory and transfer it to the staid, safe hard disk, where it would remain until you're ready to work on it some more.

However, there's a bunch of other stuff in this dialog box. Especially since this is the main cause of confusion to beginners, I think a tour of the Save File box is in order.

Navigating the Save File (and Open File) box

You've already learned about the way your computer organizes files: with folders and with folders in folders.

Well, the point of all that complicated-looking stuff in the Save File box is a miniature version of that same folder-filing system. If you haven't already done so, go to the File menu and choose Save. You should see a dialog box that looks something like this:

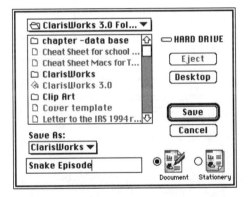

Looking at all your choices, you may decide that none of the files currently in the window suit you. But on your desktop sits the great little School Stuff folder that (I hope) you created in the beginning of this chapter (see "Supply List for Word Processing ").

To be able to use that folder to hold your Snake episode, you need go to the desktop. Click the Desktop button. You see all the items currently on your desktop. You should see your School Stuff folder. You can open this folder by either double-clicking the name or highlighting the name and then clicking the Open button. *Voilà*. Your School Stuff folder is open.

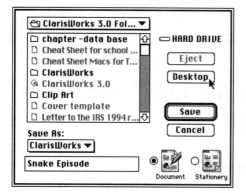

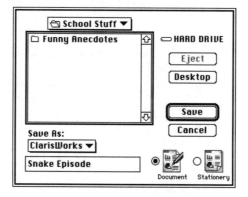

Now we see that there is a folder inside the School Stuff folder that's titled Funny Anecdotes. I think the Snake Episode is pretty darn funny, so file it there.

Highlight the Funny Anecdotes folder and click Open (or simply double-click Funny Anecdotes). If you haven't already done so, type in the name for your story, *Snake Episode*. Now click the Save button. You're done! Your document has found a home. It's been snugly tucked away in the Funny Anecdotes folder, which is inside the School Stuff folder.

I know, it's scary to put your trust in a machine; you probably feel like printing your work and running to the nearest copy machine to make five or six extra copies — but don't. Let's prove that you really did save this document.

Remember the Application menu on the upper-right side of the screen? It lists all the programs that are running at once. Choose Finder from the Application menu.

When you choose Finder, the folders, window, and Trash can pop up. And there we see our School Stuff folder.

Go ahead. Open it up (double-click). Then you'll see the Funny Anecdotes folder. Open that one too. And, if everything went well, you should now see your Snake Episode document.

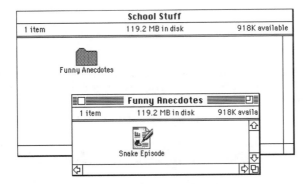

You did it! Technology can be trusted.

Closing a file, with a sigh

You've created your lesson plans, it's 5:15, and everyone has left the building. You save the work in the Lesson Plans folder and are ready to hit the road. It'll be there tomorrow, ready to print.

Click the close box in the upper-left corner of the window.

But they told me NEVER to save to the hard drive

This warning isn't an uncommon problem. Many schools request that both teachers and students refrain from saving their work on the computer's hard drive. Imagine how quickly the hard drive space of the computers would become filled with clutter in a school of more than 1,000 students and another 50 or so teachers!

It's very wise for teachers to purchase a box of disks (either pre-formatted Mac, or you can format them yourself) and use these disks to save work.

The procedure is similar to what you just learned, however. This time, after you choose Save, slide your disk into the computer. When you see the contents of the disk open, click the bottom box under Save As. Type in the name of your document. Click Save. The computer will save the information on your disk.

Now you are free to carry this disk to any computer (provided it has *ClarisWorks* loaded) and work. This practice comes in handy in schools with limited numbers of computers scattered throughout the building. (Be sure you label the outside of your disk.)

In the Mac's universal language of love, clicking the small square up there means "close the window," as you may recall. If all went well, the window disappears.

How to find out what the heck you're doing

No, I'm not going to help you re-think your career decision — although there are days when we all wonder about that mysterious force pulling us back each September.

Just because you closed your document doesn't mean you've left the program. In fact, if you pull down the Application menu on the top-right side of the screen, you'll see that *ClarisWorks* is, in fact, still running. (It's the one with a check mark beside it.)

The worrywart's balm

From the way I've described the terrifyingly delicate condition of a document that's on the screen (that you haven't *saved* yet) — that is, precariously close to oblivion, kept alive only by electric current—you may think that closing a window is a dangerous act. After all, what if you forgot to *save* some work? Wouldn't closing the window mean losing that critical memo?

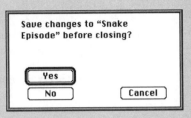

Not really. If you try to close a document, the Mac won't *let* you proceed until it asks if you're sure you want to lose all the work you've done. It will say something like:

Click Yes if you do want to save your work. Click No if you were only goofing around or showing off you Mac to somebody and don't want to preserve your labors. Click Cancel if you change your mind completely about closing the document and want to keep working on it.

You could bring the Finder to the front by choosing its name from the Application menu — without exiting the word processor. They both can be running at the same time, but only one can be in front.

In fact, that's the amazing thing about the Mac (using System 7 or higher). You can have a bunch of programs all running at once. The more memory your Mac has, the more programs you can run simultaneously.

If you want to completely quit *ClarisWorks,* make sure it's still the active program. Go to the File menu and choose Quit.

Fetch: How to retrieve a document

Let's pretend it's tomorrow. You're at school and the principal asks to have a look at your plans for next week. You are in complete control.

You turn to your Mac. Go to your hard drive and double-click *ClarisWorks.* Here's where it gets tricky, but you can handle it — if you've saved your work to a disk:

1. Click the Cancel button when the dialog box appears asking you to select a type of document.

2. The dialog box will disappear, and you'll just see your Menu bar. From the File menu, choose Open.

3. Insert your disk. The Mac will automatically read the disk and show its contents. Click the document you want to work on. When it's highlighted, click Open.

   (Or simply double-click on the document name — double-clicking accomplishes the same thing as when you highlight something and then click Open).

If you saved your work on the computer's hard disk:

1. Go to File and choose Open.

   The *ClarisWorks 3.0* folder will appear with a list of choices.

2. Locate the folder titled Weekly Lesson Plans and highlight it. Click Open.

3. The contents of the folder are listed. Find the plans you wish to work on, highlight your choice, and click Open.

There are the plans, just the way you left them (ready to be printed and handed to your principal). Hey, why does the principal want to see your plans, anyway?

Save Me Again!

To continue this experiment, you must make some changes to a document that you have already saved.

Let's try out those retrieval skills. Find the *Snake Episode* document and make some changes.

Now, if that toddler plays with the little button again (or you forgot to pay the electric bill and the electricity is shut off), you will lose all the work you've added to this priceless document.

Therefore, you have to use that trusty Save command each time you make changes that are worth keeping. The Save dialog box will *not* appear on the screen each time you use the Save command (like it did the first time). Only the very first time you save a document does the Mac ask for a title (and folder location).

You've probably heard horror stories about people who've lost hours of work when some glitch made their computers crash. Well, usually it's their own darned fault for ignoring the two most important rules of computing:

Rule 1: Save your work often.

Rule 2: Never forget Rule 1.

"Often" may mean every five minutes. It may mean after every paragraph. The point is to do it a lot. Some of the more expensive word-processing programs have *auto-save* features that complete this task for you every few minutes.

Trust me on this one. The day — no, the minute — you forget to save something you've typed, you'll get something called a *system crash* and lose your entire document to the technology wasteland.

Stationery

There's a neat feature on the Mac that allows you to save a document as Stationery. Stationery is a special type of document that allows your original saved piece to stay intact and gives you a copy of that document to add to — or alter — and then save with a different name.

This function allows you to make a document somewhat permanent. You'll be using this feature to save some of our upcoming projects, so pay attention.

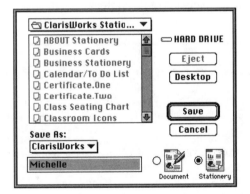

When you click the Stationery button in the Save box, that document is saved as it is and can't be altered and saved under the same name again. Let's go back to those lesson plans we were talking about. Let's say you wrote the times and activities that take place week after week. Before you filled in the specifics, you saved this "skeleton" of your plans as a stationery document. The next time you pull up this document, make changes (fill it in with specifics), and go to Save — *ClarisWorks* won't let you save it under the same name as the template. That's good news: Your template or stationery will always be there ready for you to fill in.

What you are really doing: Save As

In reality you are using the Save As command. Save As means that you are saving a document previously saved under another name with a different name this time. That sounds very confusing. Read it again slowly and raise your hand if you have questions.

We'll get into this stuff later when you create your own stationery. You'll get it — I promise.

Always Have a Backup

You know all about this rule. At my school we call it CYA (Cover Your You-Know-What). We apply this rule to notes sent by parents, memos from the county, proof of inservice credit, and so on. You have to look out for yourself in the education jungle, and I always want to have proof when a dispute arises.

The same is true in the world of computing. Only here, your protection comes in the form of backup disks. If it's important enough to spend time working on, it's important enough to make a backup disk. This means making a copy of the things you've saved on your hard disk. Yes, even your trusty hard disk can fail. Therefore, make back-ups of its contents as often as possible.

The idiot-proof guide to backing up

Put a blank floppy disk in the disk drive. (If it's a brand new disk, you'll be asked to *initialize* it; do it.)

Now select the icons of the documents you want to back up. Drag them, together or one by one, onto the floppy disk icon. If the floppy fills up, insert another one and continue. Label the floppy disks Backup (and note the date). Keep them away from magnets and telephones.

If you're a businessperson, you may even want to invest in a *backup program*, which essentially does the work for you automatically. *DiskFit, Redux,* and *Retrospect* are some popular backup programs. If you have a Performa, you already own a backup program, you lucky dog, called *Apple Backup.*

Top Ten Word Processing Tips

1. Select a word by double-clicking — and then, if you keep the mouse down on the second click and drag sideways, you select more text in complete one-word increments.

2. Never, never, never line up text using the spacebar. It may have worked in the typewriter days, but not anymore. So instead of using spaces to line up columns, use tab stops instead. Practice setting tabs and use them! It may appear fine on screen, but it won't line up correctly when you go to print.

3. You can select all the text in your document at once by using the Select All command (to change the font for the whole thing, for example). Its keyboard equivalent is ⌘-A.

4. Aesthetics Rule of Thumb: Don't use more than two fonts within a document. (Bold, italic, and normal versions of a font only count as one.)

5. Don't use underlining for emphasis. You're a typesetter now. You've got *italics!* Underlining is a cop-out for typewriter people.

6. The gray box in the scroll bar at the right side of the window tells you, at a glance, where you are in your document:

The position of the box in the scroll bar tells you whether you are at the beginning ...

... the middle ...

... or the end of your document.

By dragging this box, you can jump anywhere in the document.

There are two other ways to move around:

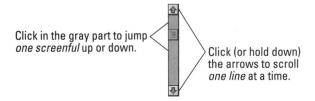

Click in the gray part to jump *one screenful* up or down.

Click (or hold down) the arrows to scroll *one line* at a time.

Click in the gray area above or below the scroll box to jump one screenful up or down.

Click or hold down the button with the up- or down-arrow to move up or down your document one line at a time.

7. You've already learned how to *copy* some text to the Clipboard, ready to paste into another place. Another useful technique is to *cut* text to the Clipboard. Cut works just like Copy except it snips the selected text out of the original document. (Cut-and-paste is how you move text from one place to another and is not to be confused with the skills required to go from kindergarten to first grade.)

8. It's considered uncouth to use "straight quotes" and 'straight apostrophes.' They harken back to the days gone by of typewriters and mimeograph machines. Instead, use "curly double quotes" and 'curly single quotes.' See the difference? In *ClarisWorks* this is an easy switch for you to make. Choose Preferences from the Edit menu. In the dialog box that appears, choose Smart Quotes.

9. If there's an element that you want to appear at the top of every page, like the page number or the date, don't try to type it onto each page. Not only is that a waste of effort, but the minute you add or delete text from somewhere else, this top-of-the-page information will become middle-of-the-page information.

   Instead, use the Insert Header or Insert Footer (for the bottom of the page) command found in the Format menu.

10. Be painfully aware that what you see on the screen isn't always what prints out. The number one source of rude surprises happens when you write with a Mac connected to *one* printer (like a StyleWriter) but print on a different one (like a laser printer). Since the typefaces are handled differently for these printers, you'll discover that sentences, lines, and pages end in different places in the printout than they did on the screen. This is another problem that I've experienced when creating documents at home and waiting to print them at school on the laser printer.

    The solution is simple. Before you print, trick the Mac into thinking it has that laser printer already attached, so you can see what it's about to do to you. From the Apple menu (), select Chooser. You should see the name of several printers there, like StyleWriter or LaserWriter (which is used for *all* brands of laser printers). Click the one you *plan* to print on, even if it's not currently connected.

    If you don't see more than one printer icon in the Chooser, you have to reinstall them from your System or printer disks.

Get Busy!

By this point, you should feel like a word-processing expert. I'm sure that you're tired of reading and practicing — so get busy!

Note: The *Macs For Teachers* Bonus Disk contains a sample letterhead that you *could* use by simply changing my name if you're not ready to learn a new skill right now.

Creating a letterhead

Every year I like to create my own personal stationery for those times when my messages need to have a more personal tone provided by (dare I say) *handwritten* notes. Yes, even I still send home handwritten notes. They are more personal and let a parent know that, in this age of technology, there's still a warm, loving individual behind the teacher's desk.

1. Open a new word-processing document.

   You remember, double-click *ClarisWorks* to open the program. When the New Document dialog box appears, choose Word Processing.

2. From the ruler, choose the alignment setting of center justification.

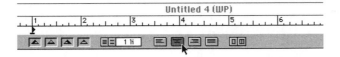

3. From the Font menu choose Times. (And choose 24 point as your Size, and then bold and italic as your Style.

4. Type your name and then press Return. Type the name of your school and then press Return again.

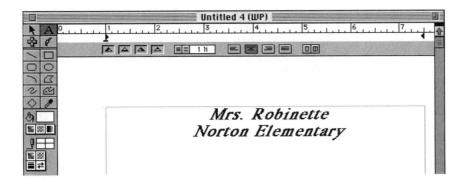

5. Now let's add another skill to our repertoire. First, click the small picture of a page that sits in the bottom-left corner of the screen (just to the left of the page number).

After you click this button, a *tool box* appears to the left of your work area. See the arrow in the top-left corner of this tool box? Click it. (It should become highlighted.)

6. If you are using *ClarisWorks 3.0,* go to the File menu and choose Insert.

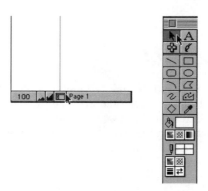

When the dialog box appears, double-click the Clip Art folder.

Take a look at that list of clip art that Claris so thoughtfully installed for you! Scroll through your choices. If you see one that makes you curious, *don't* choose it. Instead, highlight the choice and then click the Create button in the lower-left corner of the dialog box. This will create a preview of the artwork that allows you to make a choice without going back and forth between your document and the Clip Art folder. Yeah, the choices aren't that incredible — but they were free. (You can purchase clip art for very reasonable prices and easily add the images to your files.)

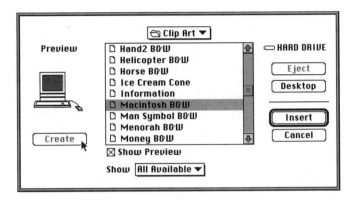

7. Highlight your Clip Art choice and click the Insert button. (I chose the Macintosh — big surprise.) The image appears on your stationery.

Can't find Clip Art?

If you are using an earlier version of *ClarisWorks* (earlier than 3.0), you won't find a Clip Art file already installed. Instead, after highlighting the arrow in the tool box, go to the Apple Menu (🍎) and open the Scrapbook.

I know, there aren't that many to choose from, but you can add to the collection later. For now, find something you can live with. When the picture you have chosen is on the screen, go to the Edit menu and choose Copy. Remember the clipboard we learned about in Chapter 4? Well, your picture is on that baby right now!

Close the Scrapbook (click the little box in the top-left corner of the window). You should see your stationery again. Go to the Edit menu and choose Paste. You've added Graphics.

8. Now, class, we should all be in the same spot at this time, looking at our document with *some type* of picture *somewhere* on the screen.

   Do you see the little squares at the corners of your picture? (If you don't see *four* black squares — the graphic's "handles" — you need to click in the graphic and start all over again. Make sure you choose the arrow in the tool box *before* you choose your picture.) These squares will help you adjust the size of your picture. Point to one of the squares; click and drag the corner. You can do some pretty strange things to your graphic.

9. Now, whenever the squares are visible, you can also move that graphic anywhere on the document. Simply click in the center of your graphic and drag to the top right corner of your stationery.

   (Click off the graphic to make the squares go away. Click on the graphic to make them appear again.)

10. Symmetry is everything, so let's put another Mac in the top left corner. Who can remember how we accomplish this amazing feat? That's right: Copy and Paste.

    If the four corners are showing around your graphic, simply go to the Edit menu, choose Copy, go back to your stationery, and choose Paste. Follow the steps mentioned previously to maneuver that baby into place. Looking good!

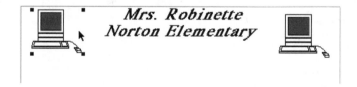

11. Now we are ready to save this as a stationery file that you can pull up quickly and easily. Go to the File menu and choose Save.

    When the dialog box comes up, notice the choices in the bottom-right corner: Document and Stationery. You want this to be saved as Stationery, so click the button. Now the Save As box is highlighted and ready for you to name your creation. Let's call it *Personal Stationery*. (Remember, just start typing over the highlighted area; your words will replace *Untitled 1*.)

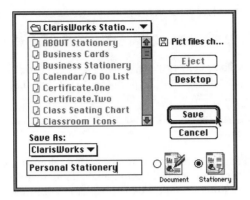

Click Save.

12. A Document Summary appears for you to make a few notes about this supreme piece of work. Type *Personal Stationery* for the title, put your name as the author, and create a name for the category.

(You can turn off the dialog box if you want.)

The rest you could fill in later if you need more detail. For now, this will do.

13. Click OK. You did it!

If you want to prove that you really have created a stationery file, go to File and choose New. When the screen appears, click Start with an Assistant or Stationery. Then, beside the word Category, you see the title General with a black arrow pointing downward. Click General and look at the list. There it is: My Stuff. Click My Stuff. Personal Stationery should come up in the scroll box. I'm proud of you.

Saving as stationery in earlier versions of *ClarisWorks*

If you are using a version of *ClarisWorks* before 3.0, saving as stationery is a little more involved. First, choose Save As from the File menu. Type a name for your document. Before clicking Save, pull down the Save As drop-down menu. Choose ClarisWorks Stationery.

The beauty of saving something as stationery is that when you open the document, *ClarisWorks* creates a copy and names it *Untitled*, thus leaving your original stationery document intact. You can rename your new document when you save it.

Turn down the corner of this page; you'll be using this function when you create a lesson plan and checklists. Think how much time you'll save by not having to set things up each time you get ready to create those required weekly communications.

Creating a lesson-plan template

This is another one of those I-should-have-done-this-a-long-time-ago things. You know what I mean — like putting up that multi-purpose bulletin board that lasts the whole year instead of coming up with a new work of art every month.

Lesson-plan templates can be used in different ways. First, you could create a standard template with all the "little details" filled in — you know, those things you write in by hand day after day, week after week: lunch times, recess duty, Special Ed times, and so on. Run the template off on your trusty copy machine and fill in the blanks by hand. This is a good option if you don't have easy access to a computer. And it still saves loads of time.

Or you could create your template, save it as a stationery document, fill it in on the computer each week, and print out your results. (This procedure does require the creation of text blocks so that you don't lose your format each time you press Return. No big deal.) Either way you choose, you will save major amounts of time, and your lesson plans will look oh-so-professional.

1. Open a new word-processing document.

2. Go to the Format menu and choose Insert Header.

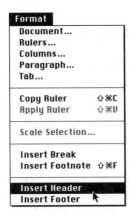

3. Set the Alignment for left justification.

4. Be creative. Choose whatever font or size you like and type your name, grade level, and the words *Day* and *Date*.

   Arrange this header anyway you feel comfortable. I always like having the day of week on my plans, because so many activities change from day to day.

5. Click below the bottom line of the header and create your plan sheet. Approximate the amount of space you'll need to fill in the lesson details and hit return to create your white space.

   Don't fill in the lesson details just yet. Remember, you are making the template first.

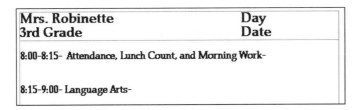

If you run out of room, don't worry about going onto a second page. If you make copies, you can make front-to-back photo copies of your plans before you fill them in.

Review steps 5 through 10 in the earlier section, "Creating a letterhead," if you'd like to add graphics to your template.

6. This might be a good time to use the Spell Check function within *ClarisWorks*. See the sidebar "Where were you when I needed you?" for details.

7. When everything looks the way you'd like, go to the File menu and choose Save.

When the dialog box comes up, notice the choices in the bottom-right corner: Document and Stationery. You want this to be saved as Stationery, so click the button. Now the Save As box is highlighted and eagerly waiting for you to name this wondrous creation. Let's call it *Lesson Plan Template*. (Remember, just start typing over the highlighted area; your words will replace *Untitled 1*.)

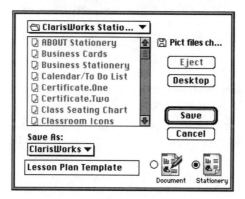

8. Click Save.

A Document Summary appears for you to make a few notes about this incredible masterpiece. Let's keep this template in the same category as the letterhead we created earlier, School Stuff.

Where were you when I needed you?

That's right. Mr. Spell Check (and for that matter, Mr. Computer), where were you when I was in college? I can't believe I went through four years of college and two graduate school degrees without either of you. Today's kids, in my opinion, are spoiled — or just lucky to be living in this age of technology.

Anyway, you'll find my favorite function of any word processing program, the Spell Checker, under the Edit menu in *ClarisWorks*. It's in the Writing Tools file. When the Spelling box comes up, the computer will begin to check the words in your document. When it comes across an unknown spelling, it will display the word and then give you a list of possible alternatives.

You then have choices. You can *Replace* the incorrect word with the highlighted alternative. If you don't agree with the alternatives, you can change your word and have the computer *Check* your new spelling. You can *Skip* the word if you know it's correct (like a strange computer-program name). Or you can have the computer *Learn* the word if it's one you use often (like your last name) and you don't want it to constantly come up as incorrectly spelled.

When the spell checking is complete, the word *Done* will flash up, and the box will tell you how many words were checked and how many had questionable spellings. Click Done — and you will be back in your document.

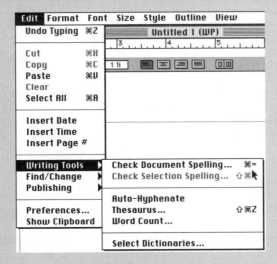

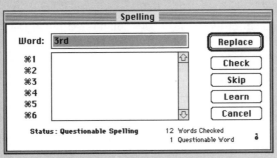

```
Document Summary
      Title: [Lesson Plan Template        ]
    Author: [Michelle Robinette           ]
   Version: [                             ]
  Keywords: [                             ]
  Category: [School Stuff                 ]
Description: [                             ]
             [                             ]

                        [ Cancel ]  [  OK  ]
```

9. Click OK.

Remember that if you are using an early version of *ClarisWorks*, saving as stationery is a little more difficult. See the sidebar, "Saving as stationery in earlier versions of *ClarisWorks*," for instructions.

Using your lesson-plan template

I told you earlier that there are two ways to use this template. The first is to simply print the blank lesson plan and fill in the blanks by hand. This option works well if you don't have a computer at home or easy access to one within your school. Don't feel like you're a computer cop-out; I, myself, used this method for a long time — even after I had a Mac at home.

Pulling up this template and typing in the information is your other option. And this option requires you to learn yet another computer skill — creating a *text block*.

1. Open up your saved lesson-plan template. Remember to choose Assistant or Stationery from the menu. Then find the My Stuff under the drop-down menu that's labeled General.

    You should see your lesson plan template in the School Stuff folder. Open it.

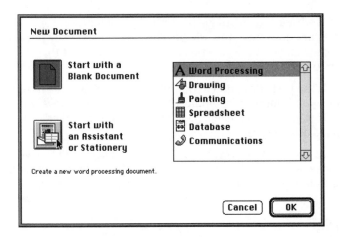

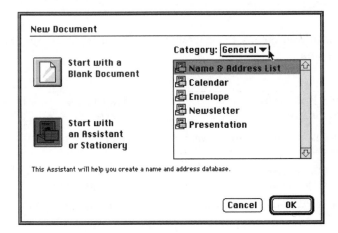

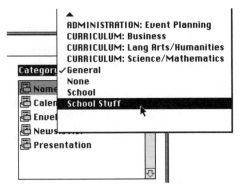

2. This is where good planning pays off. If you left an appropriate amount of space for adding text, this will be a breeze. Look at your document and decide what you want to type in. Place your cursor at the point where you wish to begin.

   Here's the trick: Hold down the Option key and click the mouse button where you want to start typing. Hold the mouse button down and drag the length of space you'll need. (Don't worry about the depth; the box will expand as you type.)

   You've just created a text block. These blocks prevent the words in your stationery from moving down each time you move to another line. In other words, it confines your typing to a certain area of the page.

Day
Date

Day Tuesday
Date

3. Type in your details. Click outside the box when you are ready to go to the next area.

Mrs. Robinette	Day Tuesday
3rd Grade	Date

   8:00-8:15– Attendance, Lunch Count, and Morning Work–
   Write spelling words 3x each in cursive. Read silently.

   8:15-9:00– Language Arts–
   1. Verbs. Read a passage in today's paper and have the students clap their hands when they hear a verb.
   2. Give each student a page from the paper and have them find and highlight at least 10 verbs.
   3. Have students use 5 of the verbs they found in sentences.

4. Continue in this manner until you fill in the entire document.

   If you find that you didn't leave enough space between time blocks, simply click outside your text block and move the next category down a little by pressing Return.

5. When you finish, save or print the day's plans. Pull up another blank lesson-plan template.

   Continue until you've completed one week's worth. If you're on a roll, plan for the entire month!

So what do you think? Isn't word processing the answer to your prayers? You'll soon be like me, wondering what-in-the-world you ever did without it. But don't stop here. Keep reading and find out about spreadsheets and databases.

Chapter 8

I May Spread a Few Sheets, but I Don't Do Windows

*W*hat I'm about to tell you is completely true. I once had a student (let's call him Johnny) whose mother was obsessed with his academic performance in first grade. Johnny was a very bright child who was already reading chapter books when he entered my class. At our first conference in November, his mother brought in a scrapbook filled with every piece of work I had sent home since the beginning of the school year. Now, I don't believe in giving letter grades in first grade, so most of the papers I'd sent home had positive images like smiley faces or checkmarks. This parent had converted these images into her own 4.0 grading scale and was concerned about her child's *grades*. I assured her that Johnny was doing fine and jokingly added that his scores in first grade would not affect his Harvard admission. She then looked at me very seriously and said, "Are you sure?"

Parents like that make us all realize how important good record-keeping can be. Most districts now require months of information tracking on a student before they'll even discuss special-area placement. I've found that good checklists can help me keep track of the important stuff (like grades and homework) and the not-so-important stuff (like ice-cream money). I'm just not the anecdotal record kind of gal — but hey, you can even create a spreadsheet for those forms.

What Is a Spreadsheet?

Spreadsheets have nothing to do with the actions you go through when making your bed. A *spreadsheet* is simply an electronic form of the old-fashioned ledger, and spreadsheets are generally used in the business arena.

Business

Our friendly businessperson uses spreadsheets to crunch numbers. You know, they take some numerical information, enter some formulas, and let the computer do their math for them. They end up with information that they put in publications they call profit and loss statements, quarterly reports, or a number of other venues — all of which are foreign to most teachers.

Education

When I first encountered spreadsheets, I didn't look at all the numbers. I only saw this wonderful layout and thought, "With a little manipulation, I can turn this into a wonderful customized checklist."

I will admit that you could take a basic spreadsheet, enter student names and grades, and then create formulas that will average your grades for you. However, it is much easier (and relatively cheap) to purchase your own gradebook program that will do your math for you and even print out a report for those documentation-crazed parents like Johnny's mom.

Let's Make a Spreadsheet!

I'm going to give you step-by-step instructions on creating your own checklist. Then I'll show you some other neat ways to use spreadsheets to keep track of classroom activities. And guess what? You can even save spreadsheets as stationery and re-customize them for other classroom needs (see Chapter 7 for details on stationery).

Note: I've added a few spreadsheet samples for you on the *Macs For Teachers* Bonus Disk.

1. Open up *ClarisWorks.*

   You remember: Go to your hard-drive icon, find *ClarisWorks,* and double-click.

2. When you see this screen, choose Spreadsheet (big surprise, right?) Then press Return (or click OK).

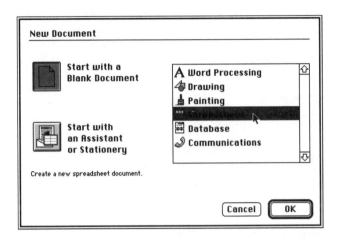

You will then be presented with a confusing-looking page full of lines, letters, and numbers. The menu-bar choices look a little different, too. Don't worry.

3. Now let's spread that sheet! First go to the View menu and choose Page View.

   This action keeps your document the size of the page you'll be printing it on. Otherwise, this sheet will scroll endlessly down the hall all the way to your principal's office.

4. Next, click in the *cell* (that's what boxes are called in spreadsheets) located at A1. It should become highlighted. Go to the Format menu and choose Column Width.

A box pops up with a space for you to type in a column width. The default is 72 pixels or screen dots. Type in 150 and press Return. The column automatically extends to a width large enough to accommodate even the longest name.

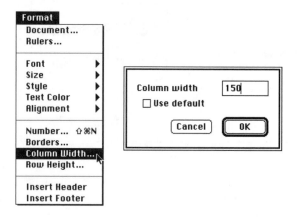

5. Cell number A1 should still be highlighted. Type the word *Name*.

What? You don't see it in the cell? That's because what you enter first appears in the box at the top of the lettered columns, called the *editing strip.* The box to the left of this space tells you what cell you are working on.

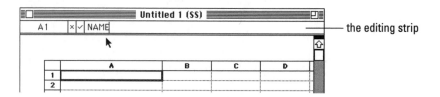

the editing strip

6. Press Return. Your typing appears in the cell. You'll notice that the next cell down is now highlighted.

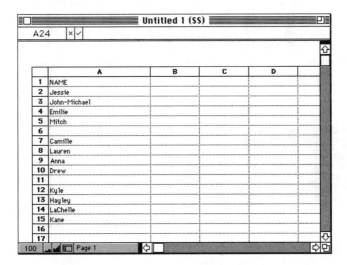

7. Now enter the names of every darling in your class. After typing each name, press Return.

I like to enter the names in clusters according to the group they sit with, because that's usually how I travel around the classroom and keep track of work.

Set up the student names in a way that best suits your style (alphabetized, first name, and so on). You can save this checklist as stationery. When you pull it up each time, all you'll have to enter is headings for your columns — not names.

Now that you've entered your names, clean this baby up and save it as stationery before putting in any specific information.

Don't waste your time!

Yes, you can format as you go — making things bold, italic, underlined — but why bother? This is definitely one of those times where formatting should take place when you've completed all your entries. Then simply go back and highlight everything you want to format. Remember to click where you want to start and drag. (The first cell you click in will be a hollowed outline; don't worry, it's selected.) When choosing cells, you need to start in a corner and drag to the opposite corner.

Once you've highlighted the area you want to format, you'll see all your choices in the Format menu. You can even use different colors for your headings (if you have a color monitor).

Don't go crazy. Choosing funky fonts or outrageous styles may make your document difficult to read — or the lettering may become too large for your column size. You want your work to be easy to read, and you don't want to reformat in order to accommodate your offbeat style choices.

Click here

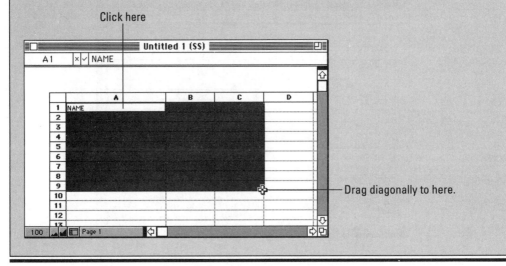

Drag diagonally to here.

8. Go to the Options menu and choose Display.

    I'm not going to explain each of the choices that now greet you — just do what I say. Choose Cell Grid and Solid Lines, and make sure the other boxes are empty. You've just eliminated any extra lines and made your work much easier to read. Click OK.

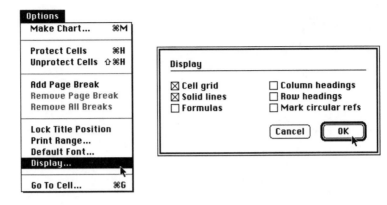

Wow! Doesn't that look a little better?

9. Before going any further, choose Save and name the spreadsheet *Blank Class List*. Be sure you click the Stationery icon in the bottom-right corner of the window. Follow all the instructions as they appear on the screen.

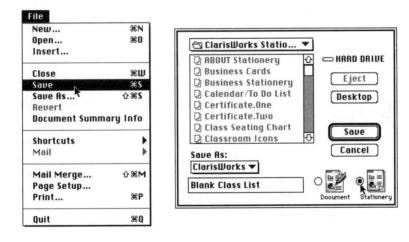

That task completed, let's go on. Your document should still be on the screen. Now you can adapt this spreadsheet for a specific use. Ready?

10. Go to the Format menu and choose Insert Header. A header appears at the top of your spreadsheet and cannot be altered by any information you put in the spreadsheet itself.

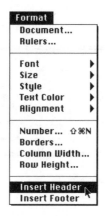

You should now see a flashing cursor in the top-left corner of your document. The next part is easy.

11. Name your checklist *Homework*. Just like in your word-processing activities, you can choose your fonts, their size, and their style.

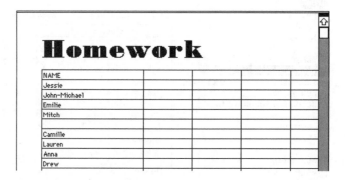

12. Now, click back on the actual spreadsheet in the cell just to the right of the word *Name*.

We need to work across this row and put in dates or assignment numbers. I'm making this a checklist for homework assignments, so at the top of each of the columns I'm putting a homework due date. Go ahead — just click in the block, type a date, and press Return. Enter all your dates.

When you press Return to enter your date, the next cell down becomes highlighted. There are two ways to navigate between the cells: Either click in the next cell you wish to work in, or use the arrow keys.

13. Now you can go back and highlight and format to your heart's content. Look in the Format menu for Font, Size, Color, and Alignment choices.

At this point, you're ready to print the checklist. You don't necessarily have to save this creation if it will be used only for this singular purpose — you have a personal stationery template waiting for you to customize for other needs.

Homework

NAME	4-1	4-7	4-14	4-21
Jessie				
John-Michael				
Emilie				
Mitch				
Camille				
Lauren				
Anna				
Drew				
Kyle				
Hayley				
LaChelle				
Kane				

14. So now go to File and then to Print.

Now That You've Done It

One wonderful thing about writing a book for educators is that I know how incredibly bright my readers are. Therefore, I'm not going to explain the steps involved in using spreadsheets in other ways; I'm simply going to throw some ideas out there. You resourceful sponges can soak it up and go from that point. Spreadsheets are fun to play with and very easy to customize.

✔ Is there a child you're trying to get placed in a Special Education program, and the psychologist wants you to track specific behaviors for a time period before placement will be considered? (Gosh, is that ever frustrating — you know the kid needs help, and they make you jump through hoops to get it!) Instead of trying to keep handwritten records on scraps of paper, create a checklist with the behaviors, along with a space in which to write stuff. Then blow Mr. or Ms. Psychologist's mind when you come back with specific dates, types of incidents, and comments!

A.D.D. CHECKLIST

(Place a Tally Mark and Date for Each Occurance)

Behavior	Tally	Dates	Notes / Details
Daydreaming			
Out of seat			
Destructive			
Harms others			

✔ The same type format could be used for a child with behavior problems that you are trying to correct. Make a form that the child could take home every day — a form showing how the behavior was during specific periods of time. I like to leave these forms on the child's desk as a visual reminder throughout the day.

✔ Projects and papers are sometimes hard for kids to conceptualize. Why not create a checklist containing each step in the process and include due dates? This form also helps parents keep track and avoid those day-before-it's-due trips to the library.

✔ How often are you asked for a list of the students in your class? Having this list saved on the computer makes it easy for you to whip that baby out at a moment's notice.

✔ When we were sharing one Mac on my grade level, I would create a checklist for each subject area and use those sheets to record grades. Then, when it was my turn for the computer, I'd enter the grades in my gradebook program (see Chapter 13, "Hot Topics in Education and the Software Solutions") for easy averaging at report card time.

Chapter 9

Databases

*H*ow many of you have parents fill out those horrible, 5 x 7-inch, white index cards on registration day? Parents hate them, you hate them, but they are necessary. Well, a database takes the place of all those awful little cards. A database is an electronic list of information that you can customize to meet your own needs.

A database is also why you get all that lovely junk mail. You see, companies sell database lists to other companies who in turn sell to two others who sell to two others, and so on and so on. Anyway, there are probably tons of companies that have the equivalent of a little index card with your vital information.

Your Class-List Database

It takes only a little time to set up the format for your database, and after that you are on your way to total (or close to total) organization. It won't do anything for that drawer in your desk where you dump everything — you get to have control, too. (Now that's a *new* concept.)

Note: If you're short on time and want to learn this skill later, try using the database included on the *Macs For Teachers* Bonus Disk.

You decide what information is important to you and how it will be displayed. Before starting, you need to find the *ClarisWorks* icon on your hard drive and open that program up.

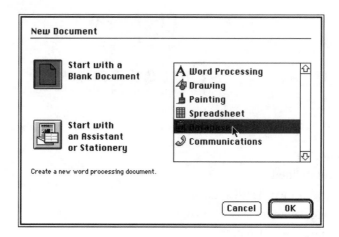

When you see the selection screen, double-click Database. Don't freak when you see the first screen!

Setting up your fields

The screen that confronts you may look confusing, but this is where you will assert control. The computer is waiting for you to tell it what blanks (*fields*) you want to fill in for each child in your class: name, address, phone, parents, and so on.

You're about to type the names for these blanks. As always, if you make a typo, just press the Delete key to backspace over it. Here we go.

1. Type *First Name*. Press the Return key.

2. Type *Last Name* and press Return.

3. Type *Parents Formal* and press Return.

   "Mr. & Mrs. Robinette" for example.

4. Type *Parents Casual* and press Return.

   "John & Michelle" for example.

5. Type *Address*. Return.

   See how each field name appears in the list above?

6. Type *Phone (H)*. Return.

7. Type *Phone (W)*. Return.

8. Type *Special Info*. Return.

9. Type *Child's Poss.* Return.

   This stands for the possessive form of the child's name. I know it sounds weird. Trust me; you'll see how we use this info later in the chapter.

10. Type *First & Last*. Press Return.

    You've entered all your fields, and your screen should look something like this:

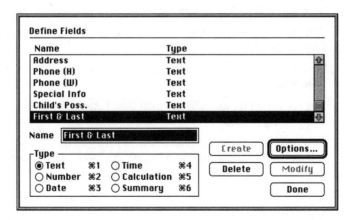

11. Click the Done button in the lower-right corner. The dialog box goes away.

    When you see what you've created, things should begin to make a little more sense. You've just created the blanks (fields) to be filled in for each person on your list. (Don't worry if the field names are too long to show up in their entirety — you still know what they are.)

First Name	
Last Name	
Parents	
Parents	
Address	
Phone (H)	
Phone (W)	
Special Info	
Child's Poss.	
First & Last	

Filling in the blanks

Computer nerds would call this next step *data entry*. Put simply, you are going to fill in the blanks you just created. To advance from one blank to another, just hit the Tab key or click inside the blank you want to work on. Are you ready?

1. Make sure you can see the dotted rectangle for each field — like the ones in the preceding figure. If not, press the Tab key. The little blinking cursor should be in the "First Name" blank. (If it's not, click there.)

2. I'll set this first one up using my daughter's info. Type *Jessie* and press the Tab key. The cursor should jump to the "Last Name" box.

3. Type *Robinette* and press the Tab key.

4. Now enter *Mr. & Mrs. Robinette* in the "Parents Formal" box and press Tab.

5. You should now be in the "Parents Casual" box. Type *John & Michelle* and press Tab.

6. You are going to enter the address in the "Address" box, so type *4705 Somewhere Drive* and press Return.

   The cursor didn't jump to the next box. Instead, you've expanded this box by pressing Return.

7. Now type *Anywhere, GA 30202* before pressing the Tab key. The box collapses back to its original size. Don't worry, your information is still there.

8. Continue now with the "Home Phone" blank. Type *963-7139* and press Tab.

9. In the "Work Phone" section you can enter two phone numbers (one for each parent or guardian): Type *M- 963-1953* and *D- 963-2159*. And yes, once again, press that Tab key.

10. You should be in the "Special Info" box. Type this word for word: *Precious child — very bright for her age.*

    Don't question it, just type. (Remember, she's a teacher's kid. Aren't they all extremely bright?) Hit the Tab key, of course.

11. In this "Child's Poss." box, you need to enter the possessive form of the child's name. Type *Jessie's* and press the Tab key.

12. Last entry. Type *Jessie Robinette* in the "First & Last" box.

    You did it! You've just filled in your first card!

    Now, if you have all the information in front of you, pull up another blank card by going to the Edit menu and choosing New Record. *Voilà* ! A new blank card appears ready for you to fill in.

    Keep filling in cards until you have entered your entire class (or all the names for your Christmas-card mailing list). Then don't forget to SAVE!

13. Choose Save from the File menu. When the dialog box appears, type in a name for your database (how about: Class List Database) and click Save.

You know what to do if you want to print a couple of copies of your class info (maybe one for home and one for your plan notebook): Go to the File menu, choose Print, and follow directions!

You may want to wait, however, and read the activities that are coming up. I'll show you a variety of ways to customize this information.

Using Your Database

So you've created this cool index file. What can you do now? Well, my friends, let me show you! The beauty of the *ClarisWorks* database is that you are never locked into one particular way to view your information. After you've created the database, you can take advantage of a number of different layout options.

You can create a list that contains only the information you need from the database. You can also print customized labels or create a *Mail Merge* document. Mail Merge allows you to customize any word-processing document with information from your database.

Making a columnar list

Just the facts, ma'am. I know you just entered lots of information that you certainly don't need on a daily basis. So why print the entire list? Let's create a list of student names with the parent names and home phone numbers.

1. If it's not already open, open your database.

    You remember. Double-click *ClarisWorks*. Choose Database, go to the File menu, choose Open, and find your database.

2. Now go to the Layout menu and choose New Layout. A layout is simply a way to view the information in your database.

3. A dialog box appears. Choose Columnar report and click OK. I know it sounds strange — but this is the one we need.

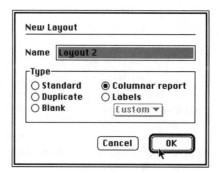

Yes, another dialog box appears. This time we are going to tell it what information (from the database) we want to include on our customized list.

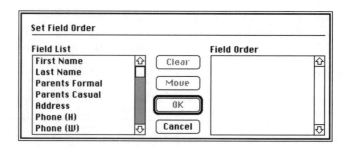

The list on the left shows the fields in your database (Field List). The empty list on the right is waiting for your information (Field Order). It is important to enter the information in the order that you want it to appear on your list.

4. Scroll down and begin with the last field on your database: "First & Last." Highlight this field. Click Move (which is no longer grayed-out, thanks to your selection). The field should move over to the Field Order list.

   Continue by adding the "Parents Casual" field and the "Special Info" field. Your screen should look like this:

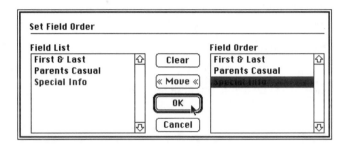

5. Click OK. The customized list should appear on your screen. Save your list and print a few copies!

Creating a Mail Merge document

Mail Merge doesn't accurately describe what we are about to do — it sounds as if we are about to mix your mail with someone else's. In reality, *Mail Merge* allows you to merge or replace general information in your letter with specific information from your database. Mail Merge doesn't have to be used for your classroom. Why not create a customized Christmas letter and have personalized greetings for each of the lucky people on your Christmas card list?

Let's start out with an easy project: a letter home to the wonderful parents of those sweet darlings you see Monday through Friday. Pretend that you've just finished a unit on Egypt and the kids have created a museum of Egyptian artifacts within your classroom. I'm going to show you how to create a customized invitation note that you could send home with each student.

Ready?

1. Leave your class-list database open. Choose New from the File menu and open a blank word-processing document.

2. Type the following standard invitation. Pretty boring? Wait and see what we are going to do to this plain Jane.

2-9-95

Dear Parents,

I'm so proud of everyone's work in our Egyptian Studies unit. We have had a wonderful time and hope that you can come visit our Egyptian Museum this Friday at 4:00. Your child is a wonderful asset to our class.

Thanks!

Mrs. Robinette

3. Go to the File menu and choose Mail Merge.

4. You will see a dialog box that looks like this:

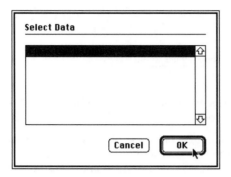

Choose your database.

5. Another (even smaller) dialog box appears. It's tiny, and it would be easier if you moved it to a corner of your screen. (Click in the title bar and drag!)

6. Now this is fun. Look at your invitation. Highlight *Parents* (but don't highlight the comma). Go to that tiny box and make a decision: Do you want this letter to be casual (calling the parents by first name) or formal?

   In the box under field name, you see all the fields you set up. Choose the way you'd like to address the parents (*Parents Formal* or *Parents Casual*) and highlight it. Then click the Insert Field button.

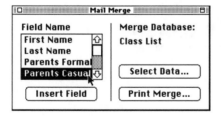

Look at your document! A place holder has taken the place of *Parents* — and in each letter you print, a different set of names will appear. (One set for each child in your database. Are you getting it?)

```
2-9-95

Dear «Parents Casual»,

I'm so proud of everyone's work in our
```

7. Now go to the words *everyone's*. Highlight the words. Go to the little Mail Merge box, and choose "Child's Poss." Press Insert Field.

   Once again, a place holder takes the place of the highlighted words, and each letter you print will have a different child's name in the possessive form in that spot! Now do you see why some of the fields that sounded strange are really very useful?

8. We'll do one more bit of customizing. Highlight the words *your child* and go to the Mail Merge box. Choose *First Name* and click Insert Field.

   You know what happens next.

9. Magic Time! Look at that Mail Merge box. See the Print Merge button? Click it. The normal print screen comes up for you to make the standard printing decisions. Go for it!

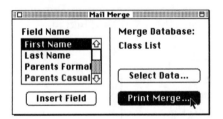

```
2-9-95

Dear John & Michelle,

I'm so proud of Jessie's work in our Egyptian Studies unit. We
have had a wonderful time and hope that you can come visit our
Egyptian Museum this Friday at 4:00. Jessie is a wonderful asset
to our class.

Thanks!

Mrs. Robinette
```

As you've probably already decided, the possibilities are endless.

Part III
Software & CD-ROM Technology

The 5th Wave   **By Rich Tennant**

"Before I go on to explain more advanced procedures like the 'Zap-Rowdy-Students-who-Don't-Pay-Attention' function, we'll begin with some basics."

In this part...

Now comes the fun part . . . sifting through the catalogs, talking to peers, and walking the aisles of the local computer stores until your mind is so full of confusing ads, misleading descriptions, and glossy packaging claims that you are beginning to wonder if all this new-found knowledge is really worth the headache.

It is worth it! Read the chapters in this part, and it will all begin to make sense — I promise.

I'll describe the different categories of software and CD-ROM programs and give you detailed lists of my favorite ones in each category.

Hot topics in education are also being addressed by many software companies. Authentic Assessment, Portfolios, and keyboarding programs are some of the biggest sellers. In Chapter 12, I discuss each of these.

So read on. Then go shopping!

Chapter 10

A Guided Tour through the Software Jungle

*S*chool administrators don't always agree on the intended outcome of their technology pursuits. Some will tell you their main goal is to raise test scores; they display class scores on overhead projectors, compare scores with rival counties, and basically make you feel like you haven't been teaching anything significant for the past year. Often these schools are looking for a quick fix and hope that technology can cure what we teachers just can't seem to get right. Other administrators take a more global approach and feel that if we use technology in teaching children to be better thinkers and problem solvers, we will produce confident and successful individuals — who in return may produce higher test scores.

The software jungle can be very confusing. It's filled with numerous products to meet the goals of a very diverse group of users; and whether you're spending your own money or the limited money provided in your school's technology budget, it's a tight squeeze. You simply don't have room for a costly purchasing mistake. In this chapter, I examine the four major types of software intended for student use. I'll give you the straight facts (and, of course, a few of my opinions on each category) while providing you with some valuable ideas for incorporating each type of software into your school setting.

Skill-and-drill and me!

Without skill-and-drill software, I may have never been accepted to graduate school. You see, I don't test well — I never have. When I found out I needed to take either the GRE or the MAT to enter grad school, I became quite the nervous teacher. (Unlike the MacGod, I did not graduate summa cum laude from Yale.) Anyway, I opted for the MAT when I found out that it lasted an hour and dealt only with analogies. I was told that the computer lab at the education school had a program to help you study for this hour-long brain burner of a test. Guess what? It was pure skill-

and-drill. As I mentioned earlier, it not only told me the correct answer, it analyzed my response and told me how I *should* have addressed the problem. I used this program for two days in a row and then went to take the test. I scored so well that the evaluator had to look at my answer sheet again. And I owe it all to our friend, Mr. Skill-and-drill. (I'm sorry to report that the university couldn't tell me the name of the program — this was in 1984. But there are many great test-preparation programs on the market covering all the major entrance exams.)

Skill-and-Drill Software

In the simplest of terms, *skill-and-drill software* is a form of electronic flash card. (The difference is you don't have to hold this software with your thumb, artfully covering the top right-hand corner, so the students can't see through to the answer on the back.) Don't misunderstand me. Today's skill-and-drill software is beautifully created, and there are some good programs out there that do a super job of reviewing skills. Most of the programs concentrate on a single skill (multiplication facts, addition, and so on) or a single subject area (math, science, or reading, for example).

The granddaddy of all skill-and-drill software is *MECC* (Minnesota Education Consulting Consortium). How's that for a name? But MECC has produced some incredible programs over the years, and many of you may be familiar with what MECC created for those wonderful — and now very lonely — Apple IIc and IIe computers.

Skill-and-drill software has its place within the school. Some things, such as multiplication facts, need to be continually reviewed — and there is no magic way to get children to memorize these facts without practice. The best forms of skill-and-drill software give *immediate feedback* and *helpful corrections*: here's what you did wrong, here's how to fix it.

The kids love drills that come in the form of a game, which most of today's programs include. But not all skill-and-drill software needs to be a game; some of the programs I enjoyed the most in those early days of MECC and the IIc were just like flash cards: They flashed up a multiplication problem, gave you so many

If you can't pay attention to me, you won't get a turn!

How often have these words come out of your mouth? I know that I should want students to be interested in the computer and begging for a turn — but not during a lesson that took me days to prepare. Let's face it: In a one-computer classroom, the whole class is intrigued by the noises coming out of the machine that you've tried to place out of their line of vision. And some of the best skill-and-drill software is usually very noisy. (The sound effects in these programs are cool and very realistic). But have no fear. Almost all these programs have control panels where you can go and switch off the sound, vary the number of problems presented, and set the level of difficulty . . . although hearing the rocket blast off or the alien capture you is half the fun. (Oh, I forgot, learning isn't supposed to be about fun!) I cured this noise problem without ruining the fun by purchasing headphones for my classroom. The cheap ones work just fine; I picked up a set for each computer in our lab at a local drugstore for $1 each.

seconds to respond, and then took away the problem. At the end of the game you were given an accuracy score. It was pure learning without the distraction of animated characters and soaring rocket ships — and it worked because kids enjoy a challenge and love to be given another chance to improve their score! This type of skill-and-drill software works especially well in the one-computer classroom where a teacher wants to give everyone a fair amount of computer time each day and is interested in monitoring progress.

But skill-and-drill software has its drawbacks. I already mentioned that most programs focus on a single skill or subject area. This restriction can prove troubling when budgets are limited and you want to purchase programs that will please the masses. Another drawback is the range of ages each program is appropriate for. Most programs are grouped by pre-school, early elementary, elementary, middle, or high school — with the majority of the software being aimed at kindergarten through grade 6. Thus, the number of kids who will benefit from the purchase is once again a problem. Finally, skill-and-drill software does very little to encourage creative thinking and problem solving (unless you count searching for the spaceship that contains the ugliest monster in the *creative-thinking* category). I feel that such skills must be encouraged in this rapidly changing world.

Productivity Software

As the name implies, when using *productivity software,* you usually walk away with a *product* of some sort. And in answer to your next question — yes, for most of the productivity software, it would be nice to have a printer attached to your computer. However, it's not a necessity. Remember the art of saving? You could have each child save work to a disk and take it at a more convenient time to a computer with a printer. (I know, there is no convenient time unless you can squeeze it in during your 30-minute "break" somewhere between using the restroom, checking out resources from the library, calling the *concerned parent*, and preparing for your next class.)

In my job as a technology coordinator, I'm required to integrate the classroom curriculum with technology. It's unrealistic to think that a school could purchase software on each individual area of the curriculum. Don't get me wrong; there are some great programs that are very specific and usually skill-and-drill. Yet I can't justify spending taxpayer dollars on a piece of software that may be used by one grade level to highlight a topic being taught for a single semester. However, by using productivity software, you can create activities for all levels and all subjects with just a single program. (I love productivity software, as you can probably tell.)

Another great benefit of productivity software is the power you give students. You are not giving them a predesigned format where they are simply participants. You are giving them the tools they need to solve their problems or interpret a topic. Look at some examples using *ClarisWorks:*

- ✔ *Second grade* students can write five sentences and then choose a way to show that they know the subject in each sentence. The opportunities are endless. They can change the font of the subject, underline the subject, type the subject in a different size, type the subject in a different color, or do any combination of these things.

- ✔ *Fifth graders* can survey the school each week and then compile the survey results on a spreadsheet. Then, using the Make a Chart command, they can turn their results into a more visual image to share in a school newspaper.

- ✔ *Middle or high school students* can use the database to enter information on a variety of environmental or social issues; later, the students can call upon this database to help find information to aid in the creation of call-to-action letters for specific causes. They can even use the database to create address labels for the envelopes.

In other words, most productivity programs are like those knives sold on late-night TV: they'll slice, dice, chop, and even julienne!

Other forms of productivity software help students create published products. These products can be based on any areas of the curriculum. Book publishing software that helps the student to write, illustrate, print (front to back, no less), fold, and staple are easy for any age to use. This type of creative involvement between the student and the computer helps make the learning more meaningful and personal.

Multimedia Software

Now we come to the kids' favorite type of productivity programs: the drawing, painting, and *multimedia* programs. I consider these programs to be a form of productivity software because a product is created. If used correctly, the product can be integrated into any area of the curriculum. Yet, to some parents and even some educators, these programs are pure fluff that should never be included in the education environment — kids shouldn't spend school time drawing and coloring.

I beg to differ. Multimedia software can be a great asset to any technology curriculum.

Multimedia programs allow for the purest form of assessment: authentic assessment. We need to allow students more chances to "show what they know" instead of prescribing a test to tell us how bright they are. Here are a few examples with students using *KidPix2:*

✔ Why not have *kindergarteners* practice letter recognition and handwriting skills by using each of the paint tools in *KidPix* to create different versions of the same letter? Then, if they are ready to extend the learning a little further, they can add stamps of pictures starting with that letter — or even better, they can use the text tools to type words starting with that letter.

✔ *Fifth graders* can create an advertisement for a product that could have been sold during the period of Westward Expansion. Using the text tool, they can add descriptive words and phrases to justify the purchase of the item. Wouldn't this activity tell a teacher if the student understood the hardships facing the travelers?

✔ *Middle school students* can create a slide show that could later be aired via closed circuit television to the entire school. Topics for the show can be based on any topics in their curriculum — or the topics can be chosen to arouse social awareness.

Once again, the multi-purpose knife has proven itself to be a good investment!

Simulation Software

This final type of software is relatively new to the market. Many of the programs have been labeled *edutainment*. That's a new word in the software industry. Yet, as contrived as it sounds, it is a very good description of the programs in this area.

Simulation software is often labeled interactive because the student becomes a part of the software. Simulation software is incredibly fun, of course, and most of the quality programs involve a very high level of thinking and reasoning. The only drawbacks involve the time necessary to complete an activity and memory requirements for your computer.

It's easy to get caught up in the activities: crossing the plains in the 1800s on the Oregon Trail, finding Carmen as she travels through history (Where in Time is Carmen Sandiego?), or building a new town that will prosper and grow in SimCity. But, before you know it, it's time to leave the lab or take the class to PE. It borders on cruelty when you ask a child to leave an adventure unsolved or incomplete, and that situation often occurs when you use these programs in the school setting.

Most of the programs are now available on disk or CD-ROM, and either way they usually require a large amount of memory. Always check the package or ad to be sure that you have the proper requirements needed to run the software. If your school is like most in the country, you're probably working on machines that have 4MB of RAM and a limited amount of hard-drive space, which will make it difficult to run some of the programs. (Some of the boxes or ads might say a program will run with a minimum of 4MB, but it won't be nearly as smooth as you'd like — and it will be *very* slow.)

A RAM Refresher

In Chapter 2 I talk about memory and I tell you that RAM stands for Random Access Memory. You pronounce this acronym the way it reads, like the goat: ram. And you will hear this word quite frequently. RAM is memory; it delivers information to your Mac's brain almost instantly.

Remember the menu? Pull down that menu and highlight About This Macintosh. Then release the mouse button. A window appears.

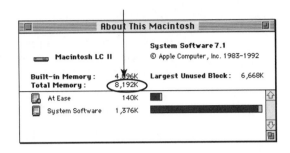

 The number shown in the preceding figure would be how much RAM your Mac has. If you lop off everything after the comma, you're left with the number of *megs* of RAM. It's probably 4, 5, 8, or 16MB. Older Macs have less. Higher-priced Macs have more. Take this opportunity to write this information on the cheat sheet in the front of this book. This number will come in handy when you're shopping for software.

Let's Be Realistic

In the ideal world, I'd have one lab for each type of software: skill-and-drill, productivity, multimedia, and simulation. I'd also like to have mini-labs within each classroom to allow small groups of students access — and possibly allow each student a fair amount of time on the computer each day. However, that's not possible within most of our schools, and time constraints often control what can be done within the labs.

So, if I had to make decisions:

1. I'd first choose to have a productivity/multimedia lab where teachers could sign up for at least an hour at a time with the freedom to come back on consecutive days to complete a project.

2. My second choice would be to have a multimedia lab like the productivity lab, where teachers could sign up for large blocks of time on continual days to complete involved multimedia projects. I'd make sure the lab was equipped with Macs with major amounts of memory (16MB of RAM and 350MB or more of hard-disk space), a scanner, a QuickTake Camera, and a video camera.

3. Then I'd choose to have a skill-and-drill lab that worked on a rotation schedule in order to give everyone in the school a chance to use the lab. Time slots for this lab could be for 30-45 minutes each.

4. And last, I'd choose to have a simulation lab where the students could sign up individually for large blocks of time (which would allow for *really* experiencing the simulation).

Media Center alternatives

The media center in your school can often be a viable alternative for a complete lab situation. Simulation programs work as a great addition to a media center in the form of a mini-lab. With a center used this way, students can come on their own, possibly after finishing required classroom work, and stay for a while.

The media center could also have a few computers set aside for skill-and-drill software that the teachers could request from the media specialist. This strategy could be a way to customize learning to meet the needs of all students.

In the media center at my school, we also have one computer that's connected to a laser printer and a modem — and is reserved solely for teachers. Teachers use this computer to create their newsletters, enter grades on gradebook programs, or use for e-mail correspondence. (I often ask teachers to preview software on this computer as well.) They like knowing that they have their own "space" to complete computing activities.

Chapter 11

The Amazing World of CD-ROM

● ●

In This Chapter

▶ CD-ROMs

▶ Requirements for using CD technology

▶ Pros and cons of using CD-ROM technology in the school setting

▶ Getting the most out of CD-ROM technology in your school

● ●

on't Throw Another Acronym at Me!

Schools are almost as notorious as computer geeks for using letters to represent inane word clusters. Let's see, in my school alone we have:

LSAC	*Local School Advisory Committee*
LSPI	*Local School Plan for Improvement*
LSTC	*Local School Technology Coordinator*
IEP	*Individual Evaluation Plan*
ILT	*Instructional Lead Teacher*

I'm sure your school is full of these sweet acronyms, and people love to use them to sound important. People think they are saving time by using these cute letter combinations when, in reality, they almost always have to say the whole phrase (because no one ever seems to know what they are talking about).

Computer heads are the same except that they don't ever break their acronyms into words. My advice? Just nod and act as if you know what they're talking about. Eventually, you'll understand, too. It took me forever to sort out the difference between RAM and ROM.

CD-ROM Explained

CD stands for *compact disc.* ROM stands for *read-only memory.* Read-only memory means that you can only read, see, or hear what's on the CD. You can't make any changes to the contents of the CD.

So what do I need in order to take advantage of this acronym?

This is one of the simpler computer feats to accomplish. The requirements are minimal, and so is the cost when compared to other add-ons in the computer universe.

You Need a CD

By now I'm sure that you've at least seen a music CD. I'm embarrassed to say this, but I only just recently purchased a CD player for my stereo system. (I'll always call new releases *albums,* and I'll never get rid of my turntable.)

Anyway, a CD is a flat, thin, shiny disk that has a diameter of about 5 inches. The ones that play music look exactly the same as the ones you use in a computer.

However, a computer CD does much more than play music. The technology behind this wondrous creation is truly amazing. You see, a CD can hold a bizillion times more information than a regular computer disk, therefore allowing it to hold animation, incredible sound, and bedazzling graphics — all of which would consume hundreds of floppy disks.

CD-ROM discs are usually a little more costly than the average computer program found in a floppy format. And many programs are available in both formats.

You Need a CD-ROM Drive

The other part of this equation is the CD-ROM drive (the $200 to $400 thing you use to play the CD). I told you in the beginning of this book that I'm not a techno-nerd, so I won't even begin to try and explain how this baby works. I *will* tell you that some machines come with CD-ROM drives built in (internal). Or you can purchase an external CD-ROM drive and plug it into the back of your Mac. (I've done it. It's *très* easy!)

If you purchase an external CD-ROM drive, you'll find some software inside the box. This software tells the Mac that it has a new neighbor sitting beside it on the desk. Don't fret; installing software is an easy task and takes less than five minutes. Simply pop the disk in your disk drive and follow the instructions for installation.

CD-ROM Technology in the School Setting

There are pros and cons to using CDs in the school setting. In our world of education, money is always a problem. If we could get over that hurdle, I'd have no problem in saying go for it! However, as you'll see, money is the root of all CD-Evil.

Pros:

- CD-ROM programs are wonderfully rich, colorful, and exciting.

- The programs are full of information that's usually arranged in a very appealing and easy-to-understand manner.

- Many of the programs are incredible research tools that not only put written information at a student's fingertips, but also include sound, graphics, and even movies.

Caddy, please!

CD-ROM drives come in two styles: caddy and caddy-less. A CD caddy is a container that protects the CD. A caddy costs about $5. Some Macs require a CD to be in a caddy before you can insert it. Other Macs and CD-ROM drives allow you to put the naked CD right into the pop-out tray, and then the Mac sucks it back in.

Personally, I like keeping the CDs in a caddy when they are being used in the classroom or lab. We all love kids. But face it — they just aren't careful sometimes. By keeping the CDs in caddies, I keep the discs away from their fingers.

I've bought enough caddies to cover every CD our school owns. Teachers or students never have to touch the CDs. I've noticed, however, that most of the newer machines are caddy-less. I'm going to have to do some training on the care and feeding of CDs.

Cons:

- ✔ CD-ROM programs are expensive. They are worth every penny, but they are expensive.

- ✔ CD-ROM programs can't be used in a network without costly special server software. Otherwise, you'll need a copy of each CD per machine. Some companies do discounts for bulk purchases. With floppy-based software, you can take advantage of a variety of pricing options (site license, lab packs, and so on). In other words, CD-ROM technology can be costly in the lab setting. However, some companies do offer discounts for bulk purchases.

- ✔ Most schools started purchasing computers in the days of the LCIIs and LCIIIs. They are great little machines, neither of which has a built-in CD-ROM drive or RAM capabilities to allow the best possible performance from a CD. Adding memory and CD-ROM drives is a costly option.

So What's the Answer, Ms. Robinette?

Gosh, I don't know if there is an answer. There are a number of options, none of which makes me totally happy. I just wish each school could be given the technology hardware needed to take advantage of all the neat stuff that's out there!

I know: reality, reality, reality.

By all means, buy CD-ROMs. Find ways to be creative with their use. Of course, I'd like each teacher to have a classroom full of computers or at least one with a CD-ROM drive and a vast library of CD titles. Here are two viable options for you to try within your own school:

- ✔ Add CD-ROM drives to a small group of computers in your media center. Or, as you purchase new computers with internal CD-ROM drives, place those computers in the media center and use this "Cluster o'ROM" as a research area.

  We use this idea in my school, and it really works well. We keep a different research CD title in each computer. The students come in on their own to do research. (We also use this area for small-group instruction on programs such as *HyperStudio* and *KidPix,* which we have loaded on the hard drives.)

- ✔ Have one computer (or more) with a CD-ROM drive per grade level. Housing the computer on a rolling cart and creating a schedule for sharing it among the teachers makes it easy for all students to have access to CD-ROM technology.

It would be nice to have one copy of each CD title for every grade level. However, keeping the CDs in the media center for checkout works just as well.

Well, those are my thoughts. Until each of us wins the lottery (it's bound to happen to one of us!), we teachers will have to use that *creativity* we're so famous for.

Where's the Card Catalog?

As I mention earlier in the book, kids today have it easy. (I never imagined I'd hear myself utter those words.) They don't even have to leave their computer to look up a term, get a good quote for an article, or find out the state flower for Georgia. It's all available on CD.

Because CDs can hold so much information, they are the perfect medium for reference software. Over the past few years, reference software has exploded onto the scene. As a matter of fact, most of what you consider *mainstream* reference materials are now available on CD.

These reference CDs can be divided into two categories: *general learning* and *specific learning*. In the general-learning CD category, you'll find the basics: dictionaries, thesauruses, encyclopedias, and an atlas or two. The specific-learning CDs target one area of learning, such as the ocean, and contain a vast array of information on that individual subject. The specific-learning tools often include fun activities that actually take the learner into the subject and involve lots of interactive aspects in the research process. The student learns from experience. (With general-reference CDs, the student is given information in more of a textual format.) There are some exceptions to this rule, as you'll see later.

The move to CDs

Recent trends have shown many software companies putting traditional productivity software on CDs instead of just on floppy disks. Many of the programs aren't intended to be run from CD each time they are used; placing a program on a CD simply makes it easier to install onto your hard drive rather than having four or five disks to switch back and forth during installation. The CDs are also easier to store than a pile of disks, and they take up less space. Please note: Most of the companies still offer disk versions of the same software for those who don't own CD-ROM drives.

Good reference CDs are easier to use than their hardcover counterparts. In the case of specific-learning software, the ease of use is immediately evident — the software manufacturer has taken information from a large variety of sources and compiled it onto one CD. This task would take a child forever to accomplish.

A good reference CD should also be easy to use and — in the case of dated material — should offer yearly updates for the information at a nominal cost.

The following lists contain some of my *favorite* reference CDs.

General learning

New encyclopedias and reference CDs are released each month. The ones listed here are my personal picks. I've chosen them based on ease of use, cost, and quality of the information found within.

Encyclopedias & General Reference

- ✔ **Encarta** (Microsoft, $99.95) This one is my favorite for many reasons: It's visually appealing, it's easy to use, and it incorporates text with graphics, sound, animation and maps. I love the timeline feature (which alone is a wonderful teaching tool).

- ✔ **Grolier's Multimedia Encyclopedia** (Grolier, $149.95) This CD has all the bells (and whistles, too). Its main attraction for me is its cross-referencing capabilities and the Knowledge-Tree feature (information webs) that allows children to take a subject from the general to the specific in no time.

- ✔ **Time Almanac Reference Edition** (Brøderbund, $59.00) I was surprised at the amount of information this one CD held! Time Almanac features information from weekly Time issues for the years 1989–1994 and then condenses information decade by decade for the years 1920–1988. The Top Stories section of each decade's screen quickly shows the students what written information, QuickTime movies, or photos are available for that time period.

Atlas

- ✔ **3-D Atlas** (Electronic Arts, $69.95) This one is a must buy! It takes the standard atlas to the mat. This program lets you rotate a 3-D version of the globe, zoom in on areas you wish to explore, and access political, geographical, and environmental data. Add to that satellite images and QuickTime movies that take you to the action — and you get the idea of how incredible this CD really is.

- ✔ **Small Blue Planet: The Cities Below** (Now What Software, $79.95) This atlas has been a top-seller for quite a while. It includes real pictures and interactive exploration. A variety of maps are also included: time, season, chronosphere, political, and topographical.

Dictionary, Thesaurus

▮ ✔ **Microsoft BookShelf** (Microsoft, $69.95) I'm amazed by this CD! It contains *The American Heritage Dictionary, Roget's Electronic Thesaurus, The Concise Columbia Encyclopedia, The Hammond Atlas, The World Almanac and Book of Facts, Bartlett's Familiar Quotations,* and *The Concise Columbia Dictionary of Quotations.* Can you believe all of that is on one CD? And not only that, this CD is easy to use. I probably would have gotten straight As in high school if I'd had access to this marvel of marvels.

Specific learning

In the area of specific learning, great programs are being released almost daily. These programs are just incredible; as a teacher, I appreciate the fact that the work has been done for me. No, these programs aren't going to eventually replace us; they're freeing up the time we used to spend tracking down books, filmstrips, and magazines — and letting us give our students real-life experiences with topics. The great classroom discussions that follow the use of these CDs just wouldn't occur if you were sitting with a group of kids holding up pictures from an old *National Geographic.*

▮ ✔ **The Rainforest** (REMedia, $59.95, grades 5 and up) This CD explores all the rainforests of the world with over 60 minutes of narrated video and animation clips.

✔ **Space Adventure** (Knowledge Adventure, $51.95, middle-high school) This CD includes simulation, sound, and full-motion video clips. Space exploration, robotics, and the solar system are explored.

✔ **The Animals!** (The Software Toolworks, $59.95, all ages) This CD takes you on a tour of The San Diego Zoo. Included are some really great video and sound clips. Great opportunities for exploration.

✔ **Art Gallery** (Microsoft, $59.95, all ages) This CD takes you through the National Gallery in London. It lets you view over 2,000 masterpieces. Along the way, you'll also pick up some interesting facts about the artists and the time periods in which they lived.

✔ **Dinosaurs** (Microsoft, $59.95, all ages) This dinosaur exploration is incredibly easy to use and full of fun facts. The ability to cut and paste the images has allowed me to create some pretty amazing presentations. The personal dinosaur dig is a favorite with kids. (My husband liked the PBS QuickTime movie.)

✔ **Prehistoria** (Grolier, $69.95, grades 3 and up) A very comprehensive exploration of prehistoric animals dating back over 500 million years. Deals with evolution.

✔ **A.D.A.M. The Inside Story** (A.D.A.M. Software, $59.95, high school and older) This one is just like those overlays that appeared in our biology books back in high school . . . only 100 times more interesting. You peel back layer after layer of Adam in this interactive anatomy lesson.

✔ **Oceans Below** (The Software Toolworks, $49.95, all ages) If you're a diver or have always wanted to go diving (or if you teach a unit on the ocean), this is the CD for you. This one takes you on trips to the great diving locations around the world. The narrated video segments are incredible!

✔ **The Way Things Work** (Dorling Kindersley, $79.95, all ages) This one is just like the best-selling book by David Macaulay. See and hear how things work. The Inventors' Workshop is loads of fun, and the Who's Who of Inventors is very educational. Great animation.

✔ **Great Literature** (Bureau Development Inc., $ 99.95, grades 7-12) Covers ancient to modern literature. Graphics and narration. Great for literary lesson plans. Not very flashy, but nice to have in the classroom for immediate access. The narrated readings are wonderful.

✔ **Adventures with Oslo** (Science for Kids, $45.95, elementary-middle school) This CD has some really cool animation to explain information on simple machines. The information is contained within a very easy-to-maneuver database, and the presentation is very entertaining. It will keep your students interested in a subject that tends to be boring in the class lecture arena.

✔ **Zurk's Rainforest Lab** (Soleil, $32.95, elementary) This CD focuses on the basic learning skills of reading, writing, and critical thinking. I loved the beautiful rainforest backdrop and the life-science information.

✔ **Counting on Frank** (EA Kids, $49.95, upper elementary-middle school) This software practices what all those math folks have been preaching: real-life problem-solving and hands-on learning. Frank is presented with a variety of problems throughout the day and needs your help to solve them. The on-line help feature is great for the more visual learner.

✔ **Maps 'n Facts** (Brøderbund, $55.95, middle-high school) This program is very straightforward and easy to use. The maps are clear and concise. Students can get detailed information quickly and can customize a map to meet their needs.

✔ **RedShift** (Maxis, $50.95, upper elementary-high school) This is a simulation that actually takes you on a space voyage. The graphics are incredible, and the astronomy information is top-notch. Many of the graphics are actual photos, while other views provide a 3-D effect.

✔ **Space Shuttle** (MindScape, $30.95, elementary-middle school) This CD has tons of video footage! Students get to participate in an actual NASA shuttle flight — as well as all the preparations prior to the flight.

Chapter 12

Hot Topics in Education: Authentic Assessment, Keyboarding, and Portfolios

● ●

In This Chapter
▶ Theories and thoughts
▶ Software solutions

● ●

*W*e all hear colleagues talking about the latest buzz words. The articles appear in the journals, and you feel a little guilty for not being an active participant in these latest trends. Yet, very few teachers are actually implementing these new-fangled approaches; we're still getting used to the *whole-language approach* — and that buzz word has been around for over ten years!

Technology's Role in Authentic Assessment

As a student, how often do you remember turning in a test and thinking, "She didn't even ask me about half the material I studied!" You felt a little cheated and were left with knowledge you were unable to express. I believe this situation happens on a daily basis in our schools today.

Theory and research

Authentic assessment is a popular educational term that has been given lip service in the both the political and academic community. However, there are very few examples of true authentic assessment currently in practice. The theory behind authentic assessment is strong: Students of all ages should be assessed in a way that best meets their individual learning style. Current practice, however, tends to rely on paper-and-pencil activities, with grades being given on a numerical basis.

To be quite honest, the current practice is much easier, less time-consuming, and more cost-effective. Authentic assessment requires dedication and time from the school faculty, students, and parents.

Educational researcher Howard Gardner has identified seven areas of intelligence within all humans: logical/mathematical, verbal/linguistic, musical, bodily/kinesthetic, spatial, interpersonal, and intrapersonal.

Most of us feel stronger about our intelligence in one or more of these areas. However, in schools, students are permitted to express their intelligence in only two areas: *logical/mathematical* (math, science, reasoning) or *verbal/ linguistic* (grammar, creative writing, language arts). That leaves many students in possession of knowledge that they are unable to express to others — and thus they have not been assessed authentically.

Potential impact

The potential impact of authentic assessment for all children is incredible. In my current position as technology coordinator, I have the opportunity to work with small groups of children. Many times I have brought a group back and said to the teacher, "Andy is very talented; the project he started in the computer lab is great!" And the teacher would be amazed. You see, Andy is his cut-up who never finishes work and has poor grades. Through innovative computer programs that allow a variety of ways to express knowledge, I was able to get a better picture of Andy's true intellectual ability. I gave him the opportunity and the means to show me what he knows in a style that best suits him. There are many bright and talented children in this country, just like Andy, who haven't been given the opportunity to *shine*.

On the other hand, Andy is still going to have to pass the SAT in order to go to Princeton. I guess what I'm worried about is what happens if Andy changes schools or moves. I'm not sure if "traditional" assessment will ever disappear.

Software connection

Today's world of technology allows each student to create a personal type of assessment instrument. From the second grade slow reader who could never "bubble in" the words that describe things you can eat (but can choose all the stamps in *KidPix2*) to the fifth grader who doesn't test well and appears to daydream in class (yet is able to create a *HyperStudio* presentation and show what it might have been like to explore the new Western Frontier), students have shown what they know in their own ways. The depth and amount of information shared are much greater than could ever be assessed through a paper-and-pencil test.

There are some wonderful computer programs out there that let students create presentations involving all aspects of creativity: video, animation, music, drawing, and audio. (See Chapter 13's list of multimedia and presentation software.) Imagine how empowered students would feel if you allowed them a variety of options to show what they know instead of presenting them with a four-page test!

This stuff all sounds so exciting on paper. However, a major educational change such as this is a huge undertaking. Everyone involved has to buy into the plan: parents, school administrators, students, and, *above all,* teachers. Learn all you can about authentic assessment before you try it. Be aware that many in the field of education still feel strongly about traditional assessment.

Here's some top-notch, authentic-assessment software. The prices are based on mail-order catalogs from *Learning Services* (800-877-3278) or *Educational Resources* (800-624-2926):

- ✔ **KidPix2** (Brøderbund, $49.95, elementary)

- ✔ **HyperStudio** (Roger Wagner Productions, $109.95, upper elementary-adult)

- ✔ **Kid's Studio** (Storm Technology, $41.95, upper elementary-middle school)

- ✔ **Multimedia Workshop** (Davidson, $84.95, middle school-college)

- ✔ **KidPix Studio** (Brøderbund, $64.95, elementary-middle school)

- ✔ **Persuasion** (Aldus, $139.95, high school-adult)

- ✔ **The Writing Center** (The Learning Company, $84.95, elementary-middle school)

- ✔ **EasyBook** (Sunburst, $39.95, elementary)

- ✔ **ClickBook** (Bookmaker Corporation, $49.95, middle school-adult)

- ✔ **Fine Artist** (Microsoft, $42.95, upper elementary-middle school)

- ✔ **Fine Writer** (Microsoft, $42.95, upper elementary-middle school)

The Keyboarding Buzz

Why should we teach keyboarding? When should you begin teaching keyboarding? How do you meet everyone's needs? School systems all over the country are asking all these questions and more.

Why?

Research has shown that keyboarding skills are important. Apple Classrooms of Tomorrow (ACOT) research proved that with as little as 15 minutes of keyboard practice daily for six weeks, second and third graders commonly typed 20 to 30 words per minute with 95 percent accuracy. In comparison, children in this same age group are only capable of writing 9-11 words per minute by hand.

Isn't that amazing? Keyboarding skills can greatly increase a student's level of self-expression by simply helping them get it down on paper — which is a major obstacle for some children.

When?

We all know that the youngest writers have incredible stories to tell. Their only problem is getting those stories on paper. Research has shown that the "hunt and peck" method is fine up until the second or third grade. By that time, their hands are large enough to accommodate the keyboard and the required range of reach. That's when keyboard instruction should begin.

Many school systems are looking into the possibility of eventually eliminating keyboard instruction from their high-school programs and concentrating on elementary- and middle-school keyboarding classes. The belief is that the students will have already mastered keyboarding skills by the time they reach high school. It makes sense — but it's hard to imagine going through high school without taking typing!

How?

The key to successful keyboarding instruction is consistency. Keyboarding instruction doesn't require large blocks of time — only 10-15 minutes. It does, however, require daily instruction and review of skills for best results. This strategy seems to be the largest stumbling block for most schools. How do you get students on the computer daily? Most schools have labs or small numbers of computers in the classrooms. The labs are used as a special area like art, music, or PE — or they're available on a sign-up basis. In either of the scenarios, it's almost impossible for a class of students to get to computers daily.

Schools are now rethinking their scheduling practices to accommodate the needs of teachers who want to include keyboarding instruction with the basic curriculum. I predict that, in the future, keyboarding skills (along with other aspects of technology) will become a part of the basic core curriculum in most school districts. It must.

Keyboarding kudos

Finding keyboard instruction programs that work, yet don't quickly become boring, used to be a challenge. However, some very high-quality programs have recently entered the arena, making it easy to find a program that you and the children will like. All the programs have tracking abilities to let students work at their own pace while giving you feedback on their progress. My advice is to purchase a variety of programs for your school to prevent boredom. We use a different program for each grade level (3-5).

Here are my favorite keyboarding programs (and all products are available in lab packs):

- ✔ **Kid Keys** (Davidson, $42.95, elementary)
- ✔ **UltraKey 2.0** (Bytes of Learning, $39.95, elementary-middle school)
- ✔ **Mavis Beacon Teaches Typing** (Software Toolworks, $32.95, middle-high school)
- ✔ **MasterType** (Mindscape, $34.95, elementary-middle school)
- ✔ **Kid's Typing** (Sierra, $30.95, lower elementary)
- ✔ **Mario Teaches Typing** (InterPlay, $34.95, elementary)

Ask for throwaways

Last year, I had a parent bring in a bunch of computer keyboards from his office. He told me that they had upgraded their computers and were throwing out the old keyboards. This was so great! I cut off all the cords and stored the keyboards in a couple of milk crates. No, they weren't Mac and they didn't connect to anything, but they gave the kids a feel for the fingering required for keyboarding and served as a great practice for those days when we couldn't get to the lab.

Portfolios, Portfolios, Portfolios

Are you tired of hearing this word? I am. I've read the articles, gone to inservices, purchased hanging files, and really tried to embrace the concept. I've seen it in practice and agree with the theory. I just don't have the time or dedication to do portfolios right!

Theory

In a nutshell, keeping a portfolio on a child allows a teacher to show *individual student growth*. The idea is to gather all types of work samples, test scores, and anecdotal records on each child (in your spare time) and store them in an easy-to-access manner. Those who have mastered this skill do a wonderful job. I'm personally in awe of these individuals. However, unless the next teacher a child has uses the portfolio practice, it's a year's worth of work that comes to a sudden halt.

The software solutions

Well, those crafty software creator types have done it again. There are a couple of software packages on the market that have taken the normal drudgery out of compiling and storing the contents of a student portfolio.

- ✔ **The Grady Profile** (Aurbach & Associates, $134.95, all grades): 314-726-5933.
- ✔ **The Portfolio Assessment Kit** (SuperSchool, $199.95, all grades): 310-594-8580.

These programs allow you to store student work samples (scanned) and subject area evaluations. You can also add extensive narrative discussions in an electronic file folder you create for each child. They will even import data from an already established database. So why retype info you've already entered? Some of the more innovative aspects of the programs include the ability to add video samples to the profile (video of Tommy giving a how-to speech on making pancakes) and the student's voice to a work sample (little Tommy reading the first poem he wrote as you see it in his handwriting).

I know this type of information gathering will be a big part of the future. I'm only concerned about accessibility to these programs. If a teacher doesn't have a computer and scanner in the classroom, maintaining the portfolios might be difficult. However, if you do have easy access to a computer and/or scanner, imagine how great it would be to have this software in combination with a good gradebook program at your fingertips — anytime you needed it. WOW!

I also question the storage and retrieval of information such as video, sound, and color graphics. For one child this is feasible. However, in large schools, the memory requirements for storage of such information is huge.

In addition to the previously listed components, The Portfolio Assessment Kit includes a daily writing journal component. I love this aspect — it not only allows students to keep track of their writing ideas, it also has areas for monthly planning, tracking assignments, and a phone directory. Students will enjoy being able to personalize the appearance of their journal screens (a race car, floral design, and so on).

One of the neatest things about each of the portfolio programs I mentioned is that their site-license prices are *very reasonable,* thus allowing everyone in the school to maintain portfolios on children who pass through from grade to grade. Another bonus is that both programs are fully networkable!

Look into these programs. Both companies have demo disks that they can send you, and both are more than happy to field any questions you might have concerning their products.

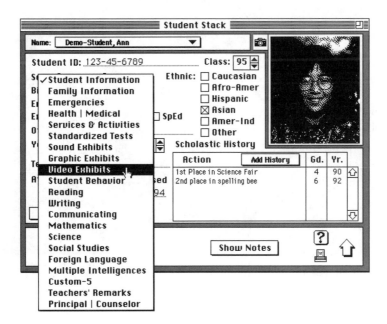

The 5th Wave
By Rich Tennant

"OH YEAH, AND TRY NOT TO ENTER THE WRONG PASSWORD."

Chapter 13

The Lists!

Remember back in Chapter 10 when I told you about the different categories or types of software? Well, in case you've already forgotten, I'll give you a quick review on each software category before listing my favorite titles.

My Disclaimer

Let me just say this up front. This list is by no means gospel — but then again, what list is? It seems to me that every review or list I read has a slant of some sort; many of the folks doing educational software reviews don't even hold degrees in education and probably haven't set foot in a classroom since they were students themselves. (The few good exceptions for reviews are listed in Chapter 22.) My most valuable advice seems to come from computing friends and colleagues who've actually used the stuff. In that respect, my list probably comes closer to being accurate than any others I've seen — I'm not employed by any of the software companies, and I make *zilch* when I mention their names!

These are *my* favorite picks based on what I've used or seen used in the school environment, what colleagues here and across the country have successfully used, and what I've used on a preview basis. Most of the prices quoted are school versions of the software from *Educational Resources* (800-624-2926) spring catalog. (A school version usually costs a little more than the home version but includes some printed material intended to help you use the software in the classroom.)

Software prices fluctuate, so call a vendor before you sit down with this list to come up with a software budget for yourself or your school.

The titles on the lists are in no specific order. All programs in each category are of supreme quality.

Skill-and-Drill

This category has gotten a bad rap over the past few years. After you take away all the bells and whistles, some say it's simply an electronic set of *flash cards*.

In reality, skill-and-drill software produces some wonderful results. And while I wouldn't rely solely on skill-and-drill software as the basis of my technology program, you simply can't beat skill-and-drill when it comes to those areas of the curriculum that require rote memorization. If you've ever taught third grade and suffered through an entire year of reminding parents to review those multiplication facts at home, you'll really appreciate skill-and-drill software.

The following works made my lists for three reasons: They're fun, they give immediate feedback, and they give helpful corrections.

Language arts

1. **Beginning Reading** (Sierra, $30.95, early elementary) This program presents a fun way for early readers to learn rhyming words, two-letter sounds, alphabetizing skills, vocabulary, and story-reading skills. All of Sierra's programs feature a "talking tutor" to enable students to work alone or get the help they need easily.

2. **Word Munchers** (MECC, $39.95, elementary) This game has been around forever and is still great. Just think of PacMan gobbling up words with a certain vowel sound and you've got a good picture of *Word Munchers*. I like the phonics link; personally, I still feel we need to be teaching those letter and vowel sounds.

3. **StickyBear's Reading Room** (Optimum Software, $39.95, elementary) Lots of neat reading and pre-reading activities are included in this piece of software. An added bonus is the Spanish version.

4. **Grammar Games** (Davidson, $52.95, middle school-high school) I've included this soon-to-be-released Mac version because the Windows version is wonderful; it's hard to find good language arts skill-and-drill stuff for upper grades. Not only will students learn basic grammar and punctuation skills, they'll have loads of fun doing it on this jungle-adventure game.

5. **Midnight Rescue** (The Learning Company, $34.95, upper elementary) This program requires students to read short passages and then recall facts, make inferences, and draw conclusions on their reading. In addition to all this school-type stuff, the game is entertaining.

6. **Word Attack 3** (Davidson, $57.95, upper elementary-middle school) This exciting game teaches students the definition and spelling of over 3,200 words and includes crossword puzzles and mazes.

7. **Reading Maze** (Great Wave, $38.95, early elementary) This program keeps records for you! Okay, it will also teach early readers basic vocabulary, too, and it has lots of different skill levels. But, as I said before, it will also keep records for you! That's right. This program keeps up with each student's progress and leaves you free to worry about whose turn is next on the computer. With the large number of skill levels, you could use this game for the entire school year, and the students would still find it challenging.

8. **SuperSolvers Spellbound** (The Learning Company, $54.95, upper elementary) This interactive program includes over 1,000 words for sharpening spelling skills. It allows teachers or students to add up to 3,000 words to the lists.

9. **Reader Rabbit 1, 2** and **3** (The Learning Company, $54.95, early elementary) This series of programs has been around a while. It has proven to be engaging and successful in teaching beginning reading skills — with stress on phonics. The Learning Company doesn't rest on its laurels, either; it is constantly making improvements to each of these programs.

10. **Spelling Blizzard** (Sierra, $30.95, upper elementary-middle school) This program not only concentrates on those words with "tricky" spellings, it also gives students some memory techniques to foster long-term retention.

Math

1. **Number Maze** (Great Wave, $38.95, elementary-middle school) As students solve math problems, they work their way through the maze. This program is very easy to customize for the difficulty level needed for your students — it ranges from picture addition to difficult division and word problems.

2. **Math Blaster Plus** (Davidson, $44.95, elementary-middle school) You can buy two different episodes in this series. (This series was one of the original skill-and-drill titles, and it's still a best seller.) The games are a fun and challenging way to review basic math skills.

3. **Turbo Math Facts** (Nordic, $41.95, elementary) Basic facts review is the cornerstone of this program. The backdrop is a race track where correct answers earn you "money"! The more money you earn, the faster the race car you can afford. This program increases in difficulty as the player advances, and it does a good job of explaining mistakes.

4. **Geometric Golfer** (MECC, $44.95, middle school-high school) Through flipping, rotating, or reflecting polygons, students try to get them in the hole with the least number of strokes.

5. **Troggle Trouble** (MECC, $44.95, elementary-middle school) Kids love to play this game because it's an exciting arcade adventure. It's so much fun that they often forget they are learning basic math skills.

6. **Tesselmania** (MECC, $46.95, middle school-high school) This program helps students understand spatial and visual relations by manipulating tessellations. The outcome is really a cool visual.

7. **Geometry, Algebra,** and **Calculus** (Brøderbund, $79.95, high school) Each program covers a full year's worth of the featured subject. The Algebra title has proven to be a big award winner. Don't expect flashy arcade graphics — just straight-forward learning tutorials.

8. **Number Munchers** (MECC, $39.95, all grades) The granddaddy of all skill-and-drill programs. And it's still fun! It's just like PacMan — only the little guy eats up factors or multiples of numbers instead of little dots.

9. **Alge-Blaster Plus** (Davidson, $39.95, middle school-high school) This program covers a full year of algebra instruction in a fun, non-threatening way. Where was this program when I was in high school?

10. **SuperSolvers Outnumbered** (The Learning Company, $55.95, upper elementary) I like this program because it incorporates word problems, charts, and graphs, in addition to basic math skills.

Science

1. **Super Solvers Gizmos and Gadgets** (The Learning Company, $54.95, upper elementary) Students must solve puzzles involving force, electricity, balance, and energy.

2 **Physics** (Brøderbund, $79.95, high school) A complete first-year course in physics. Students are allowed to manipulate vectors, interpret graphs, and solve problems.

3. **Operation Frog** (Scholastic, $99.95, middle school-high school) Simulated frog dissection is the basis of this program, and many schools have adopted it for students who refuse to take part in the actual dissection of a frog. Students have to choose the correct instruments and probe, just as they would in real dissection. Includes QuickTime movies.

4. **Where in Space is Carmen Sandiego?** (Brøderbund, $54.95, middle school-high school) This one should probably be listed with the other simulation titles, but it's hard to find a good science program — and this program is really great. Students explore the planets and constellations while searching for Carmen.

5. **BodyScope** (MECC, $44.95, upper elementary-middle school) Coloring book, puzzles, and other activities help students learn the human anatomy.

6. **Treasure Cove** (The Learning Company, $39.95, elementary) This game combines reading and beginning oceanography in an exciting adventure game.

Social studies

Most of the social studies programs are reference type CDs (see Chapter 11 for lists) or simulation games and don't contain skill-and-drill type activities.

1. **Zip Zap Map** (Scholastic, $34.95, upper elementary-high school) A fast-paced map-skill game. Students score points by placing the states, their capitals, and a variety of geographic features on a United States map.

2. **Headline Harry and the Great Paper Race** (Davidson, $42.95, upper elementary-middle school) This program borders on being simulation and could probably be included in that list as well. While learning about history, geography, and journalism, students read maps and stories to discern the truth — which encourages fact-finding and problem-solving skills.

3. **Swamp Gas Visits the United States** (Inline, $49.95, upper elementary-middle school) Students are challenged to find locations and are given a specific period of time for completing their task.

4. **Swamp Gas Visits Europe** (Inline, $49.95, upper elementary-middle school) This one is pretty much the same as *Swamp Gas Visits the United States,* but with a European twist.

Pre-School: general knowledge

All the programs in this list are superb for early-learning skills in pre-school and kindergarten. I have all of them at my house, and they've been put to good use.

1. **The Playroom** (Brøderbund, $39.95)

2. **The TreeHouse** (Brøderbund, $39.95)

3. **Sammy's Science House** (EdMark, $44.95)

4. **Baily's Book House** (EdMark, $44.95)

5. **Millie's Math House** (EdMark, $44.95)

6. **Kid's Time Deluxe** (Great Wave, $38.95)

7. **Reader Rabbit Ready for Letters** (The Learning Company, $34.95)

8. **Early Math** (Sierra, $30.95)

9. **Zurk's Learning Safari** (Soleil, $42.95)

10. **Math Rabbit** (The Learning Company, $54.95)

Productivity

This is my favorite type of software. As the name implies, you will (or should) come away with a product of some sort. Productivity software is great for addressing the technology-curriculum integration problem. One program can usually be used for a wide range of ages, thus making anything in this list a worthy purchase.

1. **ClarisWorks** (Claris, $72.95, all grades) I don't need to explain this one for you. Don't be a fool; go buy it if you haven't already.

2. **The Writing Center** and **The Student Writing Center** (The Learning Company, $84.95, elementary-middle school) *The Writing Center* is for younger students and is very easy to understand. *The Student Writing Center* builds upon the first program and includes guided report writing (bibliographies too!), a journal function, a thesaurus, and letter-writing templates.

3. **The Cruncher** (Davidson, $59.95, middle school-high school) This is a really great spreadsheet program for the junior set.

4. **EasyBook** (Sunburst, $39.95, all grades) This software allows children to write and illustrate a book on the screen. Students have control over fonts, text space, and illustration space. And, miracle of all miracles, it lets you print "front to back" — no matter what type of printer you have!

5. **ClickBook** (BookMaker Corp., $49.95, all grades) This software can take any Mac file and turn it into any of 17 sizes and styles of double-sided booklet.

6. **TimeLiner** (Tom Synder Productions, $79.95, all grades) Many schools say they couldn't do without this software. You can create timelines of various sizes and include small illustrations to accompany labels that you attach to identify time periods.

7. **PageMaker** (Aldus, $168, middle school-high school) Most high schools and colleges now use this software for their newspaper layout. Many publishing houses (IDG included) also use this software for book layout.

8. **Kid Works 2** (Davidson, $59.95, elementary) This software allows students to create and illustrate their own stories. It even has neat little "rebus type" add-in pictures and will read your story back to you.

9. **SuperPrint for the Macintosh** (Scholastic, $124.95, all grades) This program's strength is the variety of sizes and styles it allows you to print. It comes with a large graphics library, and you can also purchase add-on graphics packages.

10. **Print Shop Deluxe CD Ensemble** (Brøderbund, $79.95, all grades) Just about everyone's heard about *PrintShop* by now. This convenient CD includes all the specialty packages they've ever put out. The fonts, clip-art samples, and borders in this package are almost impossible to count. *Print Shop* allows you to make signs, posters, banners, or greeting cards.

Multimedia

As I mentioned earlier, multimedia software is a form of productivity software — yet it includes the incorporation of other media such as sound, video, photography, or electronic artwork. These programs are also a good investment for the school, because the students enjoy using them.

1. **KidPix2** (Brøderbund, $49.95, elementary-middle school) See Chapter 14.

2. **HyperStudio** (Roger Wagner Productions, $109.95, all grades) There is no way I can describe this multi-faceted program in a few sentences. This is the ultimate multi-media program.

3. **Kid's Studio** (Storm, $41.95, elementary-middle school) This is a nice program for kids who think they're too big for *KidPix2* and aren't quite ready for *HyperStudio*. It is compatible with Kodak Photo CDs.

4. **The Multimedia Workshop** (Davidson, $84.95, middle school-high school) This is a really all-inclusive program. You get a writing workshop with an easy-to-use word processor, a video workshop, a paint/draw workshop — and a library full of photos, clip art, sound clips, and QuickTime movies. By combining all these areas, students can produce some very impressive reports or presentations.

5. **HyperCard** (Apple, $99.95, all grades) This program has been around a while and used to come free with every Mac sold. It is still very popular and is similar (without all the bells and whistles) to *HyperStudio*.

6. **KidPix Studio** (Brøderbund, $64.95, all grades) This program takes *KidPix2* another step and includes animation, digital puppets, and movie clips.

7. **Persuasion** (Aldus, $139.95, high school) A very sophisticated presentation program. Much more intensive than *HyperStudio* or *HyperCard*.

8. **Amazing Animation** (Claris, $45.95, elementary-middle school) This relatively new program allows students to create interactive stories and it includes tons of cool sounds and special effects.

9. **Flying Colors** (Davidson, $71.95, elementary-middle school) This program is a *KidPix2* competitor. Variations include some neat backgrounds, gradients, kaleidoscope effects, tons of stamps, and animation.

10. **Fine Artist** (Microsoft, $42.95, elementary-middle school) This is not just another paint program. Kids can create animated pictures, comic strips, and slide shows. I especially like the artist's tips and tricks included with this program.

Simulation

Simulation software is a hard sell to parents who feel that their children shouldn't spend school time "playing a game." However, the complex thought processes that go on during a simulated game often involve all areas of learning — and the incorporation of a large amount of prior learning (something that even teachers find difficult to work into a day's lessons).

If you choose to purchase simulation programs for your classroom or lab, be sure to allow large blocks of time for students to complete their adventures. Most of the programs do allow you to save a game and return, but we all know how frustrating it can be to be pulled away from a task you find enjoyable and rewarding. (Most of these programs are now available on CD as well.)

1. **SimTown** (Maxis, $34.95, upper elementary-middle school) Students build a city from the ground up and then are challenged to make the city thrive and prosper based on the decisions they make. This version is much more "kid friendly" than *SimCity 2000*.

2. **SimCity 2000** (Maxis, $45.95, middle school-high school) This program is more intense than *SimTown*, and is played by many an adult these days. The player has more control over the environment, and the graphics are more realistic, less cartoonish.

   Be sure to check out all the other Sim titles by Maxis: *SimAnt, SimEarth, SimFarm, SimTower,* and *SimLife*. They're all super; it just wouldn't be fair to fill up my list with Sim titles.

3. **Oregon Trail** (MECC, $44.95, upper elementary-middle school) It's hard to believe, but this program has been around for over 15 years! This software simulates a westward trip across the United States in the 1800s.

4. **Crosscountry USA** (Didatech, $55.95, upper elementary-middle school) In this program, students take on the role of a truck driver assigned to deliver a load of merchandise across the country. By using maps and problem-solving skills (when to rest or eat), students try to get their cargo to its destination.

5. **Where in the World is Carmen Sandiego?** (Brøderbund, $49.95, middle-high school) By now I'm sure you've all heard of this title or seen the TV show on PBS. It's been a top-seller forever. The USA version is also just as wonderful.

6. **Nigel's Adventures in World Geography** (Lawrence Productions, $41.95, elementary-middle school) A Carmen competitor. It's actually a great choice for students who aren't old enough to enjoy Carmen. Travel with Nigel, a photographer who's searching for that perfect photo. On the way, students learn all about countries and continents.

7. **Discovering America: The Adventure of Spanish Exploration** (Lawrence Productions, $37.95, upper elementary-middle school) This is a great simulation game that helps bridge the learning gap of this historical period.

8. **Eagle Eye Mysteries** (EA Kids, $42.95, elementary-middle school) A total of 50 mysteries that get harder and harder. Students keep track of clues, interview witnesses, and read maps to solve each case.

9. **The Amazon Trail** (MECC, $47.95, middle school) Students learn navigation and map-reading skills (along with practicing decision-making in exploration while traveling through South America).

10. **DinoPark Tycoon** (MECC, $49.95, elementary-middle school) This program incorporates math, economics, business, and science to help children set up and run a theme park.

Teacher Productivity

1. **ClarisWorks** (Claris, $72.95) You need this piece of software. Read Chapters 6 through 9 if you still need to be convinced.

2. **ClarisOrganizer** (Claris, $69.95) It's like having your own computerized personal-information manager. There's a calendar program, a contacts list, and a note area. And get this: All the areas can be linked together!

3. **EasyGrade Pro** (Orbis, $47.95) This is my favorite gradebook program. It is the most user-friendly of all the programs out there, and Orbis offers a really reasonable site-license rate that allows teachers to make copies of the program for home use.

4. **The Grady Profile** (Aurbach & Associates, $134.95) This is my pick for portfolio assessment. It's got everything you or a parent would need to know about a student, and it is very easy to use, too.

5. **Print Shop Deluxe CD Ensemble** (Brøderbund, $79.95) I've already discussed this program in the Productivity section. As a teacher, I like this software for creating thank-you notes, certificates, business cards, and stationery. It also creates some great banners for birthdays and other classroom celebrations.

6. **ClickArt Cartoons** (T/Maker, $19.95) These clip-art images are funny and inexpensive. Need I say more?

7. **Norton Utilities** (Symantec, $59.95) This software helps to keep your hard drive trouble-free. It can help you recover something you threw away or fix a floppy disk that may be unreadable. Another plus is its capability to maximize your hard drive by defragmenting spaces left when you continually take software on and off the hard drive.

8. **Fool Proof** (SmartStuff Software, $39.00) This is a desktop security system that will let your class use the computer and see the desktop while enabling you to lock certain files (like your gradebook or the midterm exam) and prevent the trash can from being used. Many schools are now switching to this program instead of using *AtEase*.

9. **Test Designer Supreme** (SuperSchool Software, $79.95) Allows teachers to create essay-, multiple-choice, and true-or-false test questions. Strengths of this program are the layout choices, the ease of use, the database for storing questions, the option to take the test on the computer, and the program's support of five languages.

10. **Teacher's Tool Kit** (Hi-Tech of Santa Cruz, $63.95) Four programs that will help you create customized word searches, word scrambles, fill-in-the-blank quizzes or study sheets, and multiple-choice tests.

No, my spacebar isn't broken!

After reading this list of software titles (*ClarisWorks, PageMaker, ClickBook, EasyBook*), you probably think that I've forgotten how to spell, or that I'm fascinated with compound words. It's not me, it's those programmers and software executives. Today, having a space in your program's name just isn't cool, and it's very rarely done. Yes, it bugs me, just like those stores who use *R* instead of the word *ARE*, and the beauty salons that spell *cuts* with a *k*. And then parents complain to us that we just don't put enough emphasis on spelling these days!

Other Stuff

Some software just didn't fit into a category, so I've included it here.

Foreign-language software

This area of software is rapidly growing; many of the programs are really great (while some aren't worth the money). The best I've seen is the *Berlitz Live!* series from Sierra Software. It retails for $120 and comes in French, German, Italian, and Spanish. The best parts about this series are the critical-phrases mastery lessons and the test-your-skill questions.

Specialized reading-comprehension software

Accelerated Reader (Advantage Learning Systems, $1,723 and up) It's not really a piece of software, it's an entire learning program. In a nutshell, you get software covering a large variety of trade-book titles. Students read the book and then take a test on the computer to tell how well they understood what they read. The students are then given feedback on their test results. The computer keeps track of each child's progress and can compile a variety of reports for teachers and parents. This program is taking off like crazy and has shown great success. (Most schools house the program in the media center.)

Mind games

Thinkin' Things Collection 1 and **Thinkin' Things Collection 2** (EdMark, $54.95) These programs do a great job improving thinking skills. The option to vary difficulty levels is an added bonus. I enjoy playing these myself!

Widget Workshop (Maxis, $32.95) Build strange inventions by using a variety of out of the ordinary and realistic parts. The immediate feedback and the information for further inventing on and off the computer make this a valuable program.

E-books (electronic books)

Brøderbund's Living Books ($49.95) blow all the other companies out of the water when it comes to quality in this category. I'm serious. All the other titles that I previewed didn't even come close. Brøderbund starts with quality children's trade books and then enhances them with interactive hilarity; not only do narrators read the books, but each illustration has a variety of characters and items that can be clicked to "perform." Each story is also read in another language. In that aspect I could see these stories being used to enhance many of the foreign-language classes that are now being taught at the elementary level.

My only comment to that monster of a software company might be to include some comprehension questions at the end of each book and possibly a few "about the author" pages. Otherwise, keep up the good work.

Be aware that I could add to this list on a monthly basis. I just hope that I've helped a little in your navigation through the vast software jungle.

Part IV

How to Act Like You Know What You're Doing

"Fortunately at this grade level the Mac is very intuitive for them to use. Unfortunately so is sailing mousepads across the classroom."

In this part...

Kids do it every day in the classroom. You know what I mean: They mouth the answer to that multiplication problem as the other 85 percent of the class screams out the answer.

I'm going to help you fake it through two of the most widely used programs in educational circles: *KidPix2* and *The Writing Center*. I've tried to include programs that would be appropriate for a variety of grade levels and uses.

Take your time and see what you think.

I'm only scratching the surface on each of these programs. You can dig deeper when you have time (ha!). Or you can even do the unmentionable and read the manuals!

Chapter 14
Faking Your Way Through *KidPix2*

In This Chapter

▶ A brief history of *KidPix2*

▶ How to use the toolbox

▶ Using saved work to create a slide show

K*idPix* is the grandpappy of all drawing programs. It's been around the longest and still ranks as the most popular program in its class. This gem appeals to a wide range of ages as well, which makes it a valuable addition to most schools' software libraries. And the sound effects are awesome!

A Bit o' Confusion

Listen carefully as I explain this next bit of software rationale. Brøderbund, the company behind *KidPix* and many other successful software programs, first released *KidPix* as a stand-alone program. It was wonderfully fabulous, and everyone had to have it — but still there was a thirst for more! So Brøderbund soon came out with *KidPix Companion,* which added some neat features to your original *KidPix* purchase. Well, Brøderbund finally wised up and packaged both of these programs together under one title, *KidPix2.* Did all that make sense?

If you own or your school owns any of the programs or combination of programs mentioned in this last very confusing paragraph, you may pass GO, collect $200, and participate in all the upcoming activities.

Opening *KidPix2*

Go to your hard drive, find the *KidPix2* icon, and double-click. (If your school has installed *At Ease,* it's even easier! Look at the screen, point to the *KidPix2* icon, and click.)

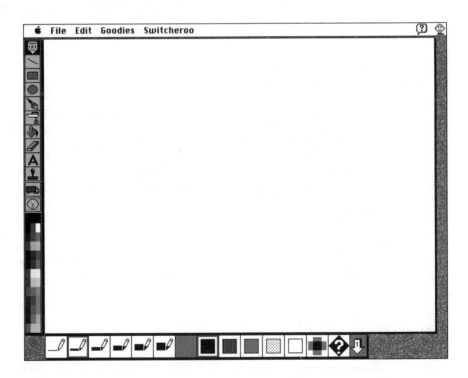

Tools of the Trade

The first screen that greets you has a blank sheet of paper and a row of interesting-looking icons down the left side (the *toolbox*) and across the bottom. What's neat about these icons is that, if you learn to use each of the tools represented by the icons, you will be able to master most of the more advanced "adult" drawing programs.

Oh no!

This little guy is a lifesaver if you remember to use him right away. When you click on him, he undoes your last action. That means, if you make a mis- take, go straight to him. Don't try to fix it in another way. Once you do something else, he will correct only the latest action.

Let's Create a Masterpiece!

The best way to learn this program is to actually do what you're talking about. I want you to create and save three pictures using *KidPix2*. Don't worry — I'm going to hold your hand along the way. After you create and save the pictures, I'm going to show you how to use them in a really super slide show.

Picture 1

You've opened up *KidPix2* and you have a blank paper (on screen) in front of you.

1. Click the pencil icon (in the top-left corner) and let go of the button.

2. Choose the color green from the color palette on the row of tools.

   Your mouse controls your pencil strokes — holding the mouse button down and moving creates a line. When you lift your finger off the mouse button, you stop drawing.

3. Now draw a line across the bottom of the page where you would want some grass. Be sure you connect up with the sides of the page.

4. Now click the paint bucket and leave the color as green.

5. Move the cursor, which now looks like a paint bucket, to the area you drew in for grass and click. That whole area should have turned green.

If the whole page turned green, that means you left an open area when you drew your first line. The paint "spilled" into the rest of the picture. If this happened, click the "Oh no!" man. That last action will be undone.

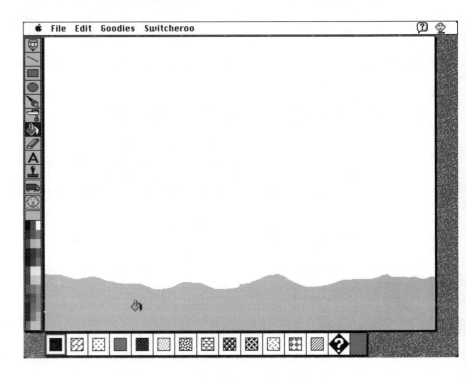

Don't spill the paint!

Notice the very tip of the spilling paint. The location of this tip of spilling paint is where the paint will be "dumped." Many children get frustrated when they can't get the paint to go where they want it. And when drawing figures that will later be filled with paint from the bucket, be sure all the lines are closed. If not, the paint will spill out of the shape and fill the entire page.

Another good tip is to have students stay away from the fine-line width when drawing. It's too difficult to be sure of closed lines when using such a fine point.

 Paint goes where tip of spilling paint is placed.

 Even a small opening will cause paint to spill.

Using thin lines to draw makes it more difficult to ensure closed lines.

6. Let's use the paint bucket again and choose sky blue as our color. Dump it above your grass. I know, I'm not the artsy type. Be more creative if you'd like.

7. Now go to the stamp icon and click.

   You should see a row of small stamps appear at the bottom of the screen. Find one you like. If you don't like any of these, click the arrow at the end of the row, and you'll see more.

8. When you see a stamp you like, click it. The image will become your cursor.

9. Move the stamp to the desired location and try this:

   a. push the option key (the stamp gets big)

   b. push the shift key (the stamp gets bigger)

   c. push the option and shift keys together (the stamp gets the biggest!)

10. Choose the location and size you want and then click the mouse.

11. Enough for this picture. Go to the File menu and choose Save. Name this work of art *picture 1*.

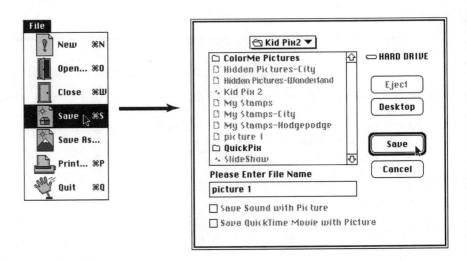

Picture 2

1. Go to the File menu and choose New.

   A nice clean sheet of paper should pop up in front of you.

2. Choose the circle tool and the color black.

   Across the bottom of the screen you should see some new choices on how your shape will be filled (or not filled). Play around. Click and drag. As you drag, you pull a circle. The same premise works with the square tool. Fill your page with shapes.

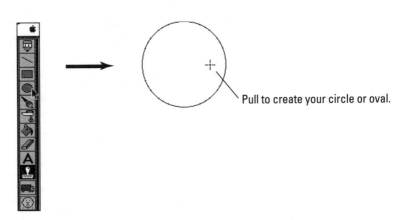

Pull to create your circle or oval.

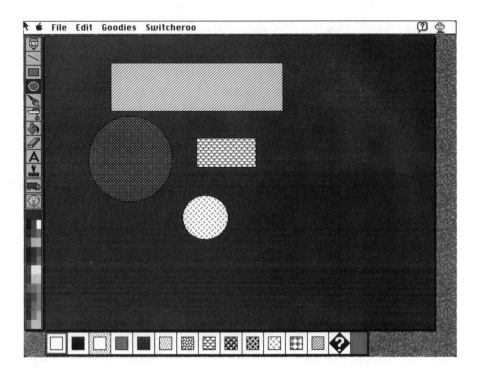

3. Choose the paint bucket and a bright color, such as red. Dump it for your background. Pretty visual, huh?

4. Go to the File menu and Save this masterpiece as *picture 2*.

Picture 3

1. Go to File and choose New.

2. This time we are going to pretend that we are Andrew Pollock. (Isn't he a modern artist?) Click the paintbrush and choose a color.

   Across the bottom of the page you see a variety of choices for your brushstrokes. Try each one of them. Alternate colors between your tries. Go ahead — fill the page!

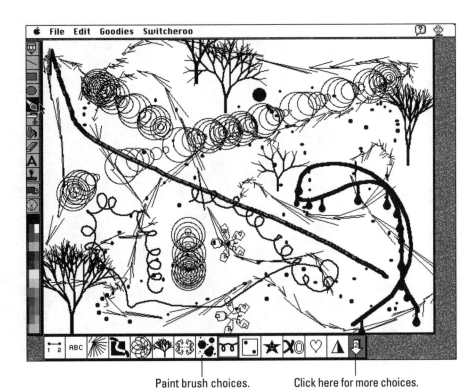

Paint brush choices.   Click here for more choices.

3. Let's say that you aren't comfortable with this wildly modern image in front of you. Go to the eraser icon and click.

   At the bottom of the screen some new choices appear once more. The first four are eraser sizes and shapes. Choose one and erase part of your masterpiece by clicking and dragging over what you want to get rid of.

As you erase, a hidden image appears.

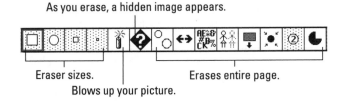

Eraser sizes.   Erases entire page.

Blows up your picture.

The dynamite explodes the whole picture. The other icons, with the exception of the question mark, also clear your entire page. (The question mark allows you to erase your picture while uncovering a hidden *KidPix2* image.)

4. Choose the dynamite, move it to the center of your picture, and click.

5. Now go back and use all of your newfound talents to create another masterpiece. This time you are going to add some words to your work of art before saving it. Go to the letter A icon and click.

   You should see some letters across the bottom of the screen.

6. Hold down the Option key and click the letter A icon again.

   Those letters are replaced with letter styles. In the first view, you could have chosen one letter at a time and placed it on your screen. In this view, you can choose the style of letter you'd like and then click where you want to begin typing on the screen. (Don't forget you have a choice in color as well!)

7. Type **The End** on your picture.

8. Go to the the File menu and Save this as *picture 3*.

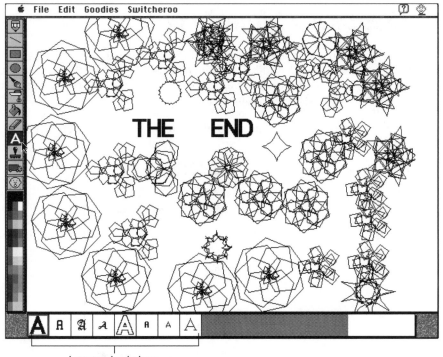

Letter style choices.

Draw Me

A neat opening activity for teaching *KidPix* to a class of readers or early readers is to choose the Draw Me option from the Switcharoo menu. A silly sentence appears and is then read aloud. Here's an example: "I'm a hairy eyeball ten feet tall on a funny fat cow that goes moo-meow and I howl at the moon." And then the program invites the student to draw what they've just read and heard described. This is also a good source to use when teaching a unit on descriptive language.

I'm sure you'd rather keep playing — this program is addictive. So do what you must. Come back to this chapter when you are ready to create a slide show to highlight your creative works.

Printing? If you'd like to print a picture, simply go to the File menu and choose Print — and make your decisions about size, number, quality, and so on. You know the dialog-box drill by now!

Creating a SlideShow

Up until this point the differences between the earlier version of *KidPix* combined with *KidPix Companion* have not made a difference in your ability to learn the program. However, getting to the SlideShow component is different in each of the programs.

In *KidPix2,* simply go to the Switcheroo menu and choose Switch to SlideShow.

In *KidPix* with the *KidPix Companion* added, you will have to quit *KidPix* and look inside the *KidPix* folder on your hard drive. You should see the SlideShow icon within the folder. Double-click the icon. The SlideShow program should open. If you don't see the SlideShow icon, you don't have *KidPix Companion* on this computer. Sorry.

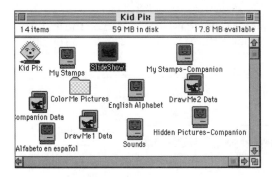

If you've opened the SlideShow program, you should now see a bunch of empty trucks staring at you. Your mission — should you choose to accept it — is to fill three of these trucks with pictures you've created.

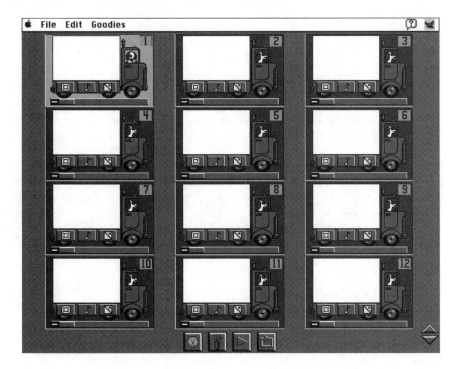

1. Click the picture frame at the base of the first truck.

   A screen pops up telling you to "Pick a Picture." You should see your saved *KidPix* masterpieces. If you don't, pull down the arrow above the scroll bar, choose Desktop and then Hard Drive. Open up your *KidPix2* file to find your pictures.

2. Choose "picture 1" and click Select.

   The picture should now be loaded on the first truck. Go ahead and load your other pictures on trucks 2 and 3 as you did in the first step.

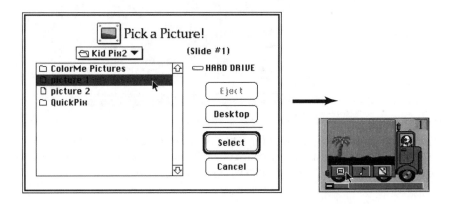

3. Now we get to add some sound! See the musical note at the base of the trucks? Click the note on the first truck.

   You should see another dialog box; this one is asking you to "Pick a Sound." Play around. Choose a few of the pictures and select Preview. You can press Select when you find one you like — or choose the microphone and record your own voice as narration! Add sounds to each of your pictures.

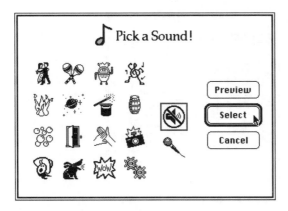

If you choose the microphone, you'll get another dialog box that works just like your tape recorder.

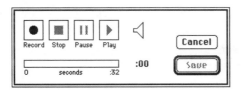

4. Click the last square to select a *transition choice*. The transition (a fade or dissolve) takes you from one slide or picture to another.

If you choose the scissors icon in the "Pick a Transition" dialog box, the transition is quick. Choose any of the others for some really neat special effects. Go ahead and pick a transition for each truck.

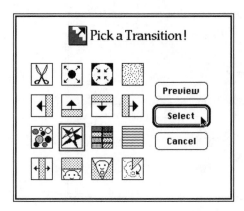

5. You've done it! Your show is complete. You'll know if you made all the necessary choices if each icon/picture, sound, and transition becomes filled with color. To view the slideshow, press the arrow at the bottom of the page.

The square arrow will play your show in a *loop* (over and over again).

6. You can Save your show, or simply choose Quit from the File menu.

Our little show was very simple and somewhat silly. However, the educational possibilities are endless! In Appendix A, you'll see ideas for using *KidPix* to enrich your curriculum.

KidPix2 tips

✔ Never use the smallest choice pencil width. It's too hard for children (and adults) to be sure they've closed all their lines. When the paint bucket is used, paint inevitably spills out.

✔ Pictures look best when the kids draw their own artwork and don't use stamps.

✔ The mixer tool will mess up your artwork fast! Be ready to use the "Oh no!" man or lose all your work.

✔ *KidPix* is not a word processor. Be sure your typing is correct before you leave the text tool. You can't just go back and insert your cursor where you want to make changes. You will have to erase, refill the background, and then retype your words. This task can be very frustrating to students who are used to word processing.

✔ Allow the kids to use the dynamite tool only twice (or so) in a sitting. Without headphones, the noise will drive you crazy. The kids tend not to get any work done because they have too much fun blowing things up!

✔ The line tool (just below the pencil) is great for those students who say they "can't draw anything." By pressing the Shift key, the line straightens even more.

✔ Put lettering on the page after the background color has been added. Otherwise, the holes in letters such as O and P are very difficult to fill with the background color.

✔ To get higher-quality sound when recording, hold down the ⌘ key as you choose the microphone icon. This cuts your recording time down to 16 seconds but greatly improves the sound quality.

✔ Saving your slideshow as a "Stand Alone" (an option when you choose Save) allows anyone with *KidPix2* to view your program without the original pictures. This option is great for teachers who want to send slide shows on a disk to class pen pals.

Chapter 15

Faking Your Way Through *The Writing Center*

• •

In This Chapter

▶ An overview of *The Writing Center's* capabilities

▶ Step-by-step instructions on creating a class newsletter

▶ Inserting graphics

• •

*T*he *Writing Center* is a great program for beginning word-processing instruction. I like to use it as the step before *ClarisWorks.* It is very user-friendly and non-intimidating; and, in addition to all these qualities, it creates some really nice stuff.

I know many teachers who use this program to create a weekly newsletter to keep parents informed on classroom activities.

That Song!

When you open *The Writing Center,* a song that at first sounds rather upbeat will greet you. This same song, when played by a lab full of computers day after day, will soon grate on your last nerve. The first chance you get, go to the Edit menu and choose Preferences. Deselect the sound box (by clicking on — and getting rid of — the *x*). Now we can continue.

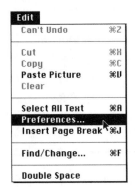
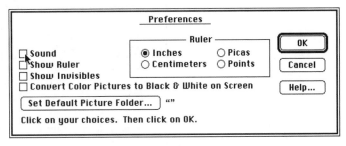

An Overview

The Writing Center offers two basic choices — a report or a newsletter. Headings are optional with both. And within a newsletter, you can determine the number of columns.

This program also comes with 17 folders full of clip art, which makes finding a graphic for your writing an easy task. Not only that, once you insert a graphic, the text automatically wraps around the image, giving the work a customized look. Look in Appendix D for printouts of all your possible picture choices.

The program comes with some standard *templates.* Just like the automatic forms you can create when word processing, a template for *The Writing Center* can do the same thing, and much more. For example, you can create awards, cards, and invitations. In addition, you can save your personal creations as templates.

Creating a newsletter

I'm not going to review word processing with you. By this point, I'm sure you're an expert. (If not, head to Chapter 7, "The Wonderful World of Word Processing.") Instead, we are going to jump into desktop publishing and create a newspaper.

My blurb about the lovely song included with every program probably made you curious, and (I hope) you've opened *The Writing Center*. But you couldn't get to the menu bar to make that adjustment, could you? That's because the program wants you to make some decisions first.

You should see this screen:

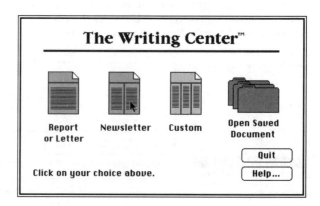

1. For our lesson you will need to choose Newsletter. This program is a little different from others. To make it more "kid friendly," there are no little boxes for you to click; simply click on top of the picture you are choosing.

2. Now you have a Newsletter Layout dialog box. Our choices are Heading or No Heading.

   Click on top of the newsletter with a Heading.

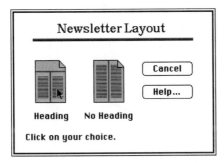

Finally, we come to a screen that looks somewhat familiar. (Oh yeah, the menu bar is usable now if you want to stop and make that little sound adjustment I mentioned earlier.)

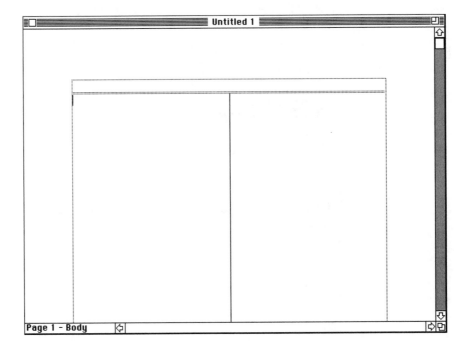

3. As you can see, the page is already divided for you. Your insertion point is located below a double row of dotted lines. The space above this set of dotted lines is called the *heading.*

   Click in this area, and your insertion point should move to the heading.

4. Now make this really look like it was created by a teacher. Go to the Picture menu and select Choose a Picture.

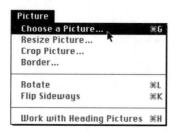

5. In the dialog box that appears, double-click the Pictures folder — or simply click the Open Folder button at the bottom of the screen.

   If your hard-drive icon appears first, open the Misc. folder. Then choose the Pictures folder.

6. A new list of folder choices appears. Use the arrow keys on the scroll bar to find the folder titled Nice for Headings and open the folder.

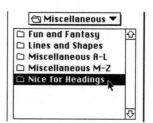

7. Once again, scroll down until you come to the title Worm in Apple. Highlight the name; the picture appears for you in the preview area to the left of the picture choices.

8. Under the picture there's a Place in Document button. Click this button.

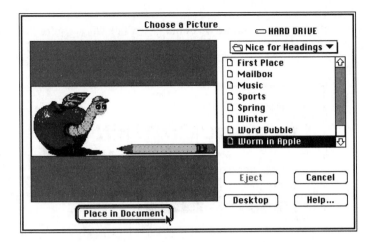

9. Looking good! Now let's think of a title for our little newsletter. Click inside the heading and your insertion point will appear in the top-left corner.

   Go to the Text menu and choose Alignment.

10. When the dialog box appears, choose Align Right and then click OK.

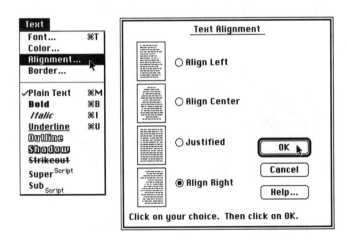

11. Now go back to the Text menu and choose Font.

   What appears is one of my favorite features within *The Writing Center*. This dialog box allows you to see what your font will look like before you use it within the document.

Choose the following: Font (Times), Size (48), and Style(s) (Bold, Italic). See how the Sample box changes? Click OK if you're pleased with the selection.

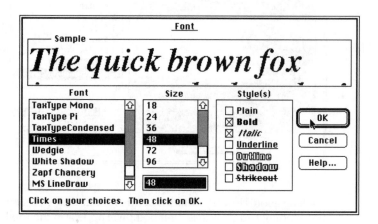

12. Now type *Robinette's* (or any other name) and press Return.

Type *Weekly* and press Return.

Type *Newsletter* and press Return. How do you like it?

13. You are ready to work on the body of the paper. Click below the heading, and your cursor moves to the left column of the paper.

I'll walk you through the creation of a story. You can then work on the remainder of the newsletter yourself. Go to the Text menu and choose Alignment. This time choose Align Center. (Notice that your cursor automatically moves to the center of the column.)

14. Now for the first headline. Go to the Text menu and select Font.

    This time choose Geneva, 14, and Bold for your font, size, and style.

15. Type *SOCIAL STUDIES.*

16. You'll need to change the font before entering your story. Make it smaller and change the alignment to Justified.

    Now type an imaginary story. Go ahead; type anything. I need you to put a couple of paragraphs down so that a picture can be inserted later.

SOCIAL STUDIES
The students have enjoyed our first week of study about the Middle Ages. We have been learning all about knights and castles this week. I'm glad they are so excited about this period in history.

17. Adding a picture is very easy. Go to the Picture menu again. Highlight Choose a Picture.

    When the dialog box appears, double-click the Picture folder. Open the Misc. folder again; this time choose the Fun and Fantasy folder.

18. Within this folder, choose the Knight. Click on the Place in Document button.

    I know this isn't where you probably want your picture. And gosh, is it big! Don't worry — we can fix everything.

    Do you see the little boxes around your graphic? This means your graphic is selected and ready for you to manipulate. Whenever you see these boxes, you can simply click in the center of the graphic and drag it to the desired position.

19. But you say it's too large? Well, you have two options. Either click on one of those little boxes and pull in on the picture to adjust the size, or go to the Picture menu and choose Resize Picture.

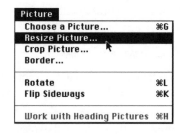

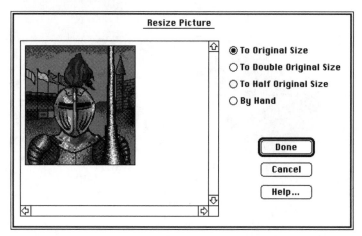

20. When you get the graphic the size you want, move it to the desired location and click outside the picture to place it.

    Here's the really cool part. If you place your graphic on top of text, the text will wrap around the picture. Go ahead, try it!

    If you decide to place the graphic somewhere else, simply click on the image. Your little boxes will reappear, indicating that the graphic is ready for you to manipulate it all over again. So resize it, move it, or even get rid of it by pressing Delete. You are in control of this situation.

SOCIAL STUDIES

The students have enjoyed our first week of study about the Middle Ages. We have been learning all about knights and castles this week. I'm glad they are so excited about this period in history.

SOCIAL STUDIES

The students have enjoyed our first week of study about the Middle Ages. We have been learning all about knights and castles this week. I'm glad they are so excited about this period in history.

That's basically all there is to know in order to fake your way through this program. When you finish with this first column, text will wrap to the top of the next column. Continue working in this same manner. Your newspaper can be as many pages as you wish.

SOCIAL STUDIES

The students have enjoyed our first week of study about the Middle Ages. We have been learning all about knights and castles this week. I'm glad they are so excited about this period in history.

Writing Center tips

✔ Use the Spell Check feature (in the Reference menu) before printing your work.

✔ Don't use too many fonts. It gets confusing for the reader. Try to limit yourself to three or four different font styles.

✔ Too many graphics clutter up your reading space. You want your newsletter to be visually pleasing — not overstimulating.

✔ Remember that the graphics on the screen will appear black and white on your page, unless you are working with a color printer.

✔ Allow students to become "columnists" and contribute weekly articles for the newsletter.

✔ The Border choice under the Text menu allows placement of a border around a selected text block.

✔ Students can draw pictures in *KidPix,* save them, and then place them in a *Writing Center* document by choosing Desktop in the Choose a Picture dialog box. They then open the hard drive and *KidPix* to find the picture. Finally, they simply place the picture in the document and manipulate it as if it were a *Writing Center* graphic.

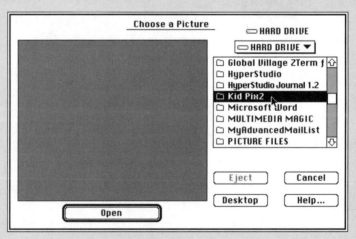

Part V
Going Online

"We're concerned—Kyle doesn't seem to be able to hot key between apps like all the other children."

In this part...

*E*verybody's talking about the Information Highway. Read on and find out what all the buzz is about. A modem is the required mode of transportation and America Online is one of the most interesting places to stop for a visit. So fasten your seat belt and start your engine!

Chapter 16

It's a Modem

*I*t's been said that a modem (a telephone hookup for your Mac) is the single most powerful (and relatively inexpensive) add-on you can buy. This inconspicuous little box is your On Ramp to the Information Superhighway. It's true — and once your students get a taste of life in the fast lane, they'll be begging for more.

What It Is

A modem is a little plastic or metal box, usually about the size of a bad paperback novel. One wire plugs into the phone jack in the wall of your classroom, home, or media center. The other wire goes into the modem port on the back of your Macintosh. (The modem port is marked, interestingly enough, with a telephone icon.)

What happens next is pure magic. Using the little box as a translator, your Mac can now speak its native Mac language to other computers worldwide. It does so the same way you would — by making a call over the phone lines and hoping that whoever answers speaks your language.

After you're connected to another computer (or *online*), you can do things you could never do before. For example, you can do the following:

✔ **Type messages back and forth to other people.**

Isn't this exciting? Instead of speaking like any normal person, you can type your thoughts — where they can be read, misinterpreted, or ignored by thousands of people at once.

✔ **Leave typed electronic-mail messages for people to find later.**

This feature is called e-mail. E-mail is actually great. It's faster (instantaneous), cheaper (essentially free), and less bother (no licking) than U.S. Mail. Yet it's better than a phone call because both you and your recipient can ignore it until you're ready for it. Nobody's ever had to get up from dinner to answer an e-mail. (Well, OK, certain pathetic people probably do.)

✔ **Send software or documents to or from your Mac.**

This is one of the biggies. Suppose you've purchased a great new portfolio-assessment software, but as soon as you double-click its icon, you get a message that says "Hardware Enabler Update Utility 3.2.1 required to run. Now Quitting."

If you had a modem, you wouldn't have to give up in disgust. You could dial up either a person or pay-by-the-hour service, for example America Online, and get that Hardware Enabler Update Utility. Within 15 minutes, you'd be setting up portfolios for each student.

With fax software added to your modem (most of them come with this tidbit), you can send any document created on your computer to anyone who has a fax machine. Most fax software lets you receive a fax (via your computer) as well.

✔ **Look something up.**

If you belong to one of the information services, (America Online, CompuServe, and so on), you can do all kinds of other things. As with other electronic bulletin-board systems (BBS), these services let you explore mountains of information. You can look up movie reviews, stock prices, ideas for using technology in the classroom, and employment opportunities. You can consult an encyclopedia, check out your astrological chart, and communicate with thousands of other educators who "surf the net" (find adventure on the network).

Where you can stick it

Boy, have I ever wanted to say that a few times during my teaching career. No, really — I have!

Anyway, location is an important consideration when using a modem in your school. Most opt for a central location, like the media center, for a number of reasons: more room, existing phone lines leading into the area, and usually a computer.

When the Mac makes a phone call, it ties up the phone line just as effectively as your teenage daughter. When your Mac is using the modem, nobody can use the phone. In the school setting, this requires installation of a *dedicated line* (a phone line that will be used only with the specified computer and modem). It's an expensive necessity.

At home, you can have this expensive dedicated line, or you can entertain one of these options:

✔ **Continually plug and unplug your phone.**

This is definitely the option of choice if you plan to use your modem only occasionally.

✔ **Buy a Y-jack.**

A Y-jack is a $3 adapter from Radio Shack that lets you plug two phones into the same wall jack. Of course, in this case, you're going to plug in one phone and one modem. If both devices are connected to the wall simultaneously, assessing the Information Superhighway involves much less time crawling around in the dust bunnies under your desk. The modem doesn't interfere at all with the normal use of your phone — and yet, when you do want to use the modem, you have no rewiring to perform.

Then again, many modem brands have a built in Y-jack. You plug the modem into the wall and plug the phone into the modem. This does mean, however, that your phone will be busy while the modem's in use.

Speed

Faster modems cost more. And who cares about speed?

You will — the moment your students try to send or receive information over the phone line and are given this horrible message, "Out of time for this month." Generally, on-line services charge by the hour, and school accounts are allotted a limited number of hours free per month. Every minute is precious in a school full of eager-to-learn students. The faster the modem, the faster you can send or receive information, thus saving valuable time and money. Buy the fastest modem your school's funds can allow.

Today's modems come in several standard speeds: 2400bps, 9600bps, 14,400bps, and 28,800bps, for example. According to the Laws of Inevitable Technological Obsolescence, each type becomes cheaper and better each year, and the "standard" speed increases each year.

TECHNO TERMS

Another acronym?

Yes, gentle reader, I again apologize for using boring techno mumbo-jumbo. I promised I'd do this as little as possible, but this term you need to know: *bps* stands for *bits per second.* The higher the bps number, the faster information flows between your modem and another. This may not seem significant to you now, but it will become very significant when you are trying to register for that graduate course via the computer and your poor, slow 2400bps modem prevents you from snagging the last open spot on the class list!

Telecommunicating

Telecommunicating is a sophisticated word for what happens once you connect your phone to your computer. In the next chapter, I'll tell you more about my favorite on-line service. For now, I'll use general terms that can be applied to any of the services you may decide to use.

Who ya gonna call?

After you're equipped with a modem and a phone jack to plug it into, you still need to get software to control it. Without some kind of modem software, you can't do much more than stare.

What software you need depends on what you plan to accomplish with your modem. The options are endless — and range from connecting to a friend with a Mac and a modem to jumping on the much misunderstood Internet.

Commercial services, also known as *on-line services*, run on a pay-by-the-hour rate and most have package prices for schools. When schools open an account, they are given a certain number of hours per month; when those hours are used up, the service is disabled until the next month. This setup prevents the school from incurring charges for time used past the prepaid limit. It also means that time is precious and needs to be used efficiently.

Shop around for the best rates. I was really fooled the first time I purchased an account for my school. Talk to friends and read Chapter 24 ("Great Deals and Great Reads") before you decide to take the on-line plunge.

Netiquette: in Cyberspace, nobody can hear you smile

Before you charge onward into modemland (called *Cyberspace* by the buzzword-crazed media), take a moment to consider this: When you type something to other people, they don't have the benefit of seeing your expression. Hearing a student say, "Mrs. Robinette asked me to stay after school" while jumping up and down excitedly has a very different implication than "Mrs. Robinette asked me to stay after school" with a lowered head and downcast eyes. Cyberspace is the only party on earth where you're judged purely by your thoughts. What a wonderful opportunity for students!

Because of all this social bizarreness, certain standards of behavior of which Emily Post never dreamed now exist. Follow the guidelines, and you're certain to make a good impression and have a good time.

Don't type in all capitals

Leave your Caps Lock key alone. All capital letters are hard to read and have a special meaning in the soundless realm of on-line speech: It means YOU'RE SHOUTING. It also means that you're a rank beginner who doesn't know this rule.

Don't worry about the flaming

Flaming means on-line ranting and raving. Being teachers, we are all quite used to this form of communication from parents. It happens a lot online. For example, you were online and left an innocent message inquiring about gradebook programs for your school. You return the next day to find that some cyberjunkie has responded with a message like this:

```
Ill informed IDIOTS like you give classroom technology a bad
name! ARE YOU CRAZY? You need to stop worrying about making
your life easier and get on with the business of TEACHING!
Use technology to help the kids — not YOU!
```

People flame a lot online for three reasons. First, they are anonymous. People are known by a nickname or a number, so they figure, "who cares if I lose my cool a little?" Second, the on-line services are filled with thousands of messages. Some people think they need to hit their point with a SCUD missile or they might not even get noticed. And third, the kinds of people who spend most of their time online usually don't have alternative outlets for their energies.

Online, no one can hear you smile

As I mentioned a moment ago, reading people's expression when they write to you online is impossible. You can't see them rolling their eyes or pretending to gag as they try to clarify what they're saying.

Therefore, some creative individuals (who, in my opinion, have more time than they know what to do with) came up with some pretty ingenious symbols for common expressions that can't be conveyed by mere words. In order to understand these gems, turn your head 90 degrees to the left.

:)	smile	:-p	sticking out tongue
:(	unhappy	=:-o	shocked
;)	sly wink	:-/	skeptical
:-*	kissing	=):-)=	I'm Abraham Lincoln.
8-)	wearing shades		

But then again, thousands of people find these faces insufferable — myself included.

Others might use acronyms to represent common phrases:

LOL	Laughing out loud.
ROTFL	Rolling on the floor laughing.
BRB	Be right back.
BAK	Back at the keyboard.
RTFM	Read the (you-know-what) manual.
IMHO	In my humble opinion.
GMTA	Great minds think alike.
@*#*&!	Golly.

Create your own Cybertalk

As you begin to get your students familiar with Cyberworld and its etiquette, have them create some signs, symbols, and acronyms of their own — symbols that represent feelings and phrases associated with the trends and ideas of their generation. It may be interesting to see what ideas your cyberkids can come up with.

Scheduling

I'm going to take this time to inform you that exploring online can be very addictive — and once you, the kids, or other teachers get a taste of what's out there, you won't be able to stop! In my school, we've had a problem with time running out before the quest for more knowledge and communication is fulfilled. It's tough to tell a group of students that they have to wait to see if someone wrote them back. Kids don't like to wait, and neither do I.

Ideally, you could purchase an account with unlimited hours of on-line time per month (or at least 25 or more hours). More than likely, your school won't be able to afford such a luxury. I sincerely believe that these services will *wise up* soon and offer substantially reduced rates to schools. Until that happens, here are few ideas for making the best use of your on-line time.

✔ Allow only supervised groups of students access to on-line time.

It's too easy for children to get off task, waste time, or (worse yet) forget to sign off. (Most services will automatically shut down when left idle for a period of time — but that's still wasted time, and on-line time is money!)

✔ Keep a log book beside the computer hooked up for telecommunication.

Have teachers keep track of their on-line time.

✔ Allow only certain grades to participate each month.

You thus give each class a larger amount of time per visit.

✔ Use the voucher system.

Create vouchers or coupons which are good for 15 minutes of on-line time. (Make sure the total of the vouchers is the same as the amount of time you are given each month.) Pass the vouchers out to the teachers and tell them they can redeem the vouchers at any time that month. We allow the teachers to exchange with each other if they want more time in a specific month. This is a fair way to give access to all — and those who don't wish to use their time can feel good about giving it to a colleague who will put it to good use.

✔ Work with small groups (six students or fewer).

This strategy allows everyone to be able to view the screen and have easy access to the keyboard.

✔ Spend the first few visits online getting acquainted with what is offered.

Don't jump into an activity before the students are familiar with the concept of telecommunications. Keeping things simple in the beginning and building an understanding of what's out there will allow them to venture in exciting directions with *confidence* later on.

An important note

Please know that this chapter gives you the very basic information on modems and that vast space known as the Information Superhighway. Bard Williams has recently completed a great book titled *The Internet For Teachers*. This is the book to buy if you are interested in an extended journey through cyberspace!

Chapter 17

A Quick Tour of America Online

• •

In This Chapter

▶ Starting your on-line journey

▶ Sending a few post cards (e-mail)

▶ Keywords for a successful journey

▶ Picking up something for the kids (on-line activities for your class)

▶ Queries for your guide

• •

L et me begin by reviewing the name of this service. It's America Online —
not Online America. Calling it by the wrong name will be an immediate clue
to all those techno-nerds that you're not really that informed. Say it with me,
"America Online, America Online, America Online." If you've mastered this, we
can go on.

All kidding aside, America Online is one of the best ways to get yourself motor-
ing down the infamous Information Superhighway.

Getting Hooked Up

Well this one's easy. Get an America Online start-up disk (call 800-827-6364 and
request a preview disk for yourself). It allows you to try America Online free for
10 hours. Remember, in order to take advantage of this service, you'll need to
have a modem connected to your computer and your phone.

I'm going to leave it up to you to follow the simple instructions presented when
you insert the disk and click the installer. But if you have any problems (or you
just want to know all the details about America Online), get yourself a copy of
America Online For Dummies (IDG Books Worldwide).

Nothing really exciting is going to happen during the first ten minutes or so. Like the first day of school, there's lots of paperwork and general information to get out of the way.

Just give them the information they ask for and be done with it.

Surfing the net

From this day forward, after you've set up your AOL (America Online) account, you'll see this screen when you open America Online:

You'll notice that, as you type, the letters (or numbers) you enter do not appear. That's how they remain a secret from people looking over your shoulder. Don't worry, the computer knows all and sees all.

The connection time is a little slow for me, so after I enter my password and hit the Sign On button, I usually go brush my teeth or get the kids something to drink (why are kids always so thirsty?).

When I return, this next screen is what I see; and if I'm in time, I'll hear an overly cheerful male say, "Welcome" and then, "You've got mail" — if someone's written to me!

This screen is called the oh-so-original *Welcome screen.* There are two major functions for this screen:

- ✔ If someone has written you, you'll see a mailbox icon in the lower-left corner.
- ✔ The other icons on the screen tell you about current events online.

For now, just click the Go To Main Menu button at the bottom of the screen.

This screen is a little more interesting. Each of the 14 decorative buttons represents a department you can visit online. Within each of these departments lies a wealth of knowledge and entertainment just waiting to be discovered.

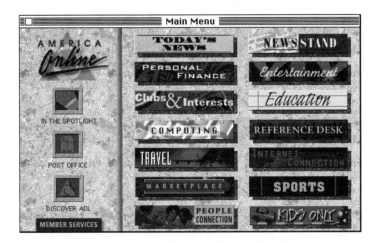

Explore if you'd like for a while. Just come back to this spot when you're ready to continue on the journey.

A stop at the post office

You've probably noticed by now that, in addition to all the neat choices appearing on the screen in front of you, there are also menus listed at the top of your screen. Let's do mail.

That's right, we are going to send some e-mail (electronic mail). It's just like sending a real letter — only it's faster and cheaper. Instead of relying on the U.S. Postal Service you're now placing all your trust in Ma Bell and your modem!

1. Go to the Mail menu.

```
Mail
  Post Office
    Compose Mail          ⌘M
    Read New Mail         ⌘R
    Check Mail You've Read
    Check Mail You've Sent

  Edit Address Book
  Address Memo

  FlashSessions...
    Activate FlashSession Now
    Read Incoming Mail
    Read Outgoing Mail

  Mail Gateway
  Fax/Paper Mail
```

Like menus in all other Mac programs, the unavailable menu commands are grayed-out. Let's send some e-mail.

Choose Compose Mail from the Mail menu. The next screen you see should look something like this:

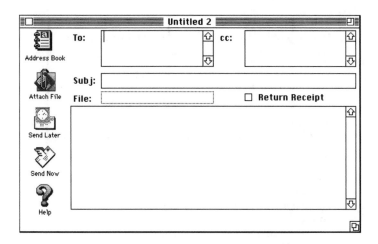

2. In the To: box you need to put the *screen name* of the person to whom you want to send e-mail. Each person using AOL has a screen name that they chose when they went through the setup procedure.

   If you don't have a friend using America Online, you can write to me. My screen name is MNette.

3. Ignore the cc: box for now unless you want to send this same letter to a few other friends.

   Remember: To move between boxes you can either use the Tab key or click inside the box with your mouse.

4. In the Subj: box, you need to type a brief description of your letter's contents. Maybe call this one *my first e-mail.*

5. Now move down to the big blank box and type your message.

6. On the left side of this window you see a column of five cute icons from which you will choose one of these activities:

   Address Book: This allows you to store frequently used e-mail addresses.

   Attach File: This allows you to attach any file from your hard drive or from a floppy disk.

If the file is long, AOL offers the option of compressing a file (making it smaller) before sending it. This saves valuable on-line time, because you are now sending a much smaller file through the phone lines.

Don't worry about your friend being able to read this "smushed" file when they go to open it. AOL has an automatic expansion feature which will decompress any compressed file that you receive.

Send Later: An important option. You see, the best time to compose mail is offline, or before your sign on. (I know what you're thinking, "Now she tells me!") By doing this you don't waste precious and costly on-line time perfecting your prose.

This function is especially important in the school setting where children are usually not the fastest or most accurate typists. Then click this button, and AOL will store the mail for you. The next time you go online, simply choose Read Outgoing Mail from the Mail menu and click the Send All button. Your message will be on it's way.

Send Now: This means just what it says. If you are already online and your message is perfected, click this button and out it will go!

?: Finally, we all know that a question mark means HELP!

That's all there is to sending mail. Let's jump back in the car and go for a little joyride!

Keywords can save time

Find your way back to the main menu. If you can't get there by closing windows, try the Go To menu and choose Main Menu.

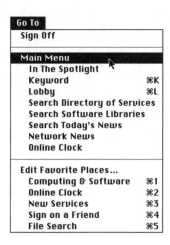

I hope that you spent some time exploring each of the departments. Now I want to tell you about *keywords,* a quicker way to access the areas you're most interested in. Keywords are AOL's way of saving you on-line time and the frustration of going from screen to screen in order to uncover your final destination.

1. From the Go To menu, choose Keyword.

   You'll want to remember the keyboard shortcut for this one: ⌘-K. You can get a list of keywords by going to Member Services in the Members menu.

2. Choose Members' Online Support, and then choose the Getting Around Icon.

   The next screen you'll see shows a List of Keywords icon. Click this icon and choose the keyword lists you'd like to view.

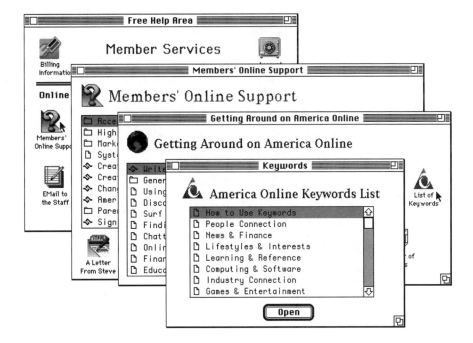

Print the lists by choosing Print Screen from the File menu.

Don't forget to enter your most used keywords on the cheat sheet in the front of this book!

A few of my favorite keywords

TIN — The Teachers' Information Network holds great lesson-plan ideas for use with your students online, for using other technology, or just for general curriculum concerns.

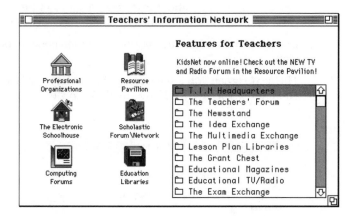

TEACHER PAGER — This service is really neat. It allows you or your students to ask for help or advice with any academic problem. You can access the service from any location online, and once you enter your question or problem, the coordinator will get you help and either get back with you — if you're still on line — or e-mail you later.

TTALK — This keyword takes you to the Teacher's Forum. This forum offers weekly live conferences that center around current issues in education. Even if you don't wish to participate, it's a lot of fun to observe.

NEAPUBLIC — This area highlights information made available by National Education Association, a national teachers' union. There's a really neat issues database that contains a wealth of interesting reading material.

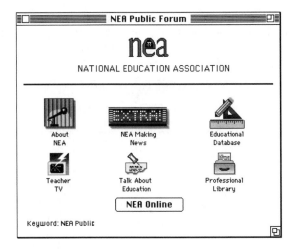

ACOT — Apple Classrooms of Tomorrow is a great place to read and share some innovative uses of technology. You'll also find reports on Apple's ongoing research programs involving classrooms across the country.

HOMEWORK — This one will take you to the Academic Assistance Center. It's a place for kids to get help online with standard homework questions or more in-depth research needs. There are teachers or assistants "live" online to give help throughout the day. There is also a message board where you can post questions and receive answers via e-mail within 48 hours.

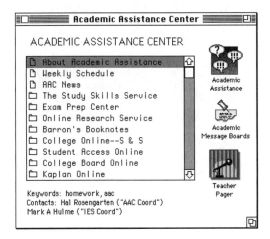

ENCYCLOPEDIA — The full series of Compton's Encyclopedia is available for you to browse or really dig into for some real research. Don't forget to print your entries — don't waste valuable on-line time reading from the screen.

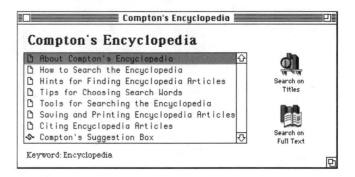

SABRE — This keyword will put one of those drinks with an umbrella in your hand and take you to faraway places. Actually, it'll take you to the exact same database used by most major travel agents. Go ahead and dream: Check out the cost for a round-trip ticket to Hawaii!

The Computing Forum (keyword: COMPUTING)

I know — why go here? This book is supposed to tell you everything you need to know, right? Well, my fellow educators, I'm taking you on this little side trip for one reason only: They've got some free (or really cheap) stuff here. We all love a good deal now, don't we?

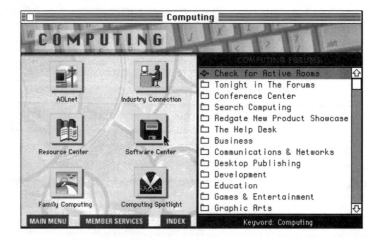

I go to the computing forum to check out the Software Center. Go ahead, click the icon. Here you will encounter a new computer skill called *downloading*. You see, programs are available for you right here on America Online. You get these programs by downloading them, or loading them down into your computer. Sounds simple, right? Well, it really is.

Before we go on, let's talk about how you pay for all these programs. It depends. Some of the programs you will download are called *freeware*. You don't pay anything! And some of the programs are *shareware*. With these programs, you'll see a name, address, and price for the program — and you are instructed to mail the creator of the program a minimal fee if you decide to keep the program.

It is important that you honor the shareware payment request if you try a program and decide to keep it. Remember that some kind, computing friend spent valuable time, energy, and brainpower to create the program. You owe this person something. Most of the shareware is under $50 — a real bargain when you consider what it would cost you in a store.

Let's download something now.

1. Click the Shareware Mac 500 icon.

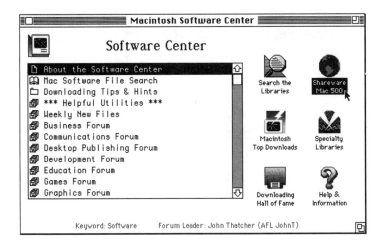

2. Choose Fonts.

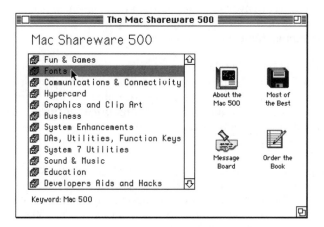

3. Now choose TrueType fonts.

The first font you'll more than likely see is Architect. Click the Get Description button. Go ahead and read the entire screen if you want — I know you'll like this one.

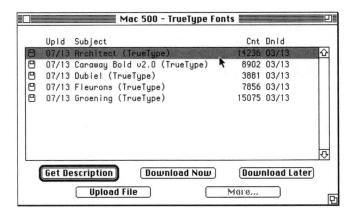

4. Click the Download Later; then click OK on the next window.

That's all there is to it. Before you sign off, simply go to the Download Manager in the File menu.

You'll see a screen that tells you what files you've selected, how long it will take you to download, and a row of icons with options. If you click Start Download, your new font will appear in your AOL Online Downloads folder when you're finished.

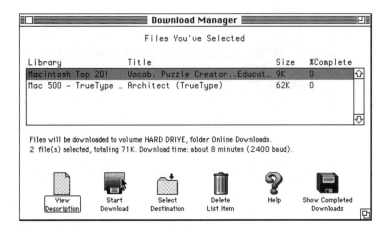

5. The next screen is great because it gives you the option of having the computer automatically sign off when it finishes the download. This means you can walk away and not worry about wasting that all important taxpayer money.

Click in the box Log off when done.

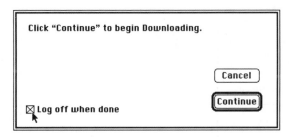

6. When your file is downloaded, go to your AOL Online Downloads folder, drag out the Architect suitcase, and drag it on top of your System folder. The computer will do the rest of the work!

Now open *ClarisWorks* or any other word-processing program you have. Try out your new font! If you need more assistance, see the Downloading Tips and Hints folder in the Software Center.

Some tips for setting up AOL

America Online can be used in a variety of ways within the school setting. School accounts are set up with a limited number of hours per month to avoid costly overtime. You'll find that once the students get online, they'll want more time than you probably purchase, so consider the following suggestions:

✔ Ask AOL for educational pricing.

✔ Buy as many hours as you can afford.

✔ Use a computer that's in a central location with easy access for all classroom teachers.

✔ Purchase a dedicated line to avoid tying up a general school line.

✔ Create some type of log to monitor usage in order to make it fair for all those who want to use the service.

Online activities for your students

CNN (keyword: **CNN**) offers a great service to America Online members. It requires a small amount of effort on your part — but it's well worth it. CNN airs a fifteen-minute, commercial-free news program each weekday at 3:45 am ET. Yes, that's AM as in who's-up-at-that-time. Hey, you're using a computer now, certainly you can learn to program a VCR.

Anyway, tape the program; then when you get to school, sign on to America Online, choose keyword **CNN** from the Go To menu, and print the daily classroom guide located in the Today's Guide folder. The guide is usually less than five pages long and is full of great ideas for discussion and worksheets based on that day's broadcast. The program is a great way to keep kids informed on world events, and the daily guides make it a real no-brainer on your part.

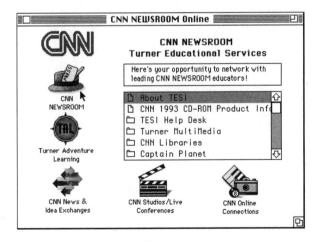

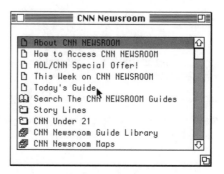

Scholastic Network (keyword: **SCHOLASTIC**) is my other favorite place for students and teachers. Take the Scholastic Network Tour the first time you visit to get a good overall picture of the resources. You'll find some stimulating reads in the Professional Development section; they have monthly focus studies, and the kids will love visiting Kids' World.

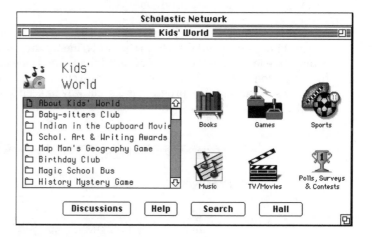

In Kids' World, the students can participate in weekly contests such as:

- **Map Man's Geography Game:** Each day a new clue is given to help identify the mysterious location.

- **History Mystery Game:** Same as **Map Man's Geography Game**, but with a history twist.

- **Math Challenge:** Each day a new clue is added to assist the students in solving a complicated, real-life math problem.

There are also areas for students to publish their written work and hook up with on-line pen pals.

Kids Only Network (keyword: **KIDS**) is, as the name implies, intended only for the eyes of children. There are a number of interesting bulletin boards for kids to post and answer messages on. Of course, Disney has an area, along with National Geographic and the Cartoon Network. The students enjoy browsing in this area if they aren't using AOL for any specific reason.

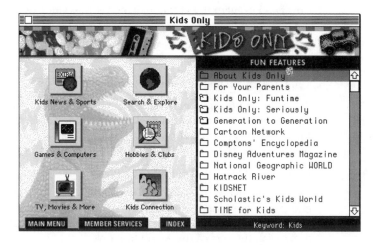

Top Ten Questions I'm Asked about AOL

1. How can I check how much time I've used?

   This is important to keep track of and it's easy to do. Go to keyword **BILLING** and choose Current Month's Billing Summary. It's a good idea to keep a check on this the first few months you have the service at your school. You don't want to end up with unused time and the end of the month (it doesn't roll over) — and you don't want to run out too quickly!

2. Where can I get help while I'm online?

   Gosh! There are help folders within just about every forum for specific guides. For general help, use keyword **HELP**.

3. Why does it sometimes take longer to get through?

   America Online has grown by leaps and bounds over the last year — all those folks like you are becoming so technically literate! Sometimes the phone lines get a little jammed. That's why you chose two numbers when you signed on. Just be patient and try again later. I've never had trouble signing on during the school day; most of the busy times occur in the evening.

4. How can I disable call-waiting on my home phone?

   Click the SetUp button in the AOL Start Up screen from the first window (before you sign on). You'll see a box that you simply check to disable call-waiting. In some areas, it may require you to dial a few numbers — don't worry, they're listed on the screen.

5. How can I prevent my students from visiting some of the adult areas?

   Most educational accounts already have these areas blocked. If not, go to keyword **HELP**, click on Member's Online Support, and open Parental Chat controls.

6. Can I use my on-line account from another location?

   If you are using someone else's Mac, choose Guest from the Screen Name pop-up menu of the Welcome window and then click the Sign On button. After you've made the connection, AOL will ask for your screen name and password. All the charges will be billed to your account.

7. How can I create my member profile?

   Once again, use keyword **HELP**, click Member's Online Support, and choose Create/Modify Your Member Profile. Take your time filling out your profile — and feel free to leave blanks if there's certain information you don't wish the rest of the world to know.

8. Where's the best place to start?

   Look at the "Hints for New Members" listed under keyword **HELP**.

9. How can I check to see if mail I've sent has been read yet?

   Go to keyword **MAIL**, choose Check Mail You've Sent, find the message in question, and then choose Status. If the mail has been read, you'll see when it was read. If it hasn't been read, you'll see that, too — and you have the option of *unsending* the mail.

10. Can I change my screen name?

    Nope. However, you can add up to four additional names and begin using one of those instead. Go to keyword **NAMES** for instructions.

Well, that's it for now. Go forth and prosper, you information-highway junkie. Be careful, it's very addictive — but big fun.

Part VI
Reality Bites

The 5th Wave   By Rich Tennant

@RICHTENNANT

PROVING THAT BIGGER ISN'T ALWAYS BEST, A CONTRACT TO BUILD A COMPUTERIZED SONAR TRACKING SYSTEM FOR THE U.S. NAVY IS AWARDED TO TROOP 708 OF THE BAYONNE, NEW JERSEY EAGLE SCOUTS.

In this part...

Well, I've teased you. I've told you all the options. I've given you extensive lists of great software. I've even taken you on a short trip down the Information Highway. Now I'm sending you back to your school — back to reality. And sometimes, reality bites!

Keep your chin up, make the most of what you've got, and be determined to strive for more.

In this part I give you some ideas on ways to get the most out of that single, lonely computer that may be sitting in the corner of your classroom. I also discuss the major components involved in creating and managing a Mac lab. And finally, I give you some great ideas on ways to keep your school and community aware of your technological accomplishments — and to convince these groups to spend more money.

Chapter 18

The One-Mac Classroom

• •

In This Chapter

▶ Why only one Mac?

▶ Mac wish list

▶ Obtaining a computer license

▶ Scheduling possibilities

▶ Managing the one-Mac classroom

• •

*T*he *Lonely Guy*. It makes me so sad to see a poor, lonely guy sitting in the corner of the room, sometimes humming quietly, other times simply cold and inactive. No, I'm not talking about a child. I'm talking about the unused Mac. I know, you don't mean for it to happen — it just does. You don't have time to preview software, make sure everyone gets a turn, and monitor progress. So you just ignore the lonely guy.

That's not good. There is nothing worse than an unused computer. It just sits there making you feel guilty for not using something that was supposed to be a valuable addition to your classroom; and it makes your students angry and frustrated because they are rarely allowed to use it. Read on and find out some easy ways to incorporate your lonely Mac into your day-to-day classroom activities.

Why Only One?

I want to begin this discussion by questioning why you have only one Mac. If your school already has a lab (or two) and is now placing computers in classrooms as it can afford the purchases, I agree with the placement of your computer. However, if your school doesn't have a lab of any sort, you may need to discuss the possibility of creating one before you get too attached to your Mac.

The generalized statement that every teacher needs a computer is overused. Teachers need a computer if they are going to use it. Studies have shown that labs are the best way to get students and teachers comfortable with computer use. It makes sense; you have a room filled with computers, an eager group of students, and their teacher. In a lab, everyone can accomplish something without having to *fit* time on the computer in with other classroom obligations. The lab gets everyone psyched about computers and wanting one for the classroom.

On the other hand, placing a single computer in a classroom with a teacher who isn't familiar with it — along with a group of kids who (for the most part) have never used one — puts everyone at a disadvantage. The teacher has to find a way to work it into her schedule, and the students end up fighting over whose turn it is.

As I step down from my soap box, I will leave you with this: Get a lab first (even a small one — kids don't mind pairing up) and then work on the computers for each classroom. Doesn't it make sense for everyone involved to be comfortable with an expensive creature before placing it in their environment?

Placement

It's the week before school starts, you've rearranged your room five or six times, and people keep dropping off more stuff for you to store: the overhead projector, the new reading series, the math manipulatives, and — oh yeah — the potting soil for your science kit. Everything is just peachy. And then in walks your media specialist with your new computer! Great, where does it fit into your interior decorating scheme?

Well, like the overhead, the tape player, the plant light, your coffee pot, and the TV, it needs a plug. You also need to make sure you put it away from the chalkboard and pencil sharpener — too much dust. And you may want to position it in a way that will allow you to continue teaching while a few children are working. (You need to remain the *main* attraction.)

Take the next few days to work out your decorating problem and then come back to this chapter.

Basic Wants and Needs

Children have a hard time discerning between wants and needs. Especially when schools sell ice cream and chips as snacks. You tell me, are those *wants* or *needs*?

A computer has very few *needs* — keep it dust free, don't turn it on and off, keep food and drink away from it, and use it.

However, there are catalogs full of *wants* for your computer! Here's the basic list for the lonely computer in your classroom.

- ✔ **set of speakers:** These are great for whole-group instruction ($20-up). But be sure to use special shielded (and self-powered) computer speakers.

- ✔ **headphones:** These are a must. They keep you from competing with the computer for attention (I've gotten these for $1 at the drugstore).

- ✔ **disks:** It's best if you buy a disk for each student so you can save space on your hard drive. You can get disks pre-formatted if you don't want to take the time to initialize one for each student, and the cost difference isn't that substantial (about $8 for a pack of 10).

- ✔ **dust cover:** This one explains itself ($12-20). They have these covers for your keyboard, too.

- ✔ **printer:** This would be a wonderful convenience for you; however, it's not a necessity. If your kids save to disks, you can take the disks later to a computer with a printer. (See Chapter 5, "A Quiet Talk about Printers," for details.)

- ✔ **CD-ROM drive:** Again, not a necessity, but it sure would be nice. (See Chapter 11, "The Role of CD-ROM Technology in Education," for more information.)

- ✔ **Software** and **CDs:** You don't need much to be productive in the class-room. If you have too many choices, the students spend all the computer time fighting over what to use! *ClarisWorks* (Chapter 6) and some type of grading program (Chapter 13) are a must.

Hey, I Want My Desktop on TV!

An *LCD panel* ($1,000) allows you to show what's on your monitor through the overhead projector, and a converter card ($400) makes it happen on your TV screen. I think they are great when you want to show a new program to the entire class. The LCD panel is portable yet fragile — and not always clear.

The LTV cards actually go inside your computer, and they aren't portable (unless you take your computer). If you have one of the new AV Macs, you are already set to display on a TV screen and don't need either of these additions.

Using your classroom TV as a monitor

There are a number of companies who produce converters that let your classroom television work as an additional monitor, which is great for whole-group instruction on a new program — much better than having 25 kids around the computer station.

Many of the converters also include remote controls that allow you to zoom in on specific areas of the screen. And some come with the capability to let you make marks (electronic) on the screen when you move the mouse — kinda like the sports guys who draw those lines showing you the football plays. What will they think of next?

I would suggest connecting one converter to a TV on a rolling cart and having it available on a check-out basis for individual classrooms. Please note that the audio portion of your program will still be heard through your computer, so external speakers might be a nice addition as well.

These convertors are manufactured by a number of different companies and have names like TelevEyes/Pro, TVAtor, AverKey, PresenterMac/PC3. They range in price from $150-$500 and can be purchased through any of the mail-order catalogs mentioned in Chapter 22.

The AV Mac

If you have an AV Mac, you don't need a converter to use your TV as a monitor. Simply run a cable from your Mac's Video Out jack to your VCR's input jack. Do the same with the sound cable.

Now here's the tricky part. Open the Monitors control panel, and click Options. You see a special box of options. Choose Display Video on Television and Flicker Free Format. Click OK. A warning dialog box appears. Click Switch. In a few seconds, your monitor will go dark — and the image will appear on your TV screen!

Understand that the picture won't be all that clear. The Mac's monitor is of much higher quality than most TV screens.

A License to Use

I always start the year by giving the class a general overview of the care and feeding of our Mac. I explain the basics and how I expect the students to treat the machine. Don't be afraid to discuss the cost and privilege of housing a computer in your classroom. Finally, I set up consequences for those who are not capable of following the rules.

At the end of our training, I have each child show me that he or she can function independently on the Mac. Each student should be able to do the following:

- ✔ open and close a program
- ✔ save work to a disk
- ✔ open work saved on a disk
- ✔ print
- ✔ shut down the computer at the end of the day

Then each child is given a *computer license* (which can be suspended, if needed).

The Scheduling Dilemma

I know. How do you determine *who* gets to use the computer and *when*? There is no easy answer to this question. I've tried just about everything. Does everyone get an assigned time? Do they get to use the computer when they finish their work? Do they get to use it when they've gotten a piece of writing through final editing and are ready to publish? All these options are viable, but I believe this choice should be up to each teacher. Just don't let the computer sit unused. Develop a system that works for you while — at the same time — you allow maximum usage of the computer.

Keep a class timeline or journal

Probably one of the best ways I've ever used the computer in my classroom was when I kept an ongoing journal of our activities. This journal can be as involved or detailed as you want. Simply have a student write a few thoughts about the day; save this to a disk or the hard drive. Take turns. Once a month you could go through the entries to edit and add graphics. At the end of the year, these thoughts can be compiled into a neat book or presentation.

Assigned times

In theory, this idea sounds great. Every child gets an assigned time on the computer every day. However, in practice, this strategy is hardly feasible. The average school day is 6 $\frac{1}{2}$ hours long. Now take out 30 minutes for lunch, 30 minutes for recess, 30 minutes for art, music, or PE, along with the 30 minutes wasted getting into class and getting ready for buses — and you are left with only 4 $\frac{1}{2}$ hours of actual classroom time. You would have to pair the students up and assign each pair a 15-minute time slot in order to accommodate the entire class.

But what about the introduction to the language arts lesson that you want everyone to hear, or the crucial math lesson? And there's always the spelling test on Friday mornings. Each of these little side trips takes someone away from computer time. Believe me, you won't hear the end of the when-can-I make-up-my-time-on-the-computer questions. And this is at the elementary level. More than likely, high school and junior high teachers see a new batch of students every 45 minutes!

An assigned time sounds great in theory, but it's difficult to make work unless you have a small class.

When you finish your work

This strategy sounds feasible. However, gifted Anna, who finishes her work in ten minutes, is on the computer every day — and she has a Mac at home — while Susie, who is slower, never seems to get time on the computer and really could use the reinforcement. I just hate these dilemmas!

AlphaSmart is very smart

AlphaSmart keyboards are one of the coolest hardware products to come along in education. These keyboards are a cross between a laptop and a simple word processor. The keyboards store information you type (they show about five lines of text before scrolling on). When you get to a computer, you simply connect the AlphaSmart with a cable and send the information to the computer. The information is then entered into your word-processing program to be edited and formatted. This is a great addition to a school that has limited access to a computer lab. Completing the text entry *before* getting to the lab gives the kids more time to do the fun stuff, such as formatting. AlphaSmart keyboards run about $250 and are worth every penny.

As a publishing center

I use the computer as an extension of the writing process — an incentive for the students to finish a written piece of work. I require their writing to be ready to publish before they go to the computer, and then I have a variety of possibilities for publishing (*Newspaper, The Writing Center, Book Version Easybook, Slide Show, KidPix2, Report, ClarisWorks,* and *Multimedia HyperStudio*). Usually, students are at different levels of the writing process, and we don't get too backed up; but, if needed, I'd have a sign-up sheet ready.

Use a chart

A pocket chart sometimes works well to make sure everyone gets a turn on the computer. Place cards with student names on them in pockets on the chart. When children have had a turn on the computer, they turn their card over so that their name doesn't show. When all the names are turned over, you flip the cards and start the rotation again. You might try keeping an egg timer at the computer and designating a certain time limit for each visit. (Try not to make it less than 30 minutes.)

These kits are incredible!

Tom Snyder Productions has created a number of all-inclusive kits that work great in the one-computer classroom. Most of the kits include workbooks to go along with the theme, as well as very detailed teacher's guides. The computer serves as an information disseminator and receiver. As the students work through the lessons, the computer also serves as a guide and keeps track of progress based on the data students enter.

This concept shows the students that the computer can't do all the work — they have to find and enter the information themselves. The cooperative learning and classroom discussions created through the use of the programs are well worth the (very reasonable) price!

One of my favorite kits is *Decisions, Decisions: The Environment.* In this program, the students are given a real-world problem to solve. The students work in teams. By reading (yes, from paper!) the advice of experts, the students decide on a course of action. They then enter their decisions, and the computer in turn gives them feedback and guidance. The computer also gives the students consequences based on their goals and the actions they decide to take. In the end, the groups are given a score based on their decisions — and the impact of those decisions on the community.

Other topics in the *Decisions, Decisions* series include: *Urbanization, Violence in the Media, Colonization* and *Revolutionary War.*

Call Tom Snyder Productions at 800-342-0236.

Numbered cups

Divide the school day into numbered blocks of time. Label plastic cups with corresponding numbers. Then, using a class list to keep track, place the cups on students' desks to show who will be using the computer that day and at what times. After completing their turn on the computer, the students place the cups on the teacher's desk to be used the next day.

Ask a friend

As you can see, there's no easy way to cure the one-Mac classroom dilemma. One solution is to get your Mac a friend. Find one or two friends who would be willing to give up their Mac for a week or two. Work out some type of rotation where each of you could have a "mini-lab" of computers in your room for a specified number of days. (It's best if you can keep the Macs on rolling carts.) By creating a rotating mini-lab, you could focus your classroom activities around the schedule and have a group of students ready to publish or create a project when the computers make their way back to your room. And by having a larger number of computers, more students will have access at a given time.

Tips for the one-computer classroom

✔ Always hold whole-class instruction on any new software you intend to have available. Your goal should be for the students to work independently while at the computer.

✔ Include keyboarding instruction or drills for the first five or ten minutes of a student's visit to the computer.

✔ Never allow students to transport the computer to or from another classroom.

✔ Never allow the students to eat or drink while working at the computer.

✔ Display student work that's been done on the computer. This shows the rest of the school (including PTA members and principals) what a great thing the computer is — and it may convince someone to spend more money!

✔ Keep track of who has time on the computer. Make sure everyone gets a chance. You don't want children or parents to complain about (lack of) time on the computer.

✔ Encourage the use of spell-check and thesaurus features found in most word-processing programs. This is a great way to incorporate language-arts instruction — and it helps perfect the students' writing.

✔ Above all, don't forget about yourself. Get on the computer and use it!

Chapter 19

The Mac Lab

*I*deally, every school should have at least one Mac lab. Two or three would be even better! If your school has a lab, I hope this chapter will give you a few new ideas or insights — and if your school doesn't have a lab, maybe this chapter can help you develop a plan to create one in the future.

The Computers

Well, of course, if you're going to create a computer lab, you'll need computers. Don't wait until you have one computer for every child in a class to create your lab. I've worked in schools where students had to double up on computers, and they did just fine. As a matter of fact, their creative writing became *incredibly creative* when they worked together.

A mini-Mac lab works well for small groups of children as well. Many schools create these smaller labs in their media center. As interest and funding grow, these labs could increase in size and eventually move to a larger area.

Networking

In simple terms, a *network* exists when you connect any two or more computers together. Businesses use networks to connect hundreds of Macs at a time. This setup allows computers to share files and send e-mail messages to one another. In the school setting, the major reason for creating a network is to be able to share printers. Connecting a network is best left to professionals.

Servers

No, you don't need one of the cafeteria workers to take time out and join the students in the lab. A *server* is a necessary part of a network if you intend to share files or printers. In regular terms, a server is an additional Mac that is dedicated to sending and receiving files for the other Macs in the network.

Printers

The printers in your lab are a vital component. Consult Chapter 5, "A Quiet Talk about Printers," for info on the various types of printers available. What I will give you now are a few tips on using printers in the lab setting.

✔ Don't allow students to always print in color. This practice becomes costly when the lab is being used daily by five or six classes. Save color for those special creations.

✔ Purchase printers that efficiently use *background printing* — which simply means that, after you press Print, you can continue working on your computer while the printer prepares your document.

✔ If students print at each visit to the lab, using a laser printer in the lab setting can prove to be costly as well. Replacing the toner cartridge in a laser printer can cost more than $75.

✔ When using paint programs like *KidPix2* or *Microsoft Fine Artist*, discourage the use of solid background colors if the pictures will be printed. The printer will have to use up loads of ink as it fills in that background. (Don't limit the use of anything if the pictures will be part of an on-screen slide show!)

✔ Purchase enough printers to have at least one for every four or five computers. Otherwise, you'll have to spend the last 15 minutes of lab time waiting for everyone to finish printing.

Lab Management

So you've got the lab, the computers, and plenty of printers. What comes next? A good plan for use and management is a must.

Staffing your lab

I'd like to see every lab staffed by a certified teacher. In today's financial crunch, this may not be realistic, so a teacher's aide or parent volunteers with extensive computer training may have to suffice. Just make sure that whoever runs your lab is ready to answer basic computing questions, troubleshoot when problems arise, or at least know where to call for the answers.

Technology Coordinators

These positions are popping up at the local school level all across the country. In my opinion, the creation of these positions shows incredible foresight on the part of the administrators at each school. The responsibilities of the technology coordinator should not include working in the lab and seeing classes during the entire school day. Instead, the technology coordinator should be free to do the following:

- ✔ train staff members on computer hardware and software
- ✔ develop lessons that integrate classroom curriculum with technology
- ✔ conduct small-group instruction with students
- ✔ preview new software and hardware
- ✔ attend technology conferences and workshops
- ✔ troubleshoot problems with lab and classroom computers
- ✔ keep administrators and the community informed on local technology activities
- ✔ create long-range and short-term technology plans and goals for the school
- ✔ oversee the technology budget
- ✔ recruit, train, and schedule volunteers to help in school computer labs

Making the lab teacher's life easier

The lab teacher's life can be improved in a number of ways. Many of these adaptations are focused on maintaining student behavior so that the lab teacher can instruct without complications. To a student, a computer is as much fun as recess — and that level of excitement needs to be maintained while learning new facets of technology usage.

The following is a list of things that will help the teacher maintain a little control while still feeding the enthusiasm of the students:

Invest in a desktop-protection program

Such programs include *At Ease* (Apple, $45.95 for single use) or *FoolProof* (SmartStuff Software, $39 single use). Both programs allow you to protect items on your hard drive. *At Ease* is good for very young children who don't need to see the desktop. (A file folder with buttons for each accessible program covers the entire desktop.)

I prefer *FoolProof* because it shows the desktop yet allows you to control what portions of the desktop are accessible (unlocked) to the students. *FoolProof* also has easy ways to set up folders for students' saved work — which isn't quite as easy with *At Ease*.

Consider a keyboard-locking program (if your lab is networked)

Purchase *ScreenShare* (White Knight Software, $249 for lab site) which allows you to lock the student keyboards as you broadcast a program to all the computers for instructional purposes. This setup allows students to pay attention instead of working ahead or experimenting on their own.

Create open communication with teachers

Come up with a system that keeps the lab teacher informed about classroom curriculum at each grade level. Use this information to plan lab activities for the students. We all know that students take away more from an activity when the learning is relevant to — or an extension of — previous learning in the classroom.

Schedule your lab wisely

Lab scheduling is an important subject, and one that causes great conflicts in most schools. Some prefer to have an open sign-up system (first come, first served); others distribute vouchers that allow teachers lab time (when your vouchers for the month are gone, you can't go), while still others use the lab as a special-area class (like art, music, or PE). My only advice is to meet as a school and come up with a plan that best suits the individual environment — just make sure the computers are always being used!

Software Selection

Personally, I'd go the productivity route. You'll be able to accommodate all grade levels and all subject areas — and you can meet those needs with a minimal amount of software. Yep, I'd say two programs (lab-pack or site-license versions) would do just fine.

Robinette's Recommendations:

✔ Elementary — *ClarisWorks* and *KidPix*

✔ Middle — *ClarisWorks* and *HyperStudio*

✔ High — *ClarisWorks* and *Persuasion*

Of course, you could add to your collection as time and money become available. I suggest becoming a master of a few really good programs before you go out searching for more ways to spend school money. Turn to Chapter 13 for my software picks broken down by type, grade level, and subject.

Chapter 20

Once They Believe You . . . Take Their Money!

● ●

In This Chapter

▶ How to show off in front of the right people

▶ Create a circle of informed friends

▶ Creativity Crash Course

▶ Beg like a child

● ●

*1*f you've gotten this far in the book, or just turned to this chapter because you're curious, I know that you are a believer! Now I want to share with you some ideas for getting others around you involved and excited — including your local administrative types. Once you've convinced some of those "significant others," it will be easier to get them to open up the checkbook and fund your cause.

Show Off Your Computer Prowess

You know it's working, the kids know it's working, so now tell the rest of the world! Keeping your local community informed is one of the best ways to get the things you want for your school.

Parents and other taxpayers have ways to get what they want from a school system by simply flexing their my-taxes-pay-your-salary muscles. For example, Tommy (fictitious name, of course) fell on the playground one afternoon and ended up with a pretty bad scrape on his knee (no stitches or anything, just a little blood). Well, the next day his father was up at our school bright and early walking around on the playground. He then came inside and informed me and my principal that his son would have never been hurt if there weren't any rocks on the playground. He then left in an angry huff, and we all had our little silent giggle — let's see, the playground's outside, there are rocks outside. Anyway, the next day the county had a crew of six — yes, six — men out on that playground picking up rocks. You see, Daddy had flexed those my-taxes-pay-your-salary muscles and called the district office, which resulted in another waste of taxpayer money to pick up less than a wheel-barrow full of pebbles. For what the county had to pay those workers, I could have probably bought a printer or two for the lab.

So let's try and redirect some of that taxpayer muscle by participating in some of the following activities.

Put out a press release

If your class just communicated with students in Russia on the Internet, put out a press release.

If little Susie's slide show won an award at a technology conference, put out a press release.

If 95 percent of your faculty participated in a technology fund raiser, put out a press release.

Get the picture? You may not always get coverage, but more than likely you'll at least get a little blurb and picture in the local paper. What may be ho-hum to you may amaze your fellow taxpayers. Amazement gains recognition . . . and recognition gains respect for your program. And remember, a little respect goes a long way when budget time rolls around.

Teach afternoon classes

Yeah, I'm sure most of you are already either teaching or taking part in a computer-literacy class. But have you ever thought of making it available to parents in your school . . . free of charge? There are lots of adults out there who are eager to learn about computers, yet they're intimidated by the whole idea. Why not give them this opportunity? Once they get excited (and, believe me, they will), they're going to be some of your biggest supporters. You won't have to convince the PTA to help pay for your on-line service or buy the laser printer you really want for the teachers. The parents will be so into computers, they'll be coming to you asking what you want them to buy next!

Use school newspapers

This one is easy. If your PTA puts out a monthly newsletter, ask for a small amount of space for a technology column. Use this space to brag about the students' accomplishments and tell about goals for the future of the technology program.

Another great newspaper idea is to have a school newspaper staff. Using the computer to create the newspaper is an education for the students. Within the paper you might have a section in which you highlight "technology stars of the month." In this section you could talk about teachers around the school who are doing great things with their computers. (We teachers love to see our name in print; recognition is so hard to get these days.)

Technology week

This new week of recognition usually falls in February. It's actually perfect timing. Everyone's over Christmas, bored with winter, and anxiously awaiting spring break. Why not add some excitement by creating a week-long celebration of technology? Invite local merchants and professionals to give presentations on ways in which they use technology.

This strategy accomplishes two goals: It lets the kids see how technology is important for their future, and it gets those oh-so-important taxpayers into your building — raising their awareness of what's going on at the local school level. Many companies end up volunteering services or supplies once they see how involved your program has become and how much you still need to make it complete.

Remember Your Friends

Don't become isolated from the rest of the world. Don't try and reinvent the wheel, as they say. I've learned more from my fellow technology coordinators than I could have ever learned on my own. Here are some great ideas for sharing with colleagues.

Throw a software party!

That's right, invite anyone who's interested to come and "play" with your new software. Only remind them of the importance of sharing when we play with our friends and require them to bring along some of their "toys." This activity is loads of fun, and it's a good way to get a look at some of the new programs you may be thinking about buying.

Have a software exchange

One of my good friends at another school came up with the idea of sharing our creative talents by putting these creations on a disk and sharing them with each other. Once a month he sends out a memo announcing a theme (forms you've created, workshop ideas, *KidPix2* lessons, and so on) and asks everyone to send him samples (on disk) along with one blank disk. He then compiles all these samples and sends you a disk with everyone's best work.

Remember: Only share *documents* you've created, not software. It is illegal to copy software.

Create a software trailer or office

At my school district's main office we have a trailer that's full of software to be checked out for preview. It's a great deal! Most of the software was given to us by the various companies in hopes that — after previewing — we'd decide to make a purchase for our school. Most of the really big companies are eager to send you their stuff.

Develop a Technology Center

This one is one of my system's goals. Plans are underway to construct a center that will house the latest in technology. Much of this work is being done in conjunction with Apple and IBM. These companies will keep the center equipped with their current products and provide training to center's staff. This center will be open to the public and will be available for teachers to visit individually or as a group for inservices. Eventually I'm sure that the software-preview trailer will be incorporated into this same facility.

Okay... You Want Cold, Hard Cash!

Yeah, yeah, yeah, everyone's informed now, and maybe a few dollars or supplies have come your way — but you want the big bucks, you say? There are ways to make money for your school without having to beg or show off.

Hold summer computer camps

The week after school's out, we hold a half-day camp for students. We have a morning and afternoon session, and parents provide the transportation. I love this idea because, unlike the school day, I get to work with the kids for an extended period of time, and we can get into more involved projects on the computer. We charge $50 a child and usually have a waiting list. Some schools turn the camp into an all-day camp and rotate the kids between computers and tennis or basketball instruction. This is a fun and easy way to make a couple thousand dollars for your technology program.

Schedule after-school clubs

This idea works something like summer camp, except that you meet with a group of kids once or twice a week. Parents like this one, too, because it gives them some time to regroup before picking up their kids — and the cost is minimal (we charge $8 a week for one two-hour session). That may not sound like much, but if you get 10-20 kids a week, it'll help buy paper, disks, and ink cartridges when you need them.

Seek parent donations

When we decided to get America Online for the school, we didn't have the funds to pay the account up front. So we devised a plan to offer access only to the fifth-grade students and in turn ask their parents to give donations in order to get the service up and running for this first year. Believe it or not, it worked. We not only got enough to prepay for one year's service, we had a little left over to buy additional time if we needed it.

Do a fund raiser

Sell something, sell anything! There are any number of fund-raiser companies that will come to your school and show you their wares. The percentage you make off of each sale is usually pretty substantial and well worth the month-long headache of arranging the whole deal.

Use Your Word-Processing Skills

You're surely a master by now. So put those skills to work and round up a little dough!

Write a grant

Every year millions of dollars in grant money goes unclaimed. I do know schools that have received huge grant awards. It's pretty incredible thinking that you could get thousands of dollars just for writing a big, thick document.

Many books on grant writing are available, and I've seen a new flood of classes on the subject. If you have the time (ha, ha!) it's worth a try. America Online has a Grant Information Center in their Scholastic Network area. The grant information is updated on a regular basis (keyword: **SN GRANTS**).

Find a corporate sponsor

What is it they say? "It never hurts to ask." Write a big company and, once again, show off. Tell them about your incredible pursuits and how their sponsorship would enable you to reach new heights. One school in my district has a division of Apple as their sponsor. They get all the new "stuff" when it comes out, and in return they act as a test audience. Another school has a local department store as a sponsor — and they've gotten all the video supplies for their multimedia pursuits *absolutely free*. I'm sure it's a big fat tax write-off for the companies, so give it a try!

Part VII
Spending Money

The 5th Wave — By Rich Tennant

KYLE AND TODDS SOFTWARE Co.

"THAT'S RIGHT, DADDY WILL DOUBLE YOUR SALARY IF YOU MAKE HIM MORE MAC APPLICATIONS."

In this part...

There's one thing that I really know how to do — spend money! In this part, I tell you about some of the really cool items you can buy. They aren't really necessary . . . but they are lots of fun. I'll also share some of my *favorite* things to spend money on: publications, organizations, and mail-order houses.

Chapter 21

Top Ten Things That Didn't Fit in the Other Chapters

*T*here just wasn't enough room to include it all. You know what I mean — the bell's about to ring, and (once again) you never got around to teaching that health lesson. Why is health so hard to work in?

Anyway, all of the "extras" mentioned in this chapter are just that — extras that aren't necessary but that would be really great to have. Now that you know the basics, adding these things to your technology base should be simple and fun.

Scanners

A *scanner* takes a picture of something and then puts it on your Mac's screen. After that, you can manipulate it any way you want (what control!). This means you can crop, erase, add to, copy, and paste.

Scanners look and act like the copy machine you probably have sitting in your work room — only they're a lot smaller, and paper never gets jammed inside. That's because your scanner consists only of the top part of your copy machine (glass top, bright light, funny hum).

What's it good for?

The uses in the school setting are incredible. You can scan a copy of Johnny's first story and then copy it into *KidPix2,* where he can add his own illustrations and print it for Mom. Or better yet, get involved in that portfolio idea we (and the whole world) discussed earlier (see Chapter 12), and keep Johnny's work in an electronic portfolio that's easy to pull up when Mom comes for a conference; the electronic portfolio takes up a lot less space than that milk crate with hanging file folders.

Another neat thing to do is scan photos or newspaper clippings to incorporate into text files. Why not add that scanned photo of your principal kissing a pig at the fall festival to the school newspaper you create with *The Writing Center?* Or the graph from the newspaper clipping showing the incredible jump in test scores since your school devoted more time and money to technology pursuits?

What'll it cost me?

Well friends, it ain't cheap. You can get black-and-white (but why bother?) or color scanners, and they come in a variety of different quality levels when it comes to resolution. They range from $500 to $4,000. My advice is to buy the best one you can afford.

And here's a hint: The higher the *dpi* (dots per inch), the better the scan will appear on the printed page. You see, the image is digitized into bunches of little dots, and the closer they are together, the clearer your scan will be.

OCR

OCR stands for *optical character recognition.* In teacher terms, this software does what we have to do on a daily basis — it interprets text (in this case, *scanned* text) and changes it into a readable and workable image. Just like we have to decipher a child's handwriting, OCR software interprets a scanned piece of text from a mere image or picture into a text-based document that you can work with.

Without this piece of software, the adjustments you can make to a scanned text image are minimal. With this piece of software you can save yourself a lot of typing if there are changes you wish to make to the document.

What's it good for?

Upper-level students may find it useful when gathering research from printed material or importing documents to be used as part of an informational presentation. The administrators within a school may find this software handy if they want to duplicate the style or format of documents and forms received from other schools.

What'll it cost me?

As you can probably imagine, this is a very sophisticated piece of software — and it's not really a necessity. I must also add that in many of the ads I've recently seen for scanners, the OCR software has been thrown in as part of the package price. If you aren't lucky enough to find one of these deals, OCR software will run anywhere between $200 to $850, depending on the level of sophistication. Take note that OCR software requires a very powerful computer.

Apple QuickTake Camera

All the schools in my area are buying these cameras as fast as they can come up with the money. These neat machines fall into the "who'd have ever thought of it" category. This camera works like any other (only no focusing), yet it doesn't use film — and even has a built-in flash. It allows you to take up to 32 pictures (in color!) and then load those digital images into your Mac by simply connecting the two with a serial cable. It's *très* easy and fun, fun, fun!

After you load the pictures into your computer, you can crop them, rotate them, scale them larger or smaller, and even zoom in on specific areas. And, of course, you can import these pictures into any of your other applications.

What's it good for?

Are you kidding? Take the camera on a field trip and then come back to create a presentation showing everything you did and learned. Or have the camera with you at the PTA performance, and then use the pictures in the PTA newsletter.

A QuickTake alternative

Connectix makes an affordable ($99) alternative to the Apple QuickTake. It's called the QuickCam. This little device is a round ball (about the size of a billiard ball) that sits on a triangular base. The QuickCam can take both video and still shots.

There are a few limitations that I must mention. You can't take this camera on the road (unless you have a laptop). Unlike the very portable QuickTake, in order for you to operate it, the QuickCam must be connected to a Mac. Also, the pictures taken with the QuickCam aren't nearly as clear as the QuickTake — and at this printing they are only black and white. (A color version will be released in late 1995.)

An electronic class scrapbook or diary could be enhanced with the addition of a few photos showing the highlights from the school year. We use the camera to take pictures of the kids who are having a birthday; we then import these into a slide show we run just before we broadcast the morning announcements on closed-circuit TV.

I'm sure by this point that you've already thought of a few more ways you could use this camera to meet your own needs.

What'll it cost me?

I've seen these cameras as low as $650, but they usually run closer to $700. Most of the schools in my area try to purchase two, because once people start using them, the cameras are always in great demand. I've also been told that it's worth the extra $80 to purchase the carrying case: Many of the teachers take the cameras of field trips or outdoors. One other accessory is a Battery Booster Pack at $50 (The battery is good for about 120 images.)

TouchWindow

This device allows children to do what we are constantly telling them not to do — touch the screen. A *touch window* is simply a screen that attaches to your computer monitor and, when you touch the screen, the computer picks up on the response as if the mouse had been clicked. By touching the screen, children can make selections, move objects, pull down menus, and even draw graphics.

Attaching the window is easy, and it's not permanent — which is a nice option if you share the computer with another class that may not need this special adaptation. Software must be installed, but this is also an easy task.

What's it good for?

The TouchWindow is ideal for special-needs children who may have limited mobility or limited fine motor skills. It's also great for pre-school and kindergarten children who may have never had exposure to the computer and are not familiar with the mouse.

Before we purchased this device, our special-needs children weren't able to use the computer. Now, they love using the Brøderbund Living Books and other interactive titles!

What'll it cost me?

To my knowledge, EdMark (the original creator of the TouchWindow) is the only manufacturer marketing to schools. The TouchWindow costs $335.

PowerBooks

I want one. I want one. I want one. I'm sure everyone has seen a laptop computer by now, and you probably thought they were mainly being used by business types on airplanes. Well, that is the way these small wonders are portrayed in commercials and magazine ads. However, the laptop is making huge headway in the education business as well.

Apple makes many different models and sizes. They come with different configurations (speed, RAM, and hard-disk space), and you also have the choice of color or black-and-white screens. There's quite a price range based on what features you desire.

A laptop doesn't have to be plugged in, thus making it portable. That's the whole deal. Once charged, most laptops will run for about three hours before needing to be recharged.

What's it good for?

Well, if you had a laptop at home and purchased some of the same software you had at school, you could take things home to edit or create. You could even enter grades on your gradebook program while sipping Kool-Aid on the deck as you watch your kids play.

Some schools are buying laptops for teacher check-out. Isn't that kind? They know they don't pay us enough to be able to purchase one of our own, so they give us loaners — it's really a wonderful idea.

I've also heard of schools purchasing class sets of laptops and storing them on a rolling cart with a printer. This makes it easy for teachers to roll the cart to their classroom and have their own lab for a period of time — an appropriate alternative these days when so many of our schools are overcrowded and space for computer labs can only be considered after regular classrooms have been created.

What'll it cost me?

The price of a laptop computer depends on the configuration, and on whether you decide on color ($2,200–$4,200) or black-and-white ($1,100–$1,700).

Like all good salespeople, I must now inform you about the additional add-ons you may want to think about when you purchase a PowerBook.

- ✔ **You really should buy a case.** With a case, you can carry your portable without risking damage. These cases are now a major fashion statement. You can go bargain basement and purchase nylon for about $39, or go high fashion with a prestigious leather case for $100–$300 that tells everyone you've arrived in the high-tech world of educational computing. Now, all kidding aside, cases are very necessary if your school plans to check computers out to teachers overnight. It would be tragic if Mr. Smith's two-year-old spilled grape juice all over the school's $3,000 PowerBook, wouldn't it?

- ✔ **You may want to buy an extra battery.** This extra battery can be had for about $70. A separate battery charger will run you an additional $70–$150.

- ✔ **You should consider an adapter.** For those long ball practices that leave you waiting impatiently in the car, or that traffic jam that goes on for miles, an adapter will let you plug your PowerBook into your car's cigarette lighter. You can get an adapter for a mere $50. What a deal!

Photo CDs

A few years back, we were all given one more option when we dropped our film off to be developed. No, I'm not talking about double prints — I'm talking CDs. Instead of simply giving you a set of prints, many photo developers will offer you the option of having your photos placed on a CD. The images on a CD are crystal clear. And — get this — you can place that trusty little CD into your computer and pull up your photos as a piece of quality clip art.

What's it good for?

What's it good for, you ask? Imagine giving a family history presentation using *HyperStudio* and being able to incorporate actual photos of the people you profile. Or imagine creating an computer class photo album with text and actual photos to describe each person!

What'll it cost me?

This figure probably varies from city to city, but it runs between $25 and $35 dollars to have a roll of 35mm color film developed onto a CD. I know — that seems pretty steep to me, too. But it's worth it when you're trying to personalize a presentation and you don't have a scanner — or you have only slides or negatives. At this time, the Photo CD service is available only through Kodak.

IIe Cards

I'll keep this one brief. There are cards that can be placed in your computer to let you run some of your old Apple IIe software. I'm not really sure why you'd want to do this with all the great Mac software out there, but I'm constantly asked this question and feel compelled to include the answer in this book. The cards run about $100.

PC Software

Another question that I'm constantly asked: Can I run my PC software on the Mac? This question is getting easier for me to answer. Apple and IBM are feverishly working on a cross-platform system and promise that we'll see it in the near future (whatever that means).

Until then, there are software programs and DOS compatibility cards that will let you run that PC software on the superior Mac. I've been told that things get slower and that all the bugs haven't been worked out just yet.

The most common software package for performing this amazing feat is called SoftWindows for the Macintosh (Microsoft), and you can get it for about $300.

Networking

 I know, you're right, I did mention this one in the Mac Lab chapter. I wanted to stress, once again, the importance of involving a professional when your school makes any attempt at becoming networked. Trying this on your own could result in large sums of wasted dollars — and labor that must be repeated.

Ideally, your school should come up with a plan for its network with the help of a professional. Then break the plan down into financially feasible parts based on the overall school plan. Many schools in my area have thrown away money and time by trying to do this on their own.

Totally networking a school with 1,000 or so students can run upwards of $400,000! Many school systems work networking costs into local bond initiatives as a way of funding the costly — but ultimately necessary — building improvement.

QuickTime Movies

This Apple invention lets you not only view digital movies on your Mac but also allows you to *create* such movies. Yes, that's right Mr. Spielberg, we teachers are soon gonna be knocking on your door.

QuickTime allows you to import movies you've created with your camcorder and insert those clips in other applications like *HyperStudio*. I know, it amazes me too — but it works.

This little invention falls under the heading of *multimedia* (incorporating sound, movies, graphics, and interactive aspects of computing). All you need to know for now is that it's the wave of the future . . . and nothing is going to stop this wave from crashing on the shores of your school.

Chapter 22
Great Deals and Great Reads

• •

In This Chapter

▶ Magazine madness: just give me something I can understand!

▶ Delectable deals

▶ Mail-order mania

• •

*W*ho doesn't love to shop (besides my husband)? Shopping for computer stuff is really fun — even if you're just browsing the aisles or thumbing through a catalog. I've discovered some really great resources over the past couple of years. Many large companies are beginning to take note of the purchasing power behind education and most are offering discounts to teachers. In this chapter, I'll share my "best picks" along with phone numbers and addresses.

I've Been to Magazine Hell and Back

When I first purchased my Mac, I immediately went to the bookstore and scooped up all the magazines (only two of them at that time — *MacWorld* and *MacUser*) that I thought would help me make the most of my new machine. I quickly became depressed when I realized that I knew *nothing* about computer technology.

Since then, I've come across some great publications that speak to me on my level. Most of these jewels aren't available at your local drugstore, so give them a call or drop a line asking for a preview copy and see what you think!

✔ **Mac Home Journal** (800-800-6542) P.O. Box 469, Mt. Morris, IL 61054

This magazine is constantly changing and improving based on the needs of its audience. The educational articles are both informative and entertaining. There are also a good number of articles written by respected professionals in the field of education.

✔ **The Computing Teacher** (800-336-5191) ISTE 1787 Agate Street, Eugene, OR 97043-1923

This magazine is a publication of the International Society for Technology in Education, a top-notch group of folks dedicated to our children. Each issue combines informative articles by respected educators with software reviews and columns that address the questions of teachers using technology.

✔ **Technology & Learning** (800-544-2917) 330 Progress Road, Dayton, OH 45449

My favorite aspect of this magazine is that they use *real* teachers as examples in their articles. This would be a great magazine for your school to get as a part of its media center collection.

✔ **Children's Software Review** (313-480-0040) 520 North Adams, Ypsilanti, MI 48197

Warren Buckleitner started this publication as a means to keep parents informed on the quality educational software available. He uses school and family testers to preview the software highlighted in each issue. The review also includes an informative software and hardware news section.

✔ **Electronic Learning** (800-544-2917)

I first found this one on America Online. The articles address all areas of technology and the product reviews are always right on target.

✔ **Club KidSoft** (800-354-6150) 718 University Avenue, Suite 112, Los Gatos, CA 95030

This magazine is aimed more at the kids in your life. What I like is that KidSoft has a team of educators — yes, former teachers and the such — who spend time previewing software and weeding through the bad stuff before they write about it or make it available for purchase. Their KidSoft catalog features great reviews, and they also have a preview CD that will give you demos of most of their approved software.

✔ **Family PC** (800- 413-9749) P.O. Box 400454, Des Moines, IA 50340-0454

Family PC highlights Mac and PC products but tends to be a little heavy on the PC side. However, this magazine's strength lies in the activities it includes to go along with a broad range of software. I've also found lots of good on-line information, and recent issues have had more articles focusing on computers in the classroom.

Did you say free?

Yes, we teachers are notorious scroungers. I've asked for display items in department stores, gotten strawberry containers from my grocer, and picked up boxes from the liquor store and covered them to use as storage. In a nutshell, if you don't have the money, just go looking for handouts.

✔ **News from the Center for Children and Technology** (212-807-4200)

This is a quarterly newsletter that highlights the role of technology in children's lives.

✔ **Edutopia** (415-662-1600)

Part of The George Lucas Educational Foundation: A newsletter dedicated to encouraging the use of multimedia and telecommunications in education.

✔ **National School Boards Association Institute for the Transfer of Technology to Education** (703-838-6722)

This group heads up the Technology Leadership Network — a project whose goal is to "promote the wise use of technology in education."

Deal me in

Now if it's not free, at least give me a good deal. You don't find many of these in the technology biz; the cost of everything is outrageous!

✔ **Apple Educator Advantage Purchase Plan** (800-959-2775)

Dial this number before you make a computer purchase for yourself. Apple offers deep discounts to educators and can usually beat those found at your local computer store. They also have a finance department.

✔ **Roger Wagner Publishing** (800-421-6526)

This is the incredible company that brings you *HyperStudio*. Roger Wagner will loan disks and manuals (you must return them later) to conduct *HyperStudio* seminars, and they are very interested in hearing about your successes and failures.

✔ **America Online** (800-827-6364)

Call America Online directly to get the best educational prices. They have deals for schools based on 10, 20, and 30 hours of usage per month.

Ask before you buy! Most large companies have discounts for educators and require no more than an ID card as proof of employment. Even Comp USA has education and government pricing.

I admit it . . . I love mail order

With a phone and a little plastic you can order just about any little "MacToy" you'd like — and, in most cases, you can have it delivered to your door the very next day. It's almost too easy.

- **MacWarehouse** (800-255-6227)

    The people are kind and helpful — and answer my queries even when I'm not ready to make a purchase. They always have a few great deals in each of their catalogs, and when you place an order, they always have a few daily specials to tease folks like me! And for only $3.00 you'll get it the next day. Be sure to ask for the educator discounts — the price cut is sometimes quite substantial.

- **MacZone** (800-248-0800)

    Same idea as MacWarehouse. Some people swear by this catalog. I guess you end up using whichever you order from first. They have very similar deals and also have $3.00 next-day shipping. Educational pricing is also available.

- **MacConnection** (800-800-0019)

    Same as MacZone and MacWarehouse. Call all three and compare prices before you make a purchase. They also offer educational pricing.

- **Educational Resources** (800-624-2926)

    This company is probably the largest national distributor of educational software. The catalog is very informative. Educational Resources also has a "Partnership Plus" program that offers discounts to schools — along with staff development kits. This program includes outstanding deals for schools that have 50 or more computers.

- **AIS Computers** (800-849-4949)

    This company does an incredible job on software review. They have an entire staff dedicated to reviewing software in order to speak informatively to educators with questions. These folks are very insightful when it comes to addressing educational needs. They totally impressed me!

- **Learning Services** (West: 800-877-9378, East: 800-877-3278)

    Learning Services is not as large as Educational Resources, but their prices are very competitive. I always like to call and compare deals before making a purchase. Go ahead, it's an 800 number. It won't cost you a thing, and you may get a better deal.

Part VIII
Appendixes

The 5th Wave

By Rich Tennant

©RICHTENNANT

"I ALWAYS BACK UP EVERYTHING."

In this part...

I've saved the best for last!

In this part you'll find all the *stuff* we teachers love to get our hands on. The lesson plans were designed to be easy to customize to fit any grade level or subject area, and the artwork contained within *KidPix2* and *The Writing Center* are great resources to keep beside your computer. My buddy David Pogue graciously gave me permission to reprint his super glossary and troubleshooting pages that I'm sure you will soon have well worn.

Appendix A
Mac Activities to Enrich Your Classroom

● ●

*W*ithin this appendix, you will find ready to use activities based around two software titles: *KidPix2* and *ClarisWorks*. That's right. With a small software investment, you can also participate in all the amazing activities found here.

Don't forget that I am a teacher, and I know how your mind works. Take these ideas and branch out on your own. We teachers are notorious for taking someone else's inspired plans and adapting them to fit our own needs. Go for it!

I've divided the lessons by curriculum area. I'm not including a grade level or age group with the activities, because — after you read through a lesson — you will more than likely think of ways to adapt it to the grade you are teaching.

If you need a quick review of the two programs used, turn to Chapter 14 for *KidPix2* questions or Chapters 6 through 9 for *ClarisWorks* help.

Language Arts: KidPix2

> ✔ Younger students may enjoy keeping a **pictorial classroom journal** or **timeline.** At the end of each week, have one student draw a picture on *KidPix2* that shows a few of the activities that have taken place over the last week. Encourage the inclusion of academic *and* nonacademic activities. Then print the picture and post it on the wall or bulletin board. Add a new image each week; soon you'll have your own visual record of your classroom activities.

We went to the zoo!

3/25/95

✔ **Letter recognition** is a big deal in kindergarten. Why not have students create their own alphabet book? Assign each student a letter of the alphabet; then have them draw or stamp the letter in the center of the page. The next step would be to draw or stamp images around that start with that letter. Finally, you could print each page and bind the book, or you could create a *KidPix2* slide show and add their voices describing the pictures.

✔ Create an original **class poem**. Write the poem together and then have each student be responsible for one line or phrase from the poem (and create a slide for a *KidPix2* slide show). Add recorded student voices and compile the pictures to create a slide show of the poem.

✔ Use the Draw Me activities found under the Switcharoo menu in *KidPix2*. Have students circle or underline a specific **part of speech** in the sentence (adjectives are a good choice), and then draw the picture.

▮ ✔ Create a **story web** using the circle and line tools.

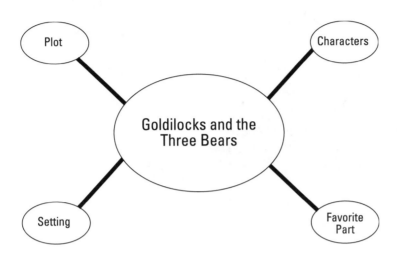

▮ ✔ Use the circle tool to draw a Venn Diagram. Use this diagram to compare two **characters** in a reading, two **plots,** or two **endings**. Save the empty diagram as stationery for students to pull up and use at different times of the year during different themes of study. After entering text, the students could use the drawing tools to add illustrations that accent the theme of the diagram.

▮ ✔ Have students use a specific number of stamps to create a **rebus story** for a younger student.

It was a ☀ day. The 🌺s were in bloom. The 🐦s were singing. I decided to take my 🐕 for a walk.

▮ ✔ Have students create a **story map** to show that they understand the setting of a story.

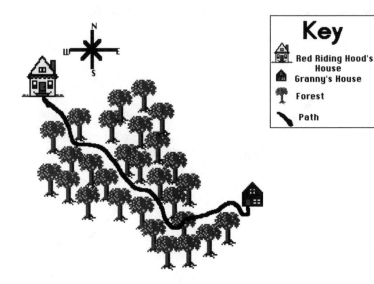

Key

Red Riding Hood's House
Granny's House
Forest
Path

Language Arts: ClarisWorks

✔ If you have frequent access to a computer, why not start a **classroom journal?** At the end of each day (or just once a week), assign a student to make a journal entry about what's happened. Be sure to include the funny, unexpected moments as well as the more academic facts. At the end of the year, you could compile the entries into a class yearbook and insert scanned photos or children's drawings.

✔ Have a prepared paragraph saved in *ClarisWorks* (on your hard drive or a disk). It might be a good idea to make the paragraph's topic one that you are currently studying in another subject area. Have the students open the paragraph. Review the different **parts of speech** and then have the students complete the following tasks:

Underline 10 adjectives.
Bold 5 adverbs.
Italicize 5 pronouns.
Shadow 5 prepositions.
Draw a ⬭circle around 10 nouns.
Outline 10 verbs.

✔ Using the **thesaurus** is an important skill for all students. Have the students type five sentences. Then copy and paste the sentences on the same page. With the thesaurus, change as many words as possible in the second set of sentences without changing the overall meaning of the sentence.

✔ Have each student type a paragraph from a book. Then have them go back and put each **adjective** in ALL CAPS (if you're in a lab), or simply delete the adjectives (if you're in a one-Mac classroom). Print the paragraph if you're in the classroom, or have students change seats in the lab and replace the original adjectives with any others they choose. For a really funny outcome, have them replace the adjectives without reading the original paragraph!

✔ Have students create a **writing-topics** database. They could create entries for different stories they'd like to write and include key phrases or ideas they want to cover. This would be a good idea for a school newspaper or magazine staff, as well.

✔ Post a list of **nouns**. Have the students create a two-column spreadsheet or word-processing document. On one side, have students list the singular form of the noun and on the other side list the plural form of the noun. Challenge them to increase the number of word pairs on their list.

✔ Review vocabulary words by having students create a **crossword puzzle.** Use a blank spreadsheet to enter the words. Then create a text block to enter the clues.

✔ Using a given list of words, students could prepare a spreadsheet with three columns. Students should place a **root word** in the first column, add a **prefix** to the word for the second column, and add a **suffix** to the word for the third column.

✔ Create a two-column document in word processing. Label the first column **present tense** and the second column **past tense.** Under each column write a sentence with the correct verb tense. Then change the tense to fit in with the next column.

Present	Past
Sally takes tap and ballet.	Sally took tap and ballet.
Today she has tap.	Yesterday she had tap.
Mrs. Smith is her teacher.	Mrs. Smith was her teacher.

✔ Adjust the columns in a spreadsheet to accommodate an **acrostic poem.**

F	FUNNY
R	REALLY NICE
I	INCREDIBLE
E	EVERLASTING
N	NICE
D	DREAMY

✔ Write a **letter** to a character from a story, a favorite author, or a person in history. Be sure to use spellcheck!

✔ Use a spreadsheet to create a chart showing proper **verb endings.**

	s	ed	ing
laugh	laughs	laughed	laughing
talk	talks	talked	talking

Math: KidPix2

✔ Give each student a **geometric-shapes list:** 3 ovals, 5 rectangles, 8 circles, 1 diamond, and so on.

Challenge the students to create a **real** or **imaginary figure** using only these shapes. If time permits, they could write descriptive sentences to accompany the picture.

✔ Give each student a package of M&Ms candy. Practice **estimation skills** by having students guess how many are in the package. Then create a graph showing how many of each color there are in the package. Allow the students to draw a bar graph or a pictograph (little drawings of the M&Ms), and then print. Compare the results with other students.

✔ Make a **shapes** booklet or slide show. Assign each student a shape and the task of filling their page with as many variations of that shape as they can think of. Encourage the use of a variety of tools, colors, sizes, and fills. Older students might enjoy doing something like this as a more professional-looking presentation for younger students in the school. They could even write an accompanying story or set of questions to go along with each slide. ("What color is the *largest* circle on the page?" "How many squares are red?")

Circles and Ovals

> ✔ **Numeral recognition** is an important skill to master before leaving kindergarten. This activity is the same as I mentioned in the language-arts section under letter recognition. Assign children a number and have them create a page depicting that number and a picture illustrating that amount. Then print the pictures and create a book — or even better, create a slide show with each picture and have the students record a sentence or cute rhyme about their visual.

✔ Patterns are fun to create and are important for students to detect. Allow the students to use any of the tools, shapes, or stamps to create **pattern strings.** After they've created a few, print the pictures — or if you're in a lab, simply have them switch seats with someone and see if they can add the next picture on each of the strings. Older students could do this same activity with number strings: factors of 5, counting by 10s, prime numbers, and so on.

What comes next?

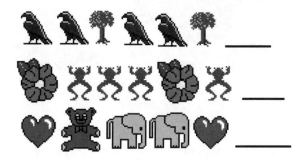

✔ **Size relationships** are easy to create with *KidPix2.* Give the students a list of relationships to depict on their page (for example: large, larger, largest).

✔ Give the students a list of **fractions** and then ask them to create illustrations of each fraction in the list.

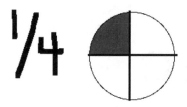

✔ Have students draw a "hidden picture" using **shapes;** then have them create a list of questions to challenge another student: Find six squares in the picture. How many circles are there? and so on.

✔ Review **geometric shapes** with older students and have them draw representations of each: point, line, segment, intersecting lines, parallel lines, perpendicular lines, right angle, acute angle, obtuse angle, parallelogram, isosceles triangle, and so on.

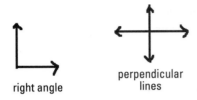

right angle   perpendicular
                        lines

✔ Create illustrated **word problems** with math facts. Print and exchange with a friend.

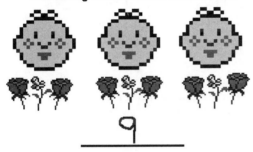

Three babies each had three flowers.
How many flowers were there in all?

Math: ClarisWorks

✔ Have each student create a spreadsheet to keep up with how many hours a day they spend on a variety of activities (sleeping, reading, watching TV, homework, chores). Have them print the spreadsheet and record the information for a week. When they return, have them record their data on their spreadsheet; then use the Make a Chart command (in the Options menu of the spreadsheet) to turn it into a **visual representation** of how they spend their time.

✔ This is the same **estimation** activity mentioned under *KidPix2* using M&Ms. But this time, instead of drawing a graph, have the students enter the information on a spreadsheet and then use the Make a Chart command to create a visual image of their results.

Candy Data

Red	Yellow	Green	Brown	Orange
3	9	9	12	7

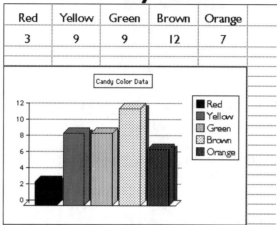

> ✔ Use an empty spreadsheet to create a **multiplication table**. Save it as stationery and then time students as they fill it in. This serves as a great timed multiplication drill.

X	1	2	3	4	5	6	7	8	9
1									
2									
3									
4									
5									
6									
7									
8									
9									

> ✔ During baseball season, have students use the newspaper and record the batting **averages** of baseball players. Enter the information in a spreadsheet; then use the Make a Chart function to create a bar graph illustrating the statistics.

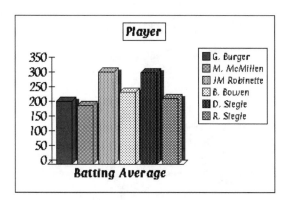

Science: KidPix2

✔ Have students illustrate the **layers of the earth's atmosphere**. Label and briefly describe each layer.

✔ Have students start with a black or dark blue screen and then use the various types of paintbrush tools to create the different **cloud types.** Label each type. (Go one step further and create a slide show with each frame containing a different cloud type! Add some ethereal music for background.)

✔ Have students use a variety of tools in *KidPix2* to illustrate and label the **three states of matter**. Add voice clips describing examples of each state, or divide your class into thirds and assign each group a state of matter to research. Then students could create a slide illustrating the state of matter they studied.

✔ Students could create an **invention**. Have each student think of a machine or appliance that might make their life easier. Name the invention, draw it, label it, and then add text telling why someone might want to buy the invention.

✔ Have students draw a **cross-section of the earth** and label each part. The colors and textures in the paint bucket make for great variations.

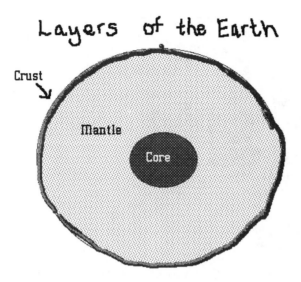

Layers of the Earth

Crust

Mantle

Core

✔ **Animal families** are always a fun unit of study. To conclude the unit, have students create a fictitious animal and then "show what they know" by classifying the animal as vertebrate or invertebrate; they could also tell its habitat, tell about its defense mechanisms, tell about its diet, describe its sleeping habits . . . . You get the picture! Students could draw on *KidPix2* and then write in *ClarisWorks* — or they could simply add small text amounts on the picture itself using *KidPix2*.

Cowrab

The cowrab hops around the pasture.
It is a herbivore. It is a vertebrate.
The cowrab's best defense is its speed.

✔ Draw a chart showing the steps in the **water cycle,** or turn each step into a slide show frame and create a looping presentation.

➤ Create a slide show on **volcanoes**. Incorporate the use of animation (the volcano erupting) by choosing no transition between frames and changing the picture slightly each time.

➤ Draw an accurate depiction of a **planet** and add text labels or information, or draw a diagram of the **solar system**.

SATURN

This is Saturn. Saturn has thin rings around it.
Saturn is the sixth planet from the sun. Its revolution
period is 29.5 years.

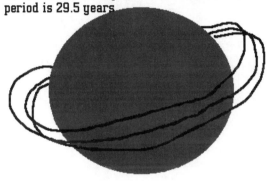

➤ Use the circle tool to draw a Venn Diagram. Use this diagram to compare two **planets**, two **continents**, two **habitats**, and so on.

Science: ClarisWorks

➤ Gather information on **weather** (date, temperature, cloudy, sunny) for a specific number of days. Then use the spreadsheet function to enter the data. Convert the data to a chart (Options menu: Make a Chart) and print. Do this same activity at different times of the year for comparison.

Social Studies: KidPix2

➤ Use the square tool and line tool to create a flowchart showing the **branches of government**. Add illustrations when complete.

➤ Create a slide show to explain the process of **how a bill becomes a law**. Each slide could illustrate a step in the process. Students could narrate.

✔ After studying a state or country, have the students create a **flag** for that country based on what they've learned about the area. Then show them the actual flag and compare the two creations.

✔ Have students use *KidPix2* to draw detailed maps of their classroom, bedroom, or neighborhood.

✔ Create a **timeline** for any period of time you are studying. Add pictures after you've entered the data.

✔ Copy the world map from the Scrapbook (under the menu) into a *KidPix2* document. Then use the pencil tool and different colors to draw the various **explorer's routes**.

Christopher Columbus
John Cabot

✔ Have each child design their own theme park, neighborhood, or shopping mall and then use the tools in *KidPix2* to make a **map** of their creation.

Social Studies: ClarisWorks

✔ After a discussion on **directional terms**, give the students a compass and have them write directions from your classroom to the front door of the school using exact directions: number of steps — along with north, south, east, west.

✔ Create a database on **state** or **country information**. Fields could include capital, bird, flower, population, nickname, major source of income, and so on.

State Name	
Capital	
Major	
Population	
Flower	
Bird	
Sports	
Historical	

✔ Create a database to highlight pertinent information about **famous historical figures**. Add to this database throughout the year; then compile and print the information as needed for booklets, study sheets, and so on.

✔ Write a convincing letter to a **local government leader** about a local environmental concern.

Health: KidPix2

✔ Use the tools and draw a diagram of a tooth. Label each part of the tooth and type in a list of **dental-care tips.**

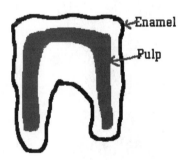

Enamel

Pulp

✔ Draw the **Food Pyramid** on the page and then insert stamps of food items in their proper position on the pyramid.

Health: ClarisWorks

✔ Write a **convincing paragraph** that deals with the dangers of drug use. Use bold or other style formats to bring the reader's attention to specific points. Compile all the paragraphs into a booklet to be shared with younger students.

✔ Divide paper into three columns and choose Landscape from the Page Layout menu. Create a three-fold brochure on a **health concern**: drug use, dental health, communicable diseases, or nutrition.

Appendix B

Troubleshooting by David Pogue

This appendix appears in *Macs For Dummies,* 3rd Edition (where it was origi-
nally Chapter 12). I've taken the liberty of lightly customizing this section,
however, so that it better meets a teacher's computing needs.

The Top Ten Beginner Troubles (That Don't Actually Need Shooting)

If you've read this book to this point, a couple of these troubles will seem
obvious. But believe me, I've seen these typical troubles zap the confidence of
many a first-timer.

1. *The screen is all gray, there's no window open, you can't find any files or folders, but the Trash can is in the corner.*

   If you want a window to appear, you have to open a disk icon. In the upper-
   right corner of your screen, there's an icon representing a disk. Point to it
   and double-click the mouse button to make it open into a window.

2. *You try to work, but nothing happens except beeping. Every time you click the mouse button, there's another beep.*

   When the Mac requests some information from you, it displays a dialog
   box — a box with some questions for you to answer. This one, for example, appears when you try to print:

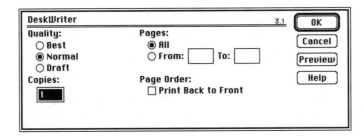

The most important factoid for troubleshooting

Get used to that computeristic-sounding word. *Extension.*

Get used to its synonyms, too: *init* (pronounced "in NIT") and *system extension.*

An *extension* is a little file that lives in your Extensions folder (which is inside your System folder). Each extension adds a specific new feature to the Macintosh: like a screen saver, fax capability, and so on. You know those little icons that march across your screen when you turn on the Macintosh? Those are your *extensions.*

An extension program runs *all the time.* It's like a program you can't quit. It gets launched when the Mac turns on, and it's running "in the background" during your entire work day.

But the people who wrote the After Dark screensaver program, for example, have never met the programmers who wrote the FaxPlus faxing extension. Suppose you have both of them in your Extensions folder. Suppose each little extension program, in the background, simultaneously reach for the same morsel of electronic memory.

"Sorry, a system error occurred."

In other words, *extension conflicts* (the technical term) are among the most common causes of problems on the Mac.

What's not very nice about dialog boxes, though, is that they commandeer your Mac. You're not allowed to do *anything* until you answer the questions and get rid of the box. If you try to keep working, the Mac will keep beeping at you, and the box will sit on your screen until doomsday.

Every dialog box, therefore, has a button you can click to make the box go away. Usually you can choose a button that says OK or one that says Cancel. (In the figure, the buttons say Print and Cancel.) Anyway, you have to click one of those buttons before the Mac will return control to you.

3. *You double-click an icon, but you get an irritating message that says "Application not found" (or something equally unhelpful).*

   This is a confounding one for beginning users. As it happens, it's also a confounding one for *experienced* users. So I'll refer you, at this point, to the same item in the section called "Error Messages."

4. *A whole document window just disappears.*

   Every now and then — and this happens even to the greats — you'll be trying to do something with the mouse, when suddenly your entire spreadsheet (or manuscript or artwork) vanishes, and you find yourself in the Finder. No message appears — no "Save changes?," no "System error," nada.

   What's probably happened is that, in the process of clicking the mouse, you accidentally clicked *outside* your document window. Of course, clicking a window (or outside a window) is the universal Mac signal that you want to bring some *other* open program to the front.

If your arrow's aim misses the document window (usually when you're trying to use a scroll bar, as shown below), you're most likely to click the gray background — the Finder.

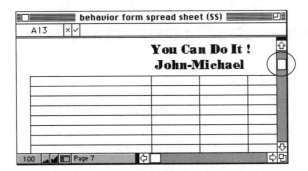

The Finder promptly jumps to the front, showing your folders and files, and the document you were working on gets shoved into the background. (All together now: "It's a feature, not a bug.")

Now you know why, in the Performa Macs and in System 7.5, Apple offers an optional feature that hides the Finder *automatically* whenever you launch a program.

To bring your original program back, choose its name from the Application menu.

5. *There's a pile of stuff next to the Trash can.*

All the Mac books and manuals tell you how to chuck a file you no longer want: drag its icon "to the Trash," meaning the Trash can icon in the lower-right corner of your screen.

What's usually not made absolutely clear is that, as you drag the icon to the Trash can, you have to place the tip of the arrow cursor directly on the Trash can icon. You have to see the Trash can itself turn black.

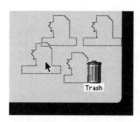 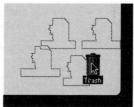

That may seem awkward, especially if you're dragging a whole group of icons at once. For example, in the illustration above at left, one of the icons being dragged is already bumping up against the edge of the screen.

You have to ignore that, though, and keep on moving the mouse until the arrow is directly on the Trash can (above right).

6. *You're word processing, and suddenly all your text disappears.*

There are two possibilities, neither of which means you've really lost your text.

First of all, not everyone is aware that, when you fill up a screenful of text, a word processor automatically shoves that screenful upward off the top of your screen, in effect advancing you to the next clean sheet of paper.

But suppose you *do* know all about scroll bars and scrolling. And you scroll, and you decide that your text really *has* disappeared.

You may well be the victim of another not-immediately-obvious Mac "feature": that any highlighted text, from a single letter to a 4,000-page encyclopedia, is *instantly replaced* by the next keystroke you type. Usually this is handy. For example, if you want to replace the word "kickback" with the words "incentive payment," you don't have to *delete* the word "kickback" first. You just select it (below, top) and then type (below, bottom):

> to accept the occasional kickback of
> to accept the occasional incentive payment of

The danger is that, if you've inadvertently (or advertently) selected a bunch of text, and you touch any key — the spacebar, Return key, or any letter — you'll replace everything you've selected with a space, a Return, or a letter.

If this happens, the solution is easy: choose Undo from the Edit menu.

If it's too late for Undo — in other words, if you've done something else *since* deleting the text (because Undo only undoes the *most* recent thing you do) — you may be able to recover some of your text. Close your document *without* saving changes. Reopen it. At least you'll see as much text as was there the last time you saved your work.

7. *There's a thin horizontal line all the way across your color monitor.*

Believe it or not, *all* Apple 13-inch and 16-inch color monitors show this faint line (it's about a third of the way up the screen). It's a shadow cast by a wire inside. Just grit your teeth and remember: "It's a Sony." (Sony makes these monitors.)

8. *You drag a file into a window, and it disappears.*

Once again, you have to watch your tip, if you'll excuse the expression. When you drag an icon, it's the cursor arrow's *tip* that actually marks where the icon is going, *not* the icon itself. What probably happened is that you accidentally released the icon when the arrow tip was on top of a *folder* within the window, as shown here:

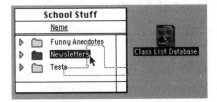

As a result, the Mac dropped the file *into* the folder, making it disappear from the screen.

9. *You can't print.*

There's a delightfully thorough discussion of printing problems later in this chapter.

10. *You become addicted to working with your Macintosh. The image of the Trash can gets burned into your corneas. Friends, family, and job seem to recede and eventually go away.*

Congratulations! You've graduated from this book.

Hardware Headaches

These aren't the most common glitches you're likely to encounter, but they're just as frustrating.

A word to writers

If you're a writer, or anybody who plans to do a lot of typing, there's a way to protect yourself against *any* of the text-loss problems described above. Even if you (1) experience a system crash before you've had a chance to save your work, or (2) accidentally replace all your text, or (3) *deliberately* delete some text, but then later wish you hadn't, there's a little piece of software that can save you. It's called Last Resort, and it lurks in the background of your Mac, silently logging everything you type into a text file. You never see it, never notice it — *but*, if the unmentionable happens, you can open the Last Resort text file and recover everything you've typed (ever since you installed Last Resort, in fact). See the Resource Resource for info. (Thunder 7 and Now Utilities have similar features.)

Mouse/trackball is jerky or sticky

This is a very common problem. Like children, mops, and mimes, a mouse does its work by rolling around on the ground. It's bound to get dirty.

To clean it, turn it upside down in your hand. Very firmly rotate the round collar counterclockwise so that you can remove it. (Same idea on a PowerBook. On a Duo, you might think the collar ring is impossible to turn, but it can be done. Push really hard against the soft curves of the ring around the trackball.)

Dump the rubber or plastic ball into your hand, wash it off under the faucet, and let it air-dry completely.

In the meantime, go to work inside the socket where the ball usually is. With tweezers or something, pull out any obvious dust bunnies and hairballs. The main thing, though, is those three little rollers inside the cavity: you'll probably see a stripe of accumulated gunk around their circumferences. With patience, a scissors blade (or a wad of sticky-side-out Scotch tape), and a good light, lift off that stuff, preferably making an effort not to let it fall inside the cavity. Keep turning the mouse right side up and tapping it on the table to dislodge stuff.

When you put it all back together, you and your mouse will both be much happier.

Double-clicking doesn't work

You're probably double-clicking too slowly, or else you're moving the mouse a little bit during the double-click process.

Cursor freezes on the screen

This is a system freeze, or system hang. Read all about it under "System Crashes and Freezes" in this appendix.

Then again, your mouse (or keyboard) cable may have come loose. Plug everything in firmly.

Menus get stuck down

If it's not your Mac, or if it *is* your Mac and you just aren't very tuned in, the culprit may be a little add-on program that makes menus jump down when the cursor touches them, even when you're *not* pressing the mouse button. I've always thought this kind of program is somewhat cruel, but some people claim that it saves them some effort.

If you're using a trackball, you may be the victim of a similarly stupid feature: a button on the trackball that, when clicked, makes the Mac think you're pressing the mouse button *all the time.* For the rest of your computing day, the Mac will think that the button is down, even if you frantically click the *regular* mouse button or try to quit the program or anything. Only when you again touch the click lock button does the Mac free the pointer from its bondage.

Nothing appears when you type

First resort: Well, obviously, you can't just type at any time and expect to see text appear. You have to be either in a word processor or in a text-editing area (like a dialog box or in the little text-editing rectangle when you're renaming an icon).

Second resort: Check the cable between the keyboard and the Mac. Make sure it's *very* firmly plugged in at both ends.

Incidentally, the keyboard and mouse cables are especially sensitive to being plugged and unplugged while the computer is on. Be religious about shutting off the Mac before plugging and unplugging them. (That's especially true of SCSI cables. The same is *not* true of modem and printer cables, though.)

Your monitor shimmers

Of course, I don't mean that your monitor *itself* jiggles; I mean the picture.

First resort: Your screen's being subjected to some kind of electrical interference, such as a lamp, a fan, or an air conditioner running on the same circuit. Try a different plug, a different monitor location, or a different career.

Last resort: You live in an earthquake zone. Move to the Midwest.

Floppy-Disk Flukes

Floppy disks are cheap and handy and make excellent coasters. But when they start giving you attitude, read on.

"File could not be copied and will be skipped."

This one's a pain, isn't it?

First resort: If you were copying a whole group of files, try dragging the troublesome file by itself.

Second resort: Make a duplicate of the file (click it and choose Duplicate from the File menu). Now try copying the duplicate.

Third resort: If the unruly file is a document, launch the program that created it. For example, if it's a Word file, launch Word.

Now go to the Open command in the File menu and try to open the file. If it opens, use the Save As command to save it onto a different disk.

Fourth resort: Eject the disk. Open and close the sliding shutter a couple times. Manually rotate the round hub. Try again.

Fifth resort: Try inserting the obnoxious floppy into somebody else's Mac.

Last resort: With a little expenditure, you can almost certainly retrieve the file. The rescue programs are called things like 911 Utilities (the best for floppies) or Norton Utilities (best for hard disks).

Mac keeps asking for a disk that you've ejected

First resort: You probably ejected the disk by using the Eject Disk command in the Special menu. In general, that's a no-no, precisely because the Mac will continually ask for it.

You can get out of this scrape by pressing ⌘-period several times. And next time, eject a disk using the Put Away command in the File menu (or by dragging the disk icon to the Trash can).

Last resort: Sometimes, even if you use Put Away, a ghost of the disk's icon remains on the screen, and the Mac keeps asking for it, and ⌘-period doesn't solve anything. In this case, you probably opened a file on that disk — and it's still open. As long as something on that disk is open, the Mac won't forget about the disk; it would be like canceling the space program while some astronauts were in the middle of a mission.

Choose the program in question from the Application menu, and make sure you close all documents. Now you should be able to drag the disk icon to the Trash can.

You can't get a floppy disk out

First resort: Press ⌘-Shift-1. That should pop out the disk, even if you can't see its icon.

Last resort: Use the paper clip trick described in *Macs For Dummies,* 3rd Edition (the sidebar "Dweebs' Corner: Alternative disk tips" in Chapter 2.)

"This disk is unreadable. Do you want to initialize it?"

If it's a brand new disk fresh out of the box, there is *no* problem. *All* brand new floppies are initially unreadable, unless they have already been initialized. Go ahead and click Erase, and follow the disk-naming process that the Mac takes you through. But if it's a disk you've used before, you certainly don't want to destroy it.

First resort: Click Eject. *No,* you do not want to initialize (that is, erase) the disk.

Second resort: Remember that there are three different kinds of floppy disks: single-sided (400K), double-sided (800K), and high-density (1400K). If you have an older Mac (say, one made before 1990), it may not have a high-density disk drive, and you may be trying to insert a high-density disk that it can't read.

Actually, it's even more complicated than *that.* Another typical problem: you insert a new 800K disk into a high-density disk drive. You go through the usual "Initialize?" routine. But then you discover that the disk won't work in somebody else's old 800K disk drive! Strange but true.

In any of these cases, again, the main thing is that you do *not* give the Mac permission to erase the disk; just take it to a more modern Mac, rescue the files, and bring them home on a kind of disk that *your* Mac can read.

Third resort: If it's a disk that you know has data on it, and you have a disk drive of the right type, then there may be something actually wrong with the disk. Eject it; shake it around a little. Try it a couple more times.

Fourth resort: There may be something wrong with your disk *drive* — and not the disk itself. That's easy enough to find out: insert the disk in another Mac's drive.

If it does turn out to be a problem with your drive, the culprit is often dust and crud. Some of my technoid friends say it's dangerous (static-wise) to use a vacuum or blower in the disk drive slot, but I've actually rescued a disk drive or two this way (and have never damaged one).

Fifth resort: Buy a recovery program like 911 Utilities. If anything can get your files off that disk, 911 can.

Sixth resort: You're not trying to insert an IBM PC disk into your Mac, are you? If you are (having read in the ads that any Mac can read a PC disk), give it up — it's not that simple. You're going to need some special software.

Last resort: If the problem is not your disk drive, and even 911 can't get your data off the disk, then the disk is really broken. Don't even erase it and reuse it: throw it away!

One occasional source of zapped floppies, by the way, is magnetic damage. Just like audio tapes, a disk stores information by magnetizing tiny particles of metal stuff. So if the disk gets magnetized by accident, the metal particles get rearranged into some random pattern that the Mac correctly deems "unreadable."

I know this sounds crazy, but *somebody* has to put this into print: Don't put refrigerator magnets on your Mac. That hard disk inside the machine is, after all, a disk, and magnets do to disks what gravity does to a watermelon dropped at 39,000 feet.

Your floppy disks don't hold the amount they're supposed to

It's true. You can't fit 800K of information on an 800K disk, nor 1.4MB on a 1.4MB disk.

The missing storage capacity is filled by an invisible file, on every disk, called the *Desktop file.* This file is the Mac's accounting department and is described in more detail under "Error Messages" later in this appendix. The point is that it takes up 7K or more on every disk. If it's taking up a lot more than that, you may have a *bloated* Desktop file; see the "Rebuilding the Desktop file" sidebar later in this appendix for instructions on slimming it down.

Hard-Disk Horrors

If you're like many Mac users, you wind up storing your whole life on that disk: appointments, finances, explosive secret diary, the works. That's a lot of trust to place in an inanimate mechanical device that's all moving parts. Back up your work all the time — and rely on this section when things go wrong.

The hard-drive icon doesn't show up

If it's an external drive, either it isn't on, it isn't plugged in right, or its SCSI setup isn't right. If we're talking about the drive inside your Mac, it's probably a SCSI problem.

It's theoretically possible that your drive is broken, too. Bummer.

Sluggish behavior

If copying, launching, and quitting programs (and opening and closing windows) seem to be taking longer than when you first bought your Mac, it's probably time to give your hard disk a physical. See the sidebar "Defragmenting your disk."

You threw something away by mistake

First resort: If you haven't chosen Empty Trash from the Special menu, you're in good shape. Just double-click the Trash icon. Its window opens so that you can rescue any files therein by dragging them back to your hard-disk icon.

Second resort: If you threw something away, emptied the Trash, and more-or-less *immediately* recognized your mistake, you're still OK. You won't find this in any manual, but it's a great trick:

Unplug your Mac.

That's right: just cut off the juice. When you restart the thing, holy moley, your Trash will be full again — and your file will have been brought back from the dead!

Last resort: If that unplugging bit didn't save your file, you're not out of luck. Chances are very good that you can still recover the last several dozen files that you threw away, using a *data-recovery program* like Norton Utilities or Mac Tools Deluxe. The more you've used your Mac since you threw something away, the less chance you have of getting it back.

Printing Problems

Compared to some other problems, these'll seem like child's play.

"Printer could not be opened." or "Printer could not be found."

First resort: These messages appear when you try to print something without turning on the printer first (or letting it warm up fully). Turn it on, wait a whole minute, and then try again.

Defragmenting your disk

Over time, you create and throw away a lot of files.

Your hard drive, if you'll indulge me, is like a closet maintained by a guy who's always in a hurry. When guests are coming over, he cleans up the living room and throws everything into the closet, although not particularly neatly. Every now and then, when he gets time, he unpacks the closet and repacks it neatly, putting everything in a tidy, organized place.

The hard drive, too, is in a hurry. When you ask it to save a file, it doesn't wait around: It shoves that file wherever it can find space. Sometimes that even means sticking the file in *two* places, splitting it up as necessary. Over time, more and more files are stored on your hard disk in pieces. It's no big deal: when you need that file again, the hard drive remembers where all the pieces are and is perfectly able to bring the file back to the screen.

But all this hunting for pieces slows the drive down. And like our busy closet keeper, it's very satisfying, every six months or so, to reorganize the files on your disk so that they're each in one piece, neatly placed end-to-end on the hard drive surface.

There are two ways to *defragment* your drive (which is the term for it). First, you can copy everything onto other disks, erase the hard drive, and copy the files back onto it. Second, you can buy a program just for defragmenting your drive. These programs are called things like Norton Utilities and DiskExpress.

Second resort: Of course, it may be that you haven't performed the critical step of selecting the printer's icon in the Chooser desk accessory. (Or even if you did, the Mac sometimes gets a little feebleminded and forgets what you selected in the Chooser. Just repeat the procedure.)

Last resort: Maybe a cable came loose. Track the cable from your Mac's printer port all the way to the printer. (Important: Make sure it's really the printer port since the modem port looks exactly like it.) If it all seems to be firmly connected, try replacing (1) the cable or (2) the little connectors.

StyleWriter II: blank pages come out

It's your cartridge.

First resort: Choose Print from the File menu. Click the Options button. Click where it says "Clean ink cartridge before printing?"

Now try to print something normally. The StyleWriter will, in effect, blow its nose before trying to print, just in case your cartridge nozzles had dried up and clogged.

Last resort: If that didn't work, your cartridge is probably empty. Buy a new one.

To replace the old one, pull open the front panel of the StyleWriter. Locate the existing cartridge, a little black square thing. Lift the blue lever to release the old cartridge; slip in the new one (after taking off the protective nozzle strip!); and lower the blue lever to lock it in.

StyleWriter II: paper jams

Some people gape in shock to hear that *other* people have endless paper problems with a StyleWriter. Either yours works like a charm, or it doesn't.

First resort: The problem is your paper. Don't try to feed single sheets; put at least 20 pages or so into the feeder. And if it's humid, fan the paper stack to separate the pages. Then re-square them and put them into the feeder.

Don't expect terrific results with stiff, textured, wedding envelopes, by the way.

Last resort: The problem is your feeder tray. On the left side is a sliding, plastic, adjustable thingy. You definitely want to slide this paper-edge-aligner right up to the paper stack's edge. Too far away, and the pages will tilt as they're pulled into the StyleWriter. Too close, and the StyleWriter will have a struggle pulling pages through.

A million copies keep pouring out

This big-time hazard for novices has to do with background printing. When you print something, *nothing happens* for a minute or two. (The Mac is storing the printout behind the scenes so that it can return control of the Mac to you.)

Trouble is, your first time at bat, you probably don't *know* what the delay is. All you know is that the printer isn't printing. So you figure you'll just try again — you pick Print from the File menu again. Still nothing: so you print *again*.

The thing is, the Mac is duly *storing* all your printing requests; at some moment when you least expect it, all of those copies will start to print!

To stop them, choose Print Monitor from the Application menu (the tiny icon at the far right of your menu bar); select each document and click Cancel Printing.

Jagged text in printouts

You'll discover that getting jagged type when you print on a laser or inkjet printer is a matter of which fonts you've used in your document.

There's only one other oddity I want to mention. If you're printing a graphic, it may be text you made in a program that has *Paint* in the title (SuperPaint, MacPaint, and so on). The trouble here is that the Mac no longer thinks of your text as *text;* it knows only about a bunch of dots in a certain pattern, and they'll never print out smoothly. See Chapter 5 of *Macs For Dummies,* 3rd Edition, for details on painting programs.

"Font not found, using Courier"

A problem unique to laser printers. Your document contains a PostScript laser font, but the Mac can't find the printer font file for the font you're using. Find the printer font (the file with the abbreviated name, like FrankGothBol) and install it into your System folder.

Nothing comes out of the printer

Sometimes the Mac fakes you out: it goes through the motions of printing, but nothing ever comes out of the printer.

First resort: Go to the menu. Select Chooser. Click the icon for the printer you're using, and make sure your actual printer's name shows up in the list on the right.

Second resort: Is there paper in the paper tray, and is the tray pushed all the way in?

Or if it's an ImageWriter: Is the little Select light on? If not, push the Select button.

Third resort: Laser printers: Alas, your document is probably overwhelming the printer's feeble memory, and the printer is giving up. You can try using fewer different fonts in the document. Try printing only a page at a time. Or try using fewer *downloadable* fonts in the document — that is, fonts that aren't built into the printer.

Fourth resort: Laser printers: If you're printing something complicated, there may be a messed-up graphic. Programs like SuperPaint, FreeHand, and Illustrator are known for generating very complex, sometimes unprintable graphics. For example, here's a graphic from SuperPaint that won't print out:

If you're printing something that includes both text and graphics, try removing your graphics and printing the same document. If it prints without the graphics, you know where the problem is. Call up the graphics program company and complain abrasively.

Last resort: Laser printers: If your printer truly has run out of memory, you can usually pay to have it upgraded with more memory. In the computer world, as always, a little cash can surmount almost any problem.

PrintMonitor won't go away

If you're using the generally wonderful Background Printing option, sometimes you may encounter the bizarro PrintMonitor program.

What's so baffling is that you never remember launching this program by double-clicking. But there it is, listed in your Application menu. And sometimes it beeps at you, demanding some intervention on your part (such as when the printer runs out of paper).

Anyway, you can't make PrintMonitor quit on cue. To make it really go away, you have to cancel any printing jobs it's still working on (by clicking the Cancel button). Then go to another program. Eventually, PrintMonitor should disappear from your Application menu.

Streaks on Laser printouts

If they're *dark* streaks, then there's some crud on some element of the paper path inside the laser printer. Open the lid. Examine the rollers (but be careful if the printer has just been on — those rollers get incredibly hot). You're looking for a single blob of grit or toner dust. Clean it off with a Q-tip, preferably damp with alcohol (the Q-tip, not you).

Also look for a series of thin, one-inch diagonal wires. Make sure those are sparkling clean.

Then again, if this streaking business just started after you've returned from a three-month trip, the cartridge probably went bad from sheer loneliness. Replace it.

If there are *light* streaks on the printouts, open the printer lid. Remove the toner drum (usually a big black plastic thing) and gently rock it from side to side. Basically, you're running out of toner dust; this procedure may give you a couple days' worth of extra time, but you'll be needing a new cartridge soon.

That stupid startup page

This is an annoying one, but easily fixed: every time you turn on your laser printer, it prints a dumb startup page with its own logo. Use the little program called LaserWriter Utility or LaserWriter Font Utility; it's on the disks that came with your Mac. (If you have some version of System 7 before System 7.5, it's on a disk called Tidbits.) Double-click LaserWriter Utility, and choose Start Page Options from the Utilities menu. Click Off.

System Crashes and Freezes

There are two scary conditions that are enough to make even semi-pro Mac jockeys swallow hard and feel a little helpless. A system *crash* is when this message appears on the screen:

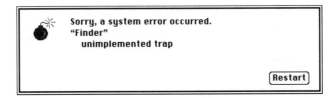

Your current work session is over, amigo. You have to restart the computer. Anything you've typed or drawn since the last time you saved your work is gone. (Safest way: Press the Restart switch, as described in "The Restart switch" sidebar at the end of the appendix.)

A system *freeze* is different — and, as horrific computer nightmares go, it's preferable. You get no message on the screen. Instead, the mouse cursor freezes into place. You can't move the cursor, and nothing you type on the keyboard changes anything. The Mac, as far as you can tell, has silicon lockjaw.

Escaping a System crash

You can't. Restart the computer. Don't even bother trying to click the Restart button on the *screen,* which doesn't do anything.

Escaping repeated System crashes

If you're crashing often, you need to get more rest.

If your *Mac* is crashing often, you need to figure out why. Ninety percent of the time, they're related either to memory or to *extension conflicts,* the dreaded topic that's looming only a few pages away.

First resort: Increase the amount of memory allotted to the program you were using. If you don't know how, you should really read the section "Out of Memory" in Chapter 12 of *Macs For Dummies,* 3rd Edition (especially the "Memory tactics" sidebar).

Second resort: Something, or several somethings, are clashing in your System Folder. See "Extension conflicts," coming up. If you're in a hurry to get your work done and can't take the time, just restart your Mac while pressing the Shift key. (That turns *all* extensions off.)

Third resort: If the crashes still haven't gone away, it's possible that something in your System Folder got gummed up. You're in for a 20-minute, but *very* effective, ritual known as a Clean Re-Install of your System Folder. See the sidebar called "The beauty of a 'clean re-install.'"

The beauty of a "clean re-install"

This procedure is just a wee bit technical. But look: if it'll save your Mac's life and not cost anything, isn't it worth slogging through?

As the gears of your System folder grind away, day after day, little corruptions and rough edges can develop. The following procedure replaces your old, possibly corroded System folder with a brand, spanking new one. It's nearly *guaranteed* to wipe out any erratic and bizarre crashes or freezes you've been having.

This process will, however, require your System installation disks: either your pile of white Apple floppy disks, or a startup CD-ROM disc, or your Apple Backup disks (Performas). If you don't have those disks ready, get them. (If you're really stuck, you can always *buy* a replacement set of system disks, in the form of System 7.1 or 7.5.)

If you have System 7.5: Insert the first installer disk (or the System 7.5 CD). Double-click the Installer. At the main installation screen — where you'd normally click the Install button — press ⌘-Shift-K, of all things. You'll be asked which you want: a *brand new System folder,* or just an updated *existing* System folder. You want the whole new one. Click your choice, click OK, click Install, and follow the directions.

If you have earlier System versions: Open your System folder. See the Finder icon?

The purpose here is to *hide* it, so it's no longer in the same folder with the System *suitcase* icon.

Drag the Finder into, for example, the Preferences folder, as shown here.

You're doing beautifully. Now close the System folder window. Press Return, and *rename* the System folder. Call it "Old System" or something.

Now, finally, take the Install Me First disk (or Apple Backup disk, or startup CD), and insert it. Double-click the icon called Installer; follow the directions on the screen, feeding floppy disks as requested.

Regardless of your System version: The result of all this is a virgin, clean System folder, free of any corruptions.

But all your customized fonts, control panels, preferences, and so on, are stranded back there in your Old System folder!

Ideally, you should install each of them from their original store-bought floppy disks. If that's too much hassle, copy them, item by item, from your Old System folder into your new System folder. Do so with care, however, so that you don't simply reinstate whatever problems you were having.

Fourth resort: You may have a SCSI conflict on your hands, especially if more than one external gizmo is plugged into your Mac.

Fifth resort: If nothing so far has stopped the crashes, there may be some weird memory-related thing going on under the hood. Some programs are allergic to virtual memory, for example; so your second step should be to turn off Virtual Memory (open your Memory control panel and hit the Off button). And if you're advanced enough to know what "32-bit addressing" is, go to the Memory control panel and turn *it* off, if your Mac lets you. A lot of older programs break out in puffy hives when *that* is on.

Sixth resort: You don't, by any chance, have *two* System Folders on your hard disk, do you? That's like throwing two baseballs at once to a Little League shortstop — chances are he'll panic and won't catch either one. Usually people have added another System Folder accidentally, in the process of copying new software onto the hard disk from a floppy. If you don't want your Mac to (forgive me) drop the ball, use the Finder's Find command and search for "system" to make sure you have only one.

Last resort: If you're *still* having system crashes, particularly if they don't seem to be related to any one program, then the fault may lie in the way your hard disk was prepared. Once again we're wading in waters too technologically deep for my comfort. But particularly if you're using a Mac purchased in 1991 or before (in other words, before System 7), frequent system crashes are a telltale sign that you need to *reformat* the hard disk.

That tiresome task involves copying *everything* off the disk (onto a million floppies, for example, or just onto another hard disk), and using a hard-disk formatting program to erase it completely. One such reformatting program is on your white Disk Tools disk that came with your Mac; it's called Apple HD SC Setup. Other popular programs are Drive 7 and FWB Hard Disk Toolkit. Or if you bought an external hard drive, you may have a drive-formatting program on a floppy disk that came with it.

In any case, the main thing is to ensure that your formatting program is *System 7-compatible.* (The programs I specifically named above are all compatible.)

When you've completely erased and reformatted your hard drive, copy all your intellectual belongings back onto it. You'll probably be amazed at how many fewer crashes you experience.

Extension conflicts

OK, here it is. The long-awaited extension-conflict discussion.

See, each *extension* (a self-loading background program that you install into your System folder, like a screen saver program) was written by a programmer who had no clue what *other* extensions you'd be using. The result: Two extensions may fight, resulting in that polite disclaimer, "Sorry, a System error has occurred."

These things are easy to fix, once you know the secret. Shut off your Mac and then turn it on again (or just press the Restart switch). But as it's starting up, hold down the Shift key. Keep it down until (1) you see the message "Extensions off," or (2) you arrive at the desktop, whichever you notice first.

Your Mac probably won't give you trouble anymore — but now, of course, you're running without *any* of your cute little extension programs. No screen saver, no macro program, and so on.

If the point of this exercise is to pinpoint *which* extensions aren't getting along, you have two choices. One is free, but takes a lot of time. One costs $50 or so, but works automatically.

The hard way: Burrow into your System folder to find the Extensions folder, where these little guys live. Drag a few of their icons out of that folder, clear out onto the gray desktop — that's how you prevent *selected* extensions from loading. You don't have to throw them away; just take them out of the System folder and restart the computer. (Use the Restart command in the Special menu.)

If the Mac doesn't crash this time, then you can pretty much bet that one of the extensions you removed was the guilty party. If it *does* crash again, repeat the whole process, but take some more extension icons out of the System folder.

Through trial and error, eventually you should be able to figure out which pair of extensions doesn't get along. Sometimes just renaming one so that it alphabetically precedes its enemy is enough to solve the problem.

The easy way: There's a program called Conflict Catcher from a company called Casady & Greene. It does many useful things for managing your extensions, but its main virtue is conflict-catching. It can figure out, all by itself, which extension (or extensions) are causing your Mac's problems. All you have to do is sit there, restarting the Mac over and over, each time telling Conflict Catcher whether or not the problem has been solved yet. By the time it's over, the program will emblazon the name of the errant extensions on your screen, so you can dismember, disembowel, or trash them as you see fit.

System freezes

If your system freezes, and your cursor locks in place, you can't save the work in the program you were working on. You don't, however, have to sell your Mac or even restart it. Instead, try this amazing keystroke: ⌘-Option–Esc. (It's about the only time you'll ever use the Esc key.)

If it works, you'll get a dialog box that says "Force [this program] to quit?" Click Force Quit, and you exit the program you were working in.

So what's the big whoop? Well, if you had several programs running, this technique only dumps the *one* you were working in — the one that crashed. You now have a chance to enter each of the *other* programs that are still running and save your work (if you haven't done so). Then, to be on the safe side, restart the Mac.

And what causes a system freeze? Pretty much the same kinds of things that cause system crashes (see above).

Error Messages

Let's start the Troubleshooting session in earnest with a few good old American Error messages. Yes, kids, these are the '90s equivalent of "DOES NOT COMPUTE." These are messages, appearing in an *alert box* like the fictional one shown below, that indicate something's wrong.

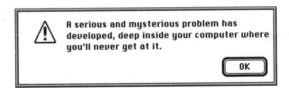

Note that these aren't the same as *System errors,* which are described later; a System error box shows a bomb with a short fuse and indicates a much graver problem.

"Application is busy or missing." or "Application not found."

I promised to return to this one: here we go.

First resort: Not everything in the Mac world is meant to be a plaything for you. The Mac reserves a few files for its own use. If it came with your Mac — like the Scrapbook file, the Clipboard file, and so on — then you at least get *something* when you double-click an icon: the Clipboard file opens up into a window where you can see the most recent stuff you copied; the Note Pad file automatically launches the Note Pad desk accessory; and extensions or control panels at least identify themselves (with a message on the screen, like "System Extension: This file adds functionality to your Macintosh").

But if you double-click a file belonging to *non*-Apple software — like any file in the Preferences folder, for example, or various other support files for non-Apple stuff — you'll just get a beep and an unhelpful error message.

That's what's going on *most* of the time.

Second resort: Every now and then, though, you'll double-click a file that you yourself created, and *still* you get the "Application not found" message. Refer back to Chapter 3, where you learned about programs and the documents they produce (like parents and children). In this case, you're trying to open a document (child), but the Mac can't find its parent (the program used to create it).

So if you double-click a *ClarisWorks* document, but the *ClarisWorks* program itself isn't on your hard disk, then the Mac will shrug its shoulders and tell you, in effect, "Yo — how am I s'posed to open this?" To remedy the situation, install the missing program back onto the hard disk.

Third resort: Sometimes you may get the "Application not found" message *even* if you're sure that the document's parent program is on the disk. (You double-click a *ClarisWorks* document, and you're told that the application — *ClarisWorks* — can't be found, even though it's *sitting right there* on the disk in plain sight!)

In a situation like this, the Mac's genealogical gnomes have become confused: the computer has lost track of which program is associated with which kinds of documents. Don't ask me how such confusions happen: just rejoice that it's an easy problem to fix. In the words of Mac gurus everywhere, "You gotta rebuild the Desktop."

Now then. Before you grope for your woodworking tools, let's analyze this concept of rebuilding the Desktop. The Desktop referred to is a very important file on your disk. So how come you've never seen it? Because the Desktop file is *invisible.* (Yes, Mac icons can be invisible. Remember that if you ever get involved in antiterrorist espionage activity.) It's something the Mac maintains for its own use.

In the Desktop file, the Mac stores two kinds of information: First, it stores the actual pictures used as icons for all your files; second, it stores information about the parent-child (program-document) relationships you're having trouble with.

If the Desktop file becomes confused (which results in the "not found" message), you have to reset it. You have to brainwash it, forcing it to unlearn the misconceptions that are giving you trouble, and relearn the correct relationships between documents and the programs that gave birth to them. See the "Rebuilding the Desktop file" sidebar for instructions.

Rebuilding the Desktop file

Turn the computer on. As it starts gearing up, press and *hold* the Option and ⌘ keys. Don't let go. Keep them down until the Mac explicitly asks you if you want to "rebuild the Desktop." (Obviously, you should click OK.)

After that's done, your document double-clicking will work if, in fact, the parent program is on the disk. And your Mac, having been cleansed of all obsolete icon pictures, will also run faster and more smoothly.

Last resort: There's one more circumstance when you'll get this message: if you try to open a generic text or graphics file that's not associated with *any* particular program.

(Sigh.) Yes, I know, this contradicts everything you've learned about programs and documents being like parents and children. But suppose that somebody wants to give you a memo she has written, yet she is not sure which brand of word processor you own. The smart thing would be to give you the memo in *text-only* format: a generic, no-frills, raw-typing format. A text file. Or, as the weenies say, an *ASCII* (pronounced ASKie) text file. No matter which program was used to create this file, *any* word processor (even on non-Mac computers, for that matter) can open it.

However, a text file isn't double-clickable. (Actually, in System 7, the Mac will offer to open it with TeachText, but let's just pretend I have a point here.) To read it, you launch your word processor *first*. Then use the Open command in the File menu (below left).

The usual list box appears, and you'll see the text file listed there (above). Double-click to open it.

The same applies to generic *picture* documents, too. The weenie-word here is *PICT* files — a PICT file is a generic, any-program-can-open-this artwork file. If you try to double-click a generic PICT file, you'll be told, "Application not found." Once again, the solution is to launch your graphics program (like MacDraw) *first* and then open the PICT file via the Open command.

"An error of Type 1 occurred." or "Bad F-Line Instruction."

This message conveys *nothing*. It's the equivalent of a 1950's-movie computer saying "Does not compute." It simply means that something has gone terribly wrong inside, and you have to start over.

Turn the Mac off, then on again. Or use the Restart switch (see "The Restart switch" sidebar later in this appendix).

As you've probably guessed, this means that anything you've typed — *and not saved* — is gone forever. Reality bites.

If you get a *lot* of these messages, however, it's time to wonder why. The Mac is not supposed to crash a lot!

Without question, the problem is your extensions. As you've read earlier, having the wrong mix of extension files inside your System folder is an invitation to conflicts and problems. Look earlier in this appendix; you'll find a section called "Extension conflicts." You'll learn how to determine which ones are responsible for ruining your life.

"Sorry, a System error has occurred."

Once again, the most likely culprit is an extension culprit, as described in the preceding paragraphs.

"You do not have enough access privileges."

First resort: Wow, does this make people mad. "Not enough *access privileges!?*" they scream. "It's *my darned computer!*"

Right you are. However, if you have a Performa or System 7.5, your darned computer has a useful feature that can actually save your Mac from the marauding actions of children or ignoramuses. It's called Protect System Folder.

Choose Control Panels from your menu. Open the control panel called General Controls — or, on a Performa, it might be called Performa. There you'll see the on/off switch for this System folder protection business. You'll see a similar checkbox for protecting your Applications folder, if you have one.

And how, you may well ask, does this feature protect anything? All it does is prevent you from *moving* any of the icons in your System folder. You can't throw them to the Trash. You can't put them into folders. You can't, in fact, do anything that would mess up your Mac.

If you try, you'll be told — yessirree — "You do not have enough access privileges." If you really do want to move something out of your System folder or Applications folder, open the control panel again and turn the Protect feature off.

Last resort: If you *don't* have a Performa or System 7.5, then there's only one possibility. You are, or have once been, connected to another Macintosh. (In the lingo, *networked.*) Which means that you, in theory, have remote-control invasion rights to somebody else's computer. Which means that they, in theory, have probably protected their stuff from over-the-network pillaging. Which means that you, sure enough, don't have enough "access privileges" (i.e., permission) to root through that other Mac via network.

If you really, really want to know more about the headachy world of networking, there are fatter, finer books than this one for that purpose.

"Not enough memory to open Word."

This is a biggie. It gets a section all by itself in *Macs For Dummies,* 3rd Edition (see "Out of Memory" in Chapter 12).

"Application has unexpectedly quit."

You're probably out of memory. Once more, see the advice in the preceding section.

However, even if your Mac has plenty of memory, the individual *program* that just "unexpectedly quit" may not have enough memory allotted to it. See the upcoming sidebar called "Memory tactics" to find out how to give your program a more generous helping of memory.

"The disk is full."

This means the disk is full.

It happens to the best of us: Over time, your hard disk gets fuller and fuller. Then, with only a megabyte of storage space to go, you try to do something (like saving an important file), and you're told there's no more elbow room.

You'll have to make some more room. From the Application menu (at the top-right corner of your screen), choose Finder. Root through your files and find some things to throw away. Drag them to the Trash can, and don't forget to *empty* the trash (using the Empty Trash command in the Special menu).

"Can't empty trash."

First resort: There's probably a locked file in the Trash can. Press Option while choosing Empty Trash from the Special menu.

Second resort: It's possible you're trying to throw away a document you're still working on. Or maybe the Mac *thinks* you're still working on it. Be sure that the file isn't open on the screen. Sometimes you even have to *quit the program* you were using before that document is considered trashable.

Third resort: Maybe the Mac has become confused about the trashability of some file in the Trash. Restart the Mac and try again.

Last resort: About once in every Mac user's life, the Mac gets *so* confused that it simply will not empty the Trash, even if you've tried all the logical things.

In this case, it's your System folder that's having the psychotic break. The trick is to start up from *some other* System folder — the handiest of which comes on your all-important Disk Tools (or Utilities) disk. This special startup disk comes with every Mac ever made, so you can't claim helplessness on this point.

Turn off the computer. Put Disk Tools (or Utilities) into the disk drive. Turn the Mac on. When the computer is running, you should at last be able to empty the Trash.

"An error occurred while writing to the disk."

Something went wrong while you were trying to save a document — probably your disk was full, or it's a flaky floppy disk. (See "Floppy-Disk Flukes" for more information on flaky floppies.)

"The file could not be copied because a disk error occurred."

Here again, see the section on disks earlier in this appendix.

"Microsoft Word prefers 2048K of memory. 2000K is available."

Once again, you're out of memory. The Mac will give you the chance to launch the program anyway — but it'll run slowly and may crash if you get too ambitious with your work.

Starting Up

Problems you encounter when you turn on the Mac are especially disheartening when you're a new Mac user. Does wonders for your self-esteem to think that you can't even turn the thing *on* without problems.

No ding, no picture

First resort: Chances are very, very, very good that your Mac simply isn't getting electricity. It's probably not plugged in. Or it's plugged into a power strip that has an On/Off switch that's currently in Off. Or, if it's a PowerBook, the battery is completely dead. (Plug in the adapter for 10 minutes before trying again.)

Second resort: If you have a two-piece Mac, you normally turn the machine on by pressing the triangle key on the keyboard — maybe the keyboard isn't plugged in. Check that.

Third resort: Here's another PowerBook possibility. It may be that the internal circuitry known as the *power manager* has gotten drunk again. Unplug the PowerBook *and* take its battery out. Let it sit like that for 10 minutes. Then put it together and try again.

Last resort: If none of those steps solved the problem, then your Mac is as dead as Elvis. Get it in for repair. But that's virtually never the actual problem.

Ding, no picture

If you hear the startup chime (or ding) but the monitor doesn't light up, then something's wrong with the monitor.

First resort: Is the screen brightness turned up? On most Macs, there's a brightness dial on the edge of the monitor. On a Classic, you have to use the Brightness control panel.

Second resort: I don't mean to insult your intelligence — but is it possible you have a screen saver program installed? (You know, like After Dark…flying toasters, all that?) To find out if that's the cause of the current blackness, click the mouse button. If the screen picture doesn't appear, read on.

Third resort: If you have a two-piece Mac, the monitor has to be (1) plugged into the Mac, (2) plugged into a power source, *and* (3) turned on. (Not everybody realizes that your monitor has an On/Off switch.) Often the monitor is plugged into the AC outlet on the Mac itself; that's OK.

Last resort: Does your monitor require a graphics card? Some old models do. Of course, if your Mac needs a graphics card, you would have discovered this problem the very first day you got your system.

Picture, no ding

Every Mac makes a sound when it's turned on. In fact, even if you've set the volume level of your Mac's speaker to zero (using the Sound control panel), you still get a sound when you start up the Mac.

First resort: Look at the little speaker jack in the back of the Mac. If there's some kind of plug in it — usually some kid's Walkman headphones, a cord connected to a stereo, a pretzel stick — then no sound can come out of the Mac speaker.

Last resort: There's a remote possibility that somebody, mucking around inside your two-piece Mac, unplugged the speaker-wire cable. Find that person, yell firmly into his or her nearest ear, and insist that the cable (inside the Mac) be reconnected.

Four musical notes (or crash sound)

If you hear an arpeggio, a lick of the "Twilight Zone" theme, or a car-crash sound, then something's seriously wrong inside the Mac. (Apple's sense of humor at work.)

Fortunately, 50 percent of the time, you hear this just after installing new memory. It means that one of the memory chips is loose or defective — something you (or whoever installed the memory for you) can fix relatively easily. And 40 percent of the time, it's a SCSI problem (covered in Chapter 12 of *Macs For Dummies,* 3rd Edition). Read on.

First resort: If you've just installed or otherwise messed around with the memory chips in your computer, that's certainly the problem. Reopen the Mac. Carefully remove each memory chip and reinstall it, checking the little centipede legs to make sure none are bent. Come to think of it, get someone who knows what he or she's doing to do this.

Second resort: The other common source of funny startup notes is a SCSI problem of some kind. Yes, I know we haven't defined this; for a quick fix, just unplug any external hard drives or scanners from the SCSI jack (the very wide one) in the back of the Mac, and try starting up again.

Last resort: If it's truly not a memory chip or a SCSI problem, call your Apple dealer. This baby's sick.

A question mark blinks on the screen

The blinking question mark is the Mac's international symbol for "I've looked everywhere, and I can't find a System Folder anywhere."

If your hard disk, like most people's, is inside the Mac, the blinking question mark means that it's not working right — or that it's working fine, but somehow your System Folder got screwed up. In either case, here's what to do.

First resort: Panic. (Who are we kidding? You're going to do this anyway.)

Second resort: After ten seconds of that, turn the Mac off and try starting again. Or just press the Restart switch (see the sidebar).

Third resort: Find a floppy disk with a System folder on it. The best bet is the white System disks (or the startup CD) that came with your Mac. The floppy called Disk Tools or Utilities usually does the trick. Put it into the disk drive. Turn the Mac on.

The Restart switch

Every Mac has this switch. Sometimes there are two buttons side by side somewhere on the Mac's casing — and the one with a left-pointing triangle is the Restart switch. Sometimes, as on older PowerBooks, there are two little back-panel *holes* you're supposed to stick a pin into.

And on all the other models, it's a *secret* Restart switch. You press Control, the ⌘ key, and the On button (or key) at the same time.

In every case, hitting Restart is the same as turning your Mac off and then on again — except that it doesn't send a wall of sudden electricity thudding into the machine's delicate electronics. Therefore, Restart is gentler to your Mac. It's good to keep the Restart switch in mind when you have a System freeze or crash, too.

If you arrive at some kind of Installer screen, then you must have used a System Software Installer disk, and (alas) it's not going to help you get going. And if it says something about needing a newer version of the System software than 7.1, the disk doesn't have the little *enabler file* your Mac needs to run.

But if the Mac happily accepts the disk, gives you the smiling Mac picture, and goes on to the familiar desktop, look for your hard disk's icon to appear. If it's there, in its customary upper-right-corner-of-the-screen position, reinstall the System software (using those same white floppies, starting with the Install disk) and start over — after first making sure you have a copy of everything useful on the disk, of course.

Fourth resort: If the hard drive icon still doesn't appear, read "Scuzzy SCSI" in *Macs For Dummies,* 3rd Edition (Chapter 12).

Fifth resort: This one is really, *really* technical. I've never even seen it work. But repair people say it could theoretically work. It's called (do *not* learn this term) *zapping the PRAM.* (They pronounce it PEA-ram.)

First, turn off (or restart) your Mac. Then turn it on again, but hold down four keys at once: ⌘, Option, P, and R; don't let go until you hear the startup chime. Supposedly, this can help.

Last resort: If nothing has worked, and you still can't make your hard-drive icon appear on the screen, then your hard drive is sick. Call up your local dealer or Mac guru, and do *not* freak out — chances are very good that all of your files are still intact. (Just because the platters aren't spinning doesn't mean they've been wiped out, just as your Walkman tapes don't get erased when the Walkman runs out of batteries.)

In fact, you can probably rescue the data from your disk yourself. Buy a disk-recovery program like Norton Utilities or MacTools Deluxe. That'll let you grab anything useful off the disk, and may even help heal what's wrong with it.

Some crazy program launches itself every time you start up

In the words of Mac programmers everywhere: "It's a feature, not a bug."

Inside the System folder, there's a folder called Startup Items. Look inside it. Somebody put a program or document in there. Anything in the Startup Items folder automatically opens up when you turn on the Mac. It's supposed to be a time-saver for people who work on the same documents every day.

Appendix C
The Techno-Babble Translation Guide

• •

accelerator — The pedal that you press while driving to pick up your very first Mac. Also, an expensive circuit board that you can install to make your Mac faster and slightly less obsolete.

active window — The window in front. Usually, only one window can be active; you can recognize it by the stripes across the title bar, like this:

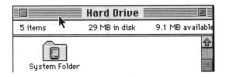

alias — A duplicate of a file's icon (not of the file itself). Serves as a double-clickable *pointer*, or reference, to the original file, folder, or disk. A feature of System 7 or later. Indicated by an italicized icon name.

Apple menu — The menu at the far left end of your menu bar, marked by the symbol — a piece of black or multicolor fruit. In the menu, you'll find a list of your desk accessories (miniprograms, such as the Calculator), as well as any files, folders, documents, control panels, and even disks (or their aliases) that you care to see there.

To add something to the menu, drop its icon into the Apple Menu Items folder within your System Folder.

AppleTalk — Another trademarked name, also having to do with Macs talking to one another. You *may* need to know this term if you have a laser printer because AppleTalk is the language that it speaks to your Mac. To print, you must make sure that AppleTalk is active. Choose the Chooser from the menu, and you'll see where you turn AppleTalk on or off.

application — Nerd word for *program*.

Application menu — The rightmost menu in the menu bar (if you have System 7), marked by an icon. This menu lists whichever programs you have open and displays a check mark next to the frontmost program. You can switch from one program to another by choosing names from the Application menu.

background printing — A feature that returns control of the Mac to you immediately after you use the Print command; the Mac will print your document, taking its own sweet time, always giving priority to what you're doing on the screen. The alternative, known as *background printing is off,* takes less time to print but takes over the Mac, preventing you from working and displaying a "now printing" message until the printing is over.

back up — To make a copy of a file for use in case some horrible freak accident befalls your original copy (such as your throwing it out).

Balloon Help — A feature of System 7 and later. See the little question mark in the upper-right corner of your screen? It's a menu. Choose Show Balloons from it; then point to various elements of your little Mac-screen world. Cartoon balloons pop out to identify what you're pointing at.

baud rate — The speed of a modem (see *modem*). Directly related to the price.

bitmap — A particular arrangement of black dots on your white screen. To your eye, a particular bitmap may look like the letter *A* (bitmapped text) or a coffee mug (a bitmapped graphic); to the computer, it's just a bunch of dots whose exact positions it has to memorize.

boot — (1) (v.) To start the computer. (2) (n.) Western footwear. (3) (v.) To fire somebody for having accidentally erased the hard drive, as in "He was booted out of here so fast, you could have heard a résumé drop."

bps — Bits per second. The technically proper way to measure the speed of a *modem* (instead of *baud,* which everybody still says out of force of habit).

bug — A programming error in a piece of software, caused by a programmer too wired on Jolt and pizza, that makes the program do odd or tragic things when you're working to beat a deadline.

button — There are two kinds of buttons that you'll have to deal with: the big square one on the mouse, and the many oval or round ones on the screen that offer you options.

byte — A piece of computer information made up of bits. Now *that* made everything clear, didn't it?

Caps Lock — A key on your keyboard that's responsible for messing up pages and pages of manuscript if you're one of those people who doesn't look up from the keyboard much. Caps Lock makes every letter that you type come out as a capital; it doesn't affect numbers. Press it to get the capitals; press it again to return to normal.

CD-ROM — A computer compact disc that requires a special $300 player. CD-ROMs can show pictures, play music or voices, display short animations and movies, and display reams and reams of text. (A typical CD holds 600 megs of information; compared with the measly 230-meg hard disks that come in the more expensive Macs.)

character — (1) A single typed letter, number, space, or symbol. (2) The scoundrel who got you into this Macintosh habit.

Chooser — A desk accessory, therefore listed in the menu, that lets you specify what kind of printer you have. Failure to use this thing when you set up your Mac is the #1 reason why beginners can't print.

click — The cornerstone of the Macintosh religion: to point the cursor at an on-screen object and then press and release the mouse button.

clip art — Instead of possessing actual artistic ability, graphic designers can buy (or otherwise acquire) collections of ready-made graphics called *clip art* — cutesy little snowmen, city skylines, Santa Clauses, whatever — that they can use to dress up their newsletters, party invitations, and threatening legal notices.

Clipboard — The invisible holding area where the Mac stashes any text or graphics that you copy by using the Copy command. The contents of the Clipboard get vaporized when you turn off the Mac (or copy something new).

close box — The little square in the upper-left corner of a window (as opposed to the little square who sold you the Macintosh), which, when clicked, closes the window.

command — Something that you'd like the Mac to do, such as Print or Save or Make Me Rich. See also *menu.*

Command key — The one on your keyboard, right next to the spacebar, that has a ⌘ (Command) symbol on it. When you press this key, the letter keys on your keyboard perform commands instead of typing letters — for example, ⌘-P = Print, ⌘-S = Save, ⌘-Q = Quit, and ⌘-Z = Undo. (Well, they can't *all* be mnemonic.)

Control key — A keyboard key that does absolutely nothing.

control panel — A little window full of settings that pertain to some aspect of the Mac's operation. There's a control panel for the mouse, another for the keyboard, another for the monitor, and so on. To view the selection of control panels, choose (what else?) Control Panels from the menu.

Copy — The command that places a copy of something (whatever text or graphics were first *selected*) in the invisible Macintosh Clipboard. Accomplishes nothing unless you then click somewhere and *paste.*

CPU — What it *stands for* is *central processing unit.* What it *means* is the actual computer — in the case of two-piece Macs, the box that contains the real brains. As distinguished from things like the monitor, the printer, and the keyboard.

crash — A very ugly moment in every Mac user's life when the Mac abruptly malfunctions, usually with scary-looking sounds and visuals. Requires restarting.

cursor — The pointer on the screen whose position you control by moving the mouse across the desk.

DA — Short for *desk accessory.*

data — Isn't he that white-makeup guy on *Star Trek: The Next Generation*?

database — An electronic list of information — for example, a mailing list — that can be sorted very quickly or searched for a specific name.

default — (1) The factory settings. For example, the *default* setting for your typing in a word processor is single-spaced, one-inch margins. (2) De blame for hooking you on de Mac hobby.

Delete key — In the typewriter days, this key was named Backspace. In my opinion, it still *should* be called that. I make it a habit to magic-marker the word *Backspace* on every keyboard that I encounter.

deselect — To *un*highlight some selected text or graphic. (You usually do it by clicking someplace else.)

desktop — (1) The top of your desk, where the Mac sits, as in "I don't want a laptop; I want a desktop computer." (2) *(Capitalized)* The home-base environment, where you see the Trash can, icons, and all that stuff. Also known as the Finder. (3) The actual (usually gray) background of that home-base view. You can drag an icon out of its window and onto this gray tablecloth, and announce to your coworker that you've just placed an icon on the Desktop.

desktop file — A file the Mac maintains for its own use, in which it stores information such as what your icons should look like and which kinds of documents can be opened by which programs. This file is invisible, but when it becomes damaged or bloated and starts causing problems, it's not quite invisible enough for most people.

dialog box — The message box that the Mac puts on the screen when it needs more information from you (for example, the one that appears when you print, asking how many copies you want). Because the Mac doesn't, thank God, actually talk back to you, and instead just listens to what *you* say, a better name might be *therapist box.*

disk — Oh, come on; you know *this* word.

disk drive — The machinery that actually reads what's on a disk. If we're talking hard disk, the disk and the drive are built into a single unit. If we're talking floppy, the disk drive is the slot in the face of the Mac into which you insert a floppy disk.

dot-matrix — A kind of low-quality printer, such as the ImageWriter, and the printouts that it makes.

dots per inch — A gauge of visual clarity, both on printouts and on the screen. The Mac's crystal-clear screen became famous for having a very high resolution — 72 dots per inch, or 72 *dpi.* A laser printer is much sharper, though, capable of printing at 300 dpi.

double-click — One of the most basic Mac skills, without which you can't do anything but stare at the blank screen. Double-clicking involves placing the on-screen pointer on an icon and, without moving the mouse, pressing the mouse button twice quickly. If you double-click an icon, it always opens into a window. In word processing, you double-click a word to select it.

download — To transfer a file from one computer to another over phone lines. If you're on the receiving end, you *download* the file. If you're on the sending end, you *upload* the file. If you're the phone company, you *love* the file.

downloadable font — Every laser printer comes with a basic set of typefaces built into it. You're welcome to use fonts that aren't in that built-in set, but the Mac has to send them to the printer (the printer *downloads* them) before the printer can start spitting out pages.

drag — (1) To position the cursor on something, hold down the mouse button, and move the mouse while the button is still down. (2) What it is when your disk drive breaks the day after the warranty expires.

drawing program — A graphics program (such as MacDraw or ClarisDraw) that creates circles, squares, and lines. The Mac stores each object that you draw as an object unto itself, rather than storing the status of each screen dot. See also *painting program* and *bitmap.*

E-mail — Electronic mail; messages that you read and write on the Mac screen without ever printing them. May also be short for *Earth-mail,* because no paper (and no rainforest acreage) is involved.

Enter key — A key (obviously) with the word *Enter* on it. It almost always does the same thing as the Return key.

expansion slot — The new notch that you have to add to your belt when you've been putting on weight. Also the connector socket for an add-on circuit board inside most Mac models.

extended keyboard — A slightly more expensive keyboard than the "standard" one. The extended keyboard has a row of function keys (F1, F2, and so on) across the top, which don't do anything, and a little bank of keys that say Page Up, Page Down, and other stuff.

extension — Miniprogram that you install by dropping it in your System Folder (whereupon the Mac puts it in the Extensions folder). From that moment on, the extension will run itself when you turn on the Mac and will be on all the time. Examples: virus protectors and screen savers.

fax/modem — Like a modem (see *modem*), but also lets you send or receive faxes from your Mac screen.

field — Computerese for *blank,* such as a blank in a form.

file — The generic word for one of the little icons in your Macintosh. There are two kinds of files: *programs,* which you purchase to get work done, and *documents,* which are created by programs. See also *program* and *document.*

file compression — Making a file take up less disk space by encoding it in a more compact format, using a *file-compression program* such as StuffIt or DiskDoubler. The trade-off: Stuffing something down (and expanding it when you need it again) takes a few seconds.

File Sharing — A built-in feature of System 7, wherein you can make any file, folder, or disk available for other people to go rooting through (as long as they're connected to your Mac by network wiring).

Finder — The "home-base" view when you're working on your Mac. It's the environment where you see the Trash, your icons, and how little space you've got left on your disk. Also known as the Desktop or "that place with all the little pictures."

floppy disk — The hard 3½-inch-square thing that you put into your disk-drive slot. Comes in three capacities: 400K (single-sided), 800K (double-sided), and 1,400K (quadruple-sided, or high-density). After being accidentally zapped by a refrigerator magnet, often used as a windshield scraper.

folder — In the Mac world, a little filing-folder icon into which you can drop other icons (such as your work) for organizational purposes. When you double-click a folder, it opens into a window. Also the name of the high-speed machine that creases and envelope-stuffs the junk mail that you're going to start getting from computer companies.

A folder

font — (1) Apple's usage: a single typeface. (2) Everyone else's usage: a typeface *family* or package.

freeze — When your cursor becomes immovable on your screen, you can't type anything, your Mac locks up, and you get furious because you lose everything you've typed in the past ten minutes.

gig — Short for *gigabyte,* which is 1,024 megabytes, or a *very* big hard drive.

grayscale — A form of color image or color monitor on which all the colors are different shades of gray, like all the images in this book.

hard copy — A synonym for *printout.* A term used primarily by the kind of people who have car phones and say, "Let's interface on this."

hard disk — A hard drive.

hard drive — A hard disk. That is, the spinning platters, usually inside your Mac but also available in an external form, that serve as a giant floppy disk where your computer files get stored.

hardware — The parts of your computer experience that you can feel, and touch, and pay for. Contrast with *software.*

header — Something that appears at the top of every page of a document, such as "Chapter 4: The Milkman's Plight" or "Final Disconnection Notice."

highlight — To select, usually by clicking or dragging with the mouse. In the Mac world, text and icons usually indicate that they're selected, or highlighted, by turning black. In the barbecue world, things indicate that they're *ready* by turning black.

icon — A teensy picture used as a symbol for a file, a folder, or a disk.

ImageWriter — A low-cost, low-speed, low-quality, high-noise Apple dot-matrix printer.

initialize — To prepare a new disk for use on your computer. Entails *erasing it completely.*

insertion point — In word processing, the short, blinking vertical line that's always somewhere in your text. It indicates where your next typing (or backspacing) will begin.

the insertion point is right before this word.

K — Short for *kilobyte,* a unit of size measurement for computer information. A floppy disk usually holds 800K or 1,400K of data. All the typing in this book fills about 1,500K. A full-screen color picture is around 1,000K of information. When your hard disk gets erased accidentally, it's got 0K (that's not OK).

landscape — Used to describe the sideways orientation of a piece of paper. Also the natural environment outdoors that you gradually forget about as you become addicted to the Mac.

laser printer — An expensive printer that creates awesome-looking printouts.

launch — To open a program, as in "He just sits at that computer all day long, moving icons around, because he hasn't figured out how to launch a program yet."

LocalTalk — The hardware portion of a Macintosh network: the connectors and cables that plug one Mac into another.

logic board — The main circuit board inside your Mac. Often at fault when your Mac refuses to turn on.

macro — A predefined series of actions that the Mac performs automatically when you press a single key — such as launching your word processor, typing **Help! I'm being**

inhabited by a Mac poltergeist!, and printing it — all by itself. Requires a special macro program such as QuicKeys or Tempo.

mail merge — Creating personalized form letters with a word processing program. Considered to be perfectly polite unless somebody catches you.

MB — Short for *megabyte.*

megabyte — A unit of disk-storage space or memory measurement (see *K*). Used to measure hard disks, memory, and other large storage devices. There are about 1,000K in a megabyte.

memory — The electronic holding area that exists only when the Mac is turned on; where your document lives while you're working on it. Expensive and limited in each Mac.

menu — A list of commands, neatly organized by topic, that drops down from the top of the Mac screen when you click the menu's title.

menu bar — The white strip, containing menu titles, that's always at the top of the Mac screen. Not to be confused with *bar menu*, which is a wine list.

modem — A phone attachment for your Mac that lets you send files and messages to other computer users all over the world, and to prevent anyone else in the house from using the phone.

modifier keys — Keys that mess up what the letter keys do. Famous example: the Shift key. Other examples: ⌘ (Command), Option, Control, and Caps Lock.

monitor — What you should do to your blood pressure when you find out how much computer screens (*monitors*) cost and weigh.

mouse — The little hand-held gray thing that rolls around on your desk, controls the movement of the cursor, and is such an obvious target for a rodent joke that I won't even attempt it.

mouse button — The square or rounded plastic button at the far end of the top of the mouse.

mouse pad — A thin foam-rubber mat that protects the mouse and desk from each other and that gives the mouse good traction. Often bears a logo or slogan, such as "Sony Disks: We're always floppy."

multimedia — Something involving more than one medium, I guess. Mainly an advertising gimmick. On the Mac, anything that gives you something to look at *and* listen to, such as a CD-ROM game.

native software — Specially written programs that run amazingly fast on a Power Macintosh.

network — What you create when you connect Macs to each other. A network lets you send messages or transfer files from one Mac to another without getting up and running down the hall with a floppy disk in your hand (a networking system fondly called *SneakerNet*).

NuBus — The special kind of expansion slot (see *expansion slot*) found in any Mac II-style computer and most Quadra-style computers. Contrast with *PDS,* the slot in a Macintosh LC. (And no, there was never an OldBus.)

OCR — Short for *optical character recognition.* You run an article that you tore out of *Entertainment Weekly* through a scanner, and the Mac translates it into a word processing document on your screen, so you can edit it and remove all references to Cher.

online — Hooked up, as in "Let's get this relationship online." In Mac lore, it means hooked up to another computer, such as America Online.

painting program — (1) A program with the word *Paint* in the title (for example, MacPaint or UltraPaint) that creates artwork by turning individual white dots black on the screen. (2) An adult-education course for would-be watercolorers.

paste — To place some text or graphics (that you previously copied or cut) in a document.

PC — Stands for *personal computer,* but really means any non-Macintosh (i.e., inferior) computer; an IBM clone.

peripheral — (1) Any add-on: a printer, scanner, CD-ROM drive, dust cover, and so on. (2) The kind of vision by which you'll see your spouse leave you forever because you're too consumed by the Mac.

PICT — A confusing-sounding acronym for the most common kind of picture file, as in "Just paste that image of Sculley's head into your word processor, Frank; it's only a PICT file, for heaven's sake."

pixel — One single dot out of the thousands that make up the screen image. Supposedly derived from *pi*cture *el*ement, which still doesn't explain how the *x* got there.

pop-up menu — Any menu that doesn't appear at the *top* of the screen. Usually marked by a down-pointing black triangle. Doesn't actually pop *up;* usually drops down.

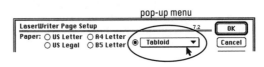

port — (1) A jack or connection socket in the back of your Mac. (2) Where boaters dock so that they can recharge their PowerBook batteries.

portrait — A right-side-up piece of paper; the opposite of *landscape* (see that entry). Also a right-side-up monitor that can display a full page (as in "a portrait display monitor").

PowerBook — A Mac laptop and the first of many Apple trademarks to contain the word *Power*.

Power Macintosh — A Mac whose primary brain is the PowerPC chip.

PowerPC chip — The very fast main processor chip inside a Power Macintosh.

PRAM — *P*arameter *RAM*: the little piece of memory maintained by your Mac's battery. Helps explain why the Mac always knows the date and time even when it's been turned off.

PrintMonitor — A program that launches itself, unbidden, whenever you try to print something when background printing is turned on (see *background printing*). Print Monitor is also the program that tries to notify you when something goes wrong with the printer, such as when a piece of paper gets horribly mangled inside.

program — A piece of software, created by a programmer, that you buy to make your Mac do something specific: graphics, music, word processing, number crunching, or whatever.

QuickTime — The technology (and the little software extension) that permits you to make and view digital movies on your Mac screen. Does nothing by itself; requires QuickTime recording, playing, and editing programs.

quit — To exit or close a program, removing it from memory. Or to exit or close your job, having gotten sick of working in front of a computer all day.

radio button — What you see in groups of two or more when the Mac is forcing you to choose among mutually exclusive options, such as these:

> A System error has occurred. What result would you like?
>
> ○ Loud, static buzzing
> ◉ Quietly blink to black
> ○ A two-minute fireworks display

RAM — Term for memory (see *memory*) designed to intimidate non-computer users.

RAM disk — A way to trick the Mac into thinking that it has an extra floppy disk inserted. The RAM disk is actually a chunk of memory set aside to *resemble* a disk (complete with an icon on the screen). A built-in option on most Macs and PowerBooks.

reboot — Restart.

rebuilding the Desktop — One of several desperate methods that you can use in the event that something screwy goes wrong with the Mac. Involves holding down the ⌘ and Option keys while the Mac is starting up.

record (n.) — Other than its obvious definitions, the computer word *record* refers to one "card" in a database, such as one person's address information. Contrast with *field,* which is one *blank* (such as a ZIP code) within a record.

removable cartridge — Like a hard drive with free refills: a storage device (usually made by SyQuest or Bernoulli) that accepts huge-capacity disks, so you never run out of disk space (until you run out of the ability to buy more cartridges).

resize box — The small square in the lower-right corner of a window that, when dragged, changes the size and shape of your window.

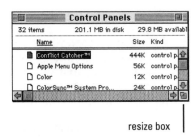

resize box

resolution — (1) A number, measured in dots per inch, that indicates how crisply a printer or a monitor can display an image. (2) A New Year's vow, such as "I will spend five minutes away from the computer each day for family, exercise, and social activity."

restart switch — A little plastic switch, marked by a left-pointing triangle, on the case molding of most Macs that, when pressed, safely turns the Mac off and on again.

ROM — A mediation mantra that you can use when contemplating the ROM chips, where the Mac's instructions to itself are permanently etched.

sans serif — A font, such as Helvetica or Geneva, with no little "hats" and "feet" at the tip of each letter. See Chapter 4.

scanner — A machine that takes a picture of a piece of paper (like a Xerox machine) and then displays the image on your Mac screen for editing.

Scrapbook — A desk accessory, found in your menu, used for permanent storage of graphics, text, and sounds. (Not the same as the Clipboard, which isn't permanent and holds only one thing at a time.) To get something into the Scrapbook, copy it from a document, open the Scrapbook, and paste it. To get something out of the Scrapbook, use the scroll bar until you see what you want, and then copy it (or cut it).

screen saver — A program (such as After Dark) that darkens your screen after you haven't worked for several minutes. Designed to protect an unchanging image from burning into the screen, but more often used as a status symbol.

scroll — To bring a different part of a document into view, necessitated by the fact that most computer monitors aren't large enough to display all 60 pages of your annual report at the same time.

scroll bar — The strips along the left and right sides or bottom of a Mac window. When a scroll bar's arrows, gray portion, or little white (or gray) square are clicked or dragged, a different part of the window's contents heaves into view (*scrolls*).

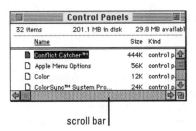

scroll bar

SCSI — Stands for Small Computer [something] Interface. The second *S* may stand for *standard, system,* or *serial,* depending on whom you ask. Used only in the following five terms.

SCSI address — Refers to a number that you must give each SCSI device (see *SCSI device*) that's plugged into your Mac, using a little switch or thumbwheel on the back. The address can be between 0 and 7, except that the Mac is always 7 and the internal hard disk is always 0. If two SCSI devices have the same SCSI address, you're in big trouble.

SCSI cable — A fat cable with a 25- or 50-pin connector at the end, used to join SCSI devices. The total length of all your SCSI cables can't be more than about 20 feet, or you're in big trouble.

SCSI device — A scanner, CD player, external hard drive, printer (sometimes), removable-cartridge drive, external floppy-disk drive (sometimes), or other piece of equipment that you attach to the wide SCSI port in the back of your Mac. When you attach more than one of these devices (by plugging each into the back of the preceding one), you have to obey certain rules (outlined in Chapter 12), or you're in big trouble.

SCSI port — The wide connector in the back of your Mac.

SCSI terminator — A plug that is supposed to go into the last SCSI device attached to your Mac. If you don't use one, you're in big trouble; although sometimes you're in big trouble if you *do* use one. See Chapter 12.

serif (n., adj.) — A term used to describe a font that has little ledges, like little "hats" and "feet," at the tip of each letter, such as Times or this font.

shareware — Programs that are distributed for free, via an electronic bulletin board or on a floppy disk, from user groups. The programmer requests that you send $10 or $20 to him or her, but only if you really like the program.

Shut Down — The command in the Special menu that turns off your Mac.

SIMM — Stands for *Single In-line Memory Module*, which I suggest that you immediately forget. It refers to the little epoxy mini-circuit board that you install into your Mac when you decide you need more memory.

sleep — A command, and a condition, that applies only to PowerBooks or the Mac Portable. Sort of like Off, except that the Mac remembers everything that you had running on the screen. When you want to use the computer again, you just touch a key; the whole computer wakes up, the screen lights up, and you're in business again. Used to conserve battery power.

slot — An *expansion slot* (see that entry).

software — The real reason you got a computer. Software is computer code, the stuff on disks: programs (that let you create documents) and documents themselves. Software tells the hardware what to do.

spooler — A program that allows *background printing* (see that entry).

spreadsheet — A program that's like an electronic ledger book; you can type columns of numbers in a spreadsheet program and have them added automatically.

stack — A document created by the HyperStudio program.

startup disk — *A* startup disk is a floppy or hard disk that contains a System Folder (including a particular set of fonts, desk accessories, and settings for running your Mac). *The* startup disk is the one that you've designated to be in control (in the event that you have more than one to choose among). The Startup Disk *control panel* is what you use to specify *the* startup disk.

stationery pad — A System 7 feature. Click a document icon, choose Get Info from the File menu, and select Stationery Pad. Thereafter, when you double-click that icon, it won't open; instead, an exact *copy* of it opens. This saves you the hassle of pasting the same logo into every memo that you write because you can paste it into your Stationery Pad document just once.

StyleWriter — A quiet, low-cost, high-quality, slow-speed Apple inkjet printer.

submenu — In some menus, you're forced to choose among an additional set of options, which are marked in the menu by a right-pointing triangle. When your pointer is on the main menu command, the submenu pops out, like this:

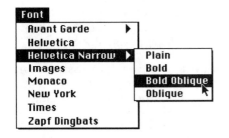

System 6 — One version of the Mac's controlling software. Faster, but harder to use, than System 7. Requires 1MB of memory or less.

System 7 — The more recent version of the Mac's controlling software. More attractive, easier to use, more powerful, and slower than System 6. Requires at least 2MB of memory and, because it's a lot of software, a hard disk (it doesn't fit on a floppy). Generically, refers to any flavor of System 7: version 7.0, 7.1, 7.5, or whatever.

System 7.1 — The first version of the Mac System software that's not free; you have to buy it. Adds two features to System 7: a Fonts folder, which contains all manner of font files (TrueType, screen fonts, and printer fonts); and WorldScript, which enables you to convert all Mac screen elements to a different language, such as Japanese. (WorldScript requires special drop-in language modules.) System 7.1 is also modular; you can add new features to it just by dropping in plug-in software tidbits as they become available.

System 7.5 — Yet another version of the System Folder, which, again, you must purchase unless your Mac came with it. Under the hood, System 7.5 is much the same as System 7.1. But it comes with about 50 new control panels and extensions that perform stunts such as giving submenus to your menu to providing a floating "control strip" for your PowerBook. Has one huge new feature: AppleGuide, which walks you through basic Mac functions (such as printing). Also has PowerTalk and QuickDraw GX, which take major computer geniuses to figure out.

System crash — When something goes so wrong inside your Mac that a bomb appears on the screen with the message "Sorry, a System error has occurred" — or not. Sometimes, the whole screen just freaks, fills with static, and makes buzzing noises, like a TV station that's going off the air.

System disk — A *startup disk* (see that entry).

System file — The most important individual file inside a System Folder. Contains the Mac's instructions to itself, and stores your fonts, sounds, and other important customization information. A Mac without a System file is like a broke politician: it can't run.

System Folder — The all-important folder that the Mac requires to run. Contains all kinds of other stuff that's also defined in this glossary: the System file, the Finder, fonts, desk accessories, printer fonts, and so on. Always identified by this special folder icon:

System Folder

telecommunication — Communicating with other computers over the phone lines. Requires a *modem* (see that entry).

TIFF — Stands for *tagged image file format* and is the kind of graphics-file format created by a scanner.

title bar — The strip at the top of a window where the window's name appears. Shows thin horizontal stripes if the window is *active* (in front of all the others).

toner — The powder that serves as the "ink" for a laser printer. Runs out at critical moments.

trackball — An alternative to the mouse. Looks like an 8-ball set in a pedestal; you roll it to move the pointer.

upload — To send a file to another computer via modem. See also *download*.

user group — A local computer club; usually meets once a month. Serves as a local source of information and as a place to unload your obsolete equipment to unsuspecting newcomers.

video card — A circuit board that most Mac II-series Macs need to display anything at all on the monitor.

virtual memory — A chunk of hard-disk space that the Mac sets aside, if you want, to serve as emergency memory.

virus — Irritating, self-duplicating computer program designed (by the maladjusted jerk who programmed it) to gum up the works of your Mac. Easily prevented by using Disinfectant or another virus barrier.

volume — A disk of any kind: floppy, hard, cartridge, or anything represented on your Desktop by its own icon.

VRAM — Stands for *video RAM.* Memory chips inside your Mac that are dedicated to storing the screen picture from moment to moment. The more VRAM you have, the more colorful your picture (and the more you paid for your Mac).

window — A square view of Mac information. In the Finder, a window is a table of contents for a folder or a disk. In a program, a window displays your document.

word wrap — A word processing program's ability to place a word on the next line as soon as the current line becomes full.

zoom box — The tiny square in the upper-right corner of a window (in the title bar) that, when clicked, makes the window jump to full size.

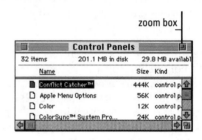

zoom box

Appendix D
CLKBC (Copy, Laminate, and Keep Beside Computer)

• •

*O*n the next few pages you'll find all the graphics included with each of the programs mentioned in Part IV (How to Act Like You Know What You're Doing).

You and your students will find it very convenient to have these graphics close at hand when planning a project or report. It will save needless time spent opening and closing files to look at the graphics within each one.

So, as the title states, go forth and COPY! Then laminate and keep these handy visuals beside your computer.

KidPix2

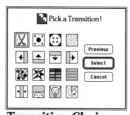

Transition Choices

Prince

Parchment

KidPix2

Painter's Easel

Ocean

Mutant Bugs

Monster

Lion

Jungle

Dream

Dog Biscuit

KidPix2

Disco Party

Cowboy

Chickie

Acrobat

Sailboat

Surprise

Space Surfer

Sound Choices

KidPix2

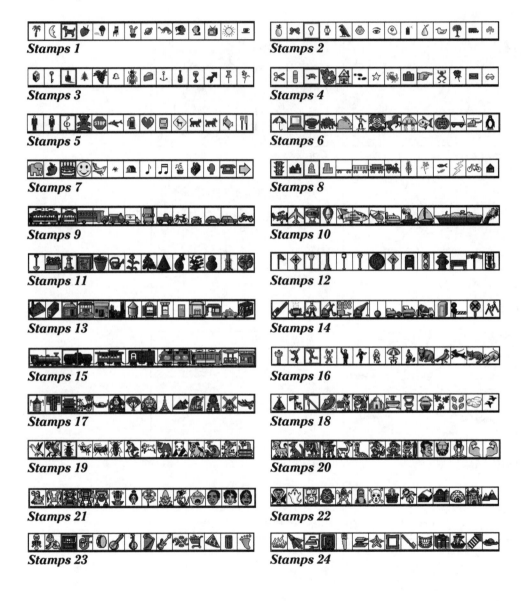

Stamps 1

Stamps 2

Stamps 3

Stamps 4

Stamps 5

Stamps 6

Stamps 7

Stamps 8

Stamps 9

Stamps 10

Stamps 11

Stamps 12

Stamps 13

Stamps 14

Stamps 15

Stamps 16

Stamps 17

Stamps 18

Stamps 19

Stamps 20

Stamps 21

Stamps 22

Stamps 23

Stamps 24

The Writing Center

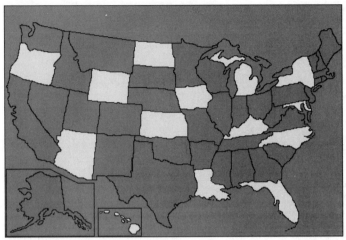

USA

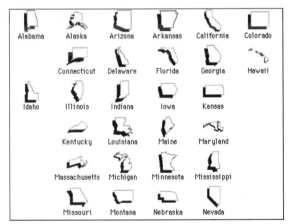

US Maps

Flags

The Writing Center

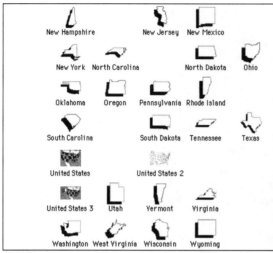

US Maps 2

World Maps

People

Weather

Nature

The Writing Center

Mammals

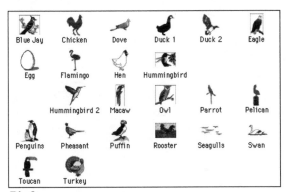

Birds

Other Animals

The Writing Center

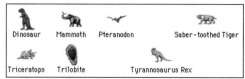

Extinct

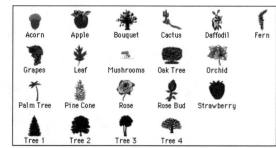

Plants

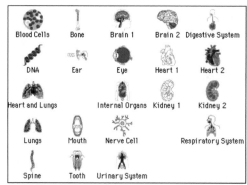

Anatomy

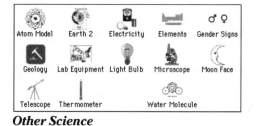

Other Science

Ecology

Activities

Holidays

Fun & Fantasy

The Writing Center

Burrito & Taco · **Cake** · **Can** · **Eggs & Fish** · **Fast Food**

Fruits · **Fruits 2** · **Grains** · **Hamburger** · **Hot Dog**

Ice Cream · **Jam** · **Legumes** · **Milk & Cheese** · **Pizza**

Popcorn · **Popcorn & Ice Cream** · **Punch Bowl**

Rice & Beans · **Taco, Drink, Nachos** · **Vegetables**

Food

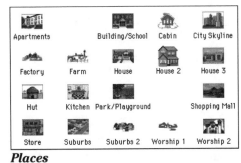

Apartments · **Building/School** · **Cabin** · **City Skyline**

Factory · **Farm** · **House** · **House 2** · **House 3**

Hut · **Kitchen** · **Park/Playground** · **Shopping Mall**

Store · **Suburbs** · **Suburbs 2** · **Worship 1** · **Worship 2**

Places

Books · **Cafeteria** · **Classroom** · **Graduation** · **Hallway/Lockers**

Library · **Teacher 1** · **Teacher 2**

School

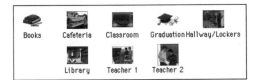

Apollo · **Astronaut** · **Jupiter** · **Lunar Module** · **Lunar Rover** · **Mercury**

Moon Phases · **Observatory** · **On the Moon** · **Satellite 1** · **Satellite 2**

Satellite 3 · **Saturn** · **Shuttle 1** · **Shuttle 2**

Solar System · **Space Lab** · **Space Shuttle**

Space

747 · **Balloon—Hot Air** · **Bicycle** · **Blimp** · **Boat—Canoe**

Boat—Motor · **Boat—Row** · **Boat—Sail** · **Bulldozer** · **Bus**

Bus 2 · **Cable Car** · **Car** · **Container Ship** · **Cruise Ship**

Helicopter · **Jeep** · **Jet 1** · **Jet 2** · **Limousine**

Mobile Home · **Motorcycle** · **Plane** · **Police Car** · **Race Car**

Ship—Tanker · **Submarine** · **Taxi** · **Train** · **Train 2**

Truck · **Truck 2** · **Truck 3** · **Tug Boat** · **Van**

Transportation

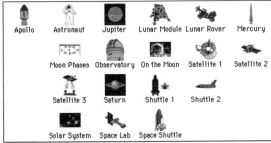

Baseball · **Basketball** · **Bowling** · **Field Hockey** · **Football** · **Golf**

Ice Skates · **Runners** · **Skiing** · **Soccer** · **Sports Bag**

Swimming Pool · **Tennis** · **Volleyball** · **Wrestling**

Sports

The Writing Center

US History

World History

The Writing Center

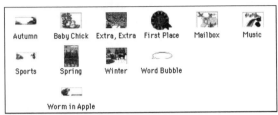

Nice for Heading

Miscellaneous A–L

Miscellaneous M–Z

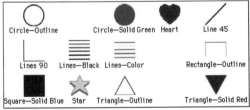

Lines and Shapes

Index

Subscribe to Club KidSoft today!

TRY THE TOP 40
Sample more than 40 of the top programs for kids on the Club KidSoft CD. Sample the best reading, math, science, and other educational software. (No shareware.)

BUY THE TOP 40
Purchase full versions of top kids' programs—right off the Club KidSoft CD! All it takes is one toll-free call to KidSoft. (No modem!). We'll give you a code that lets you unlock the program and it's yours.

EXPLORE THE EXTRAS
The Club KidSoft CD is filled with special surprises. Just for kids. There's an art gallery of kids' computer creations. Multimedia stories. Plus, contests, activities, cool music, and lots more.

SPECIAL BONUS
Each Club KidSoft CD also comes with the first software magazine for kids. Learn about the newest software and cool ways to use it. Plus, fun computer activities, contests, and more.

FREE ISSUE

Introducing **FamilyPC** — the fun, new computer magazine for teachers, parents and kids! **FamilyPC** is filled with creative ways to use technology at home and in the classroom. And now you can try **FamilyPC** FREE — just clip out the coupon below and return to the address in the arrow or call toll-free **1-800-444-2638**.

Family PC

FREE TEACHER HOME TRIAL

Published jointly by Disney (the world's leading expert on fun) and Ziff-Davis (the worlds's leading publisher of computer magazines), **FamilyPC** is dedicated to maximizing the computer advantage. Every issue includes:

- *Ratings & Reviews*
- *Creative Projects*
- *Deals & Discounts*
- *Mini-magazine just for kids*

MAIL COUPON TO:
FamilyPC
P.O. Box 400453
Des Moines, IA 50350-0453

☑ To receive your FREE Trial Issue of **FamilyPC**, just mail this coupon or call **1-800-444-2638**. If you like **FamilyPC**, you'll receive 9 more issues (for a total of 10) for the special Educator rate of $9.95. If **FamilyPC** is not for you, simply returh the bill marked "Cancel." The free issue is yours to keep.

NAME

ADDRESS

CITY

STATE   ZIP

Canadian and foreign orders, enclose U.S. funds and add $10 for GST and postage. FamilyPC's annual newsstand price is $29.50. ©1995 FamilyPC

CE91AAC

ADD YOUR *Handwriting* TO THE FONT MENU!

Signature Software

PenFont™

Personal Printed Handwriting Font

Arial
Courier
▶Your Font
Helvetica
Times

Available for MAC or WINDOWS

With PenFont you can add your handwriting and signature to the Font Menu!

Special Offer!! 10% discount on your own custom handwriting & signature font!

Signature Software will convert your best printed handwriting into a custom font that you can use with any of your Macintosh or Windows applications. Imagine running your spell checker on your handwriting! Or how about using your word processor's cut and paste features to polish up handwritten letters? Sign your FAX-modem messages. Design worksheets using your own handwriting! With PenFont you can combine the convenience and power of your computer with the personal impact of your own handwriting. All for the special discounted price of only **$44⁹⁵** (regularly $49⁹⁵)!

Order your font today!

To obtain your own PenFont, fill in the order blank on the bottom of this page and send it in to Signature Software. We will send you a custom PenFont kit including a handwriting sample form, pen, instructions and a free PenFont to use. Once you return the form to Signature Software, our font designers will convert your handwriting into a unique TrueType font. After thorough testing, this font is shipped to you along with easy-to-use installation software. Your PenFont includes your signature and two symbol characters (like your initials or a personal logo) along with a complete set of 98 US keyboard characters including the upper and lower case letters, numbers and punctuation. Or call to order the International Version which includes 62 additional accented characters for just $99⁹⁵. Contextual, cursive fonts also available; call for details.

THERE'S NO OTHER FONT LIKE YOUR OWN PENFONT, AND HERE'S HOW TO ORDER!

ORDER YOUR FONT!

Send this order blank to:

**Signature Software, Inc.
489 N. 8th St. Suite 201
Hood River, OR   97031**

Please allow 2 to 4 weeks for processing of final custom font. Rush processing is available.

Special Offer!
~~$49⁹⁵~~
$44⁹⁵
10% savings!

+ shipping and handling*
(Note: all prices $US)

Signature Software
PenFont™
Personal Printed Handwriting Font

- Call for International version ($99⁹⁵)
- For more information call
  1-800-925-8840 (in USA) or
  503-386-3221 or FAX 503-386-3229

System Requirements:

Mac - System 6.05 or higher, including System 7
PC - Windows 3.1 or above

NAME

COMPANY

ADDRESS

CITY   STATE   ZIP   COUNTRY

 CARD NUMBER
(circle one or enclose check)

CARD EXPIRATION   PHONE

CARDHOLDER'S SIGNATURE

O 3.5"
O 5.25"

(circle format desired)

ORDER FORM	Price	Total
PenFont™ (reg.$49⁹⁵) #1215 - custom printed handwriting font	$44⁹⁵	$44⁹⁵
Shipping/Handling* (see below)		_____
Grand Total		_____

——— Shipping and Special Handling* ———

United States	International
☐ Regular $7⁵⁰	☐ Regular $15⁰⁰
☐ Express 48 State $15⁰⁰	☐ Express $40⁰⁰
☐ Express AK, HI, PR $25⁰⁰	Express shipping requires street address and phone #

MacHome Journal······

Your #1

Teaching

and

Learning

Resource

Every issue is jam-packed with groundbreaking coverage of Education, the Information Superhighway, Home Office, Entertainment, Multimedia and beyond! In addition to plain-English articles and product information, MacHome Journal provides straightforward reviews of the best learning software (_and_ what to avoid!)

For work, play or education **MacHome Journal puts you at the top of the class!**

To order please call
800-800-6542
and mention code DMFTA

MAC HOME
J O U R N A L

(Ask us about our classroom past-issues program! 415-957-1911 ext. 36)